DOG
CATALOG

COPY EDITOR
Tia Schneider Denenberg

CAPTIONS
Gary Hoenig

ACKNOWLEDGEMENTS

The drawings of E. M. Stevenson on pages 84 to 105 are reproduced from the "Gaines Guide to American Dogs" by permission of the General Foods Corporation.

The dog food sales data on pages 184 to 185 are reprinted with permission from the April 25, 1977 issue of Advertising Age. Copyright 1977 by Crain Communications, Inc. Also reprinted with permission from John C. Maxwell Jr.

The excerpt on page 66 from Lassie Come-Home by Eric Knight is reprinted by permission of Holt, Rhinehart and Winston, Publishers. Copyright 1940, © 1968 by Jere Knight.

The excerpt on Page 220 from Thirteen by Corwin by Norman Corwin is reprinted by permission of Holt, Rhinehart and Winston, Publishers. Copyright 1942, © 1970 by Norman Corwin.

The excerpt from the Dear Abby column on page 233 is reprinted by permission of Abigail Van Buren.

The excerpt on page 61 by James Thurber from the Fireside Book of Dog Stories is reprinted by permission of Mrs. James Thurber.

The article "Obituary" on page 226 from Ouo Vadimus? by E.B. White originally appeared in the New Yorker and is reprinted by permission of Harper & Row, Publishers, Inc. Coypright 1932 by E.B. White.

SPECIAL THANKS

The American Kennel Club generously permitted the use of its library facilities, and the library staff, Aida Ferrer, Marie Fabrizi and Ann Sergi, were unfailingly helpful.

Thanks are also due to the following for their assistance: Lillian and Sidney Schneider, Michael Sigall, W.N. Chimel, Sid Weber, Charles F. Levine, Susan Mackenzie, Jerry Edgerton, Mimi E.B. Steadman, Jane Barbara, Mark Renovitch, Pat Cortese, Edward Levin, Susan Brooks, Alan D. Sisitsky, Sally and Murray Cohen, Wolfgang M., Monica Rochford, Mrs. Cheever Porter, Harold Malley, Joyce Frommer and Joel & Ketch.

PHOTO CREDITS
Pages: 26, 35, 187, 241, 245, 260 U.P.I.

Pages: 26, 28, 29, 64, 130, 228, 242, 243 Wide World Photos.

Pages: 92, 93, 113, 115, 117, 118, 121, 129, 192, 193, 219, 220, 221, 224, 255, 256 By Tia Schneider Denenberg.

Pages: 154, 161, 185, 203, 206, 211, 212, 252, 253, 254 By Scott MacNeill

Pages 4, By Elliot Erwitt, Page 9 By Richard Kalvar/ Magnum, Page 37 Culver Pictures, Page 55 By Robert Walker/New York Times, Page 149 By Neal Boenzi/New York Times, Page 156 By Ernest Sisto/New York Times, Page 202 By Romero/New York Times, Page 210 By Gary Settle/New York Times, Page 251 By Harry Benson, Page 261 By Arthur Brower/New York Times

DOG CATALOG

Written and Edited by
R.V. DENENBERG

Produced by
ERIC SEIDMAN

Technical Editor
WALTER R. FLETCHER

Designed by
SCOTT A. MACNEILL

Illustrations by
VICTOR JUHASZ
KIMBLE P. MEAD
DEBBIE HALL
LAUREL DOTY

Contributing Editors
HAROLD M. ZWEIGHAFT, D.V.M.
JUDITH S. STERN, Sc.D.

Researcher
MIREILLE GRANGENOIS

Cover by
VICTOR JUHASZ

Publishers · GROSSET & DUNLAP · New York
A FILMWAYS COMPANY

CONTENTS

Chapter 4 BREEDING: CULTIVATING THE FAMILY TREE

Chapter 5 SHOWING: WHERE THE COMPETITION IS DOG-BEAT-DOG

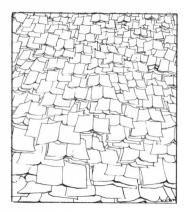

Chapter 6 TRAINING: WHEN NATURE MEETS NURTURE

Chapter 7 HEALTH: TROTTING ALONG WITH THE MARCH OF MEDICINE

Chapter 8 REPRODUCTION: GIVING THE CREATIVE URGE AN OUTLET

Chapter 9 NUTRITION: VITAMINS, MINERALS AND THAT CERTAIN SOMETHING

Chapter 10 THE LAW: PRIVATE PETS AND PUBLIC ENEMIES

Chapter 11 THE AFTERLIFE: LEAVING THE SURVIVORS IN LIMBO

Chapter 12 THE DOG'S BEST FRIEND: LIFE AT THE UPPER END OF THE LEASH

Chapter 13 GOODS AND SERVICES: TO BUY OR NOT TO BUY

FOREWORD

BY WALTER R. FLETCHER
FORMER DOG COLUMNIST OF THE NEW YORK TIMES

In my 50 years with *The New York Times,* I amassed quite a library about dogs. Whenever a dog book was published, a copy would be sent to me for review. A point finally came when my wife pleaded with me to give the volumes away to dog clubs lest we be crowded out of our apartment. Most of these books were rather poor reading. Frequently, they had been researched badly, and I'd find errors and omissions. It always amazed me that a person could write so much and say so little.

So it was a pleasure to help in the preparation of the *Dog Catalog.* This is definitely a work with a difference. Not only has it been carefully researched, but it is written in a light, readable style, has numerous explanatory charts and illustrations, and covers a wide range of subjects—from epitaphs in pet cemeteries to dogs as artillery spotters to Laika, the space traveler.

The book touches all the bases. For example, "What kind of dog should I buy?" was the question most often asked of me when I was writing dog columns and covering shows for *The Times.* If the *Dog Catalog* had been available then, it would have made life much easier for me. I could have directed the would-be owner to this book, and he could have turned to the chart describing the origins and characteristics of each breed. If he were considering exhibiting his pride and joy, he could have consulted the step-by-step description of how a dog show works, read about how much

a championship would cost him and studied the specialized vocabulary of the judges.

While choosing the breed may be difficult, if you have ever had a dog, deciding whether to get another is not hard. Owning a dog is habit forming, although such an addiction is hardly hazardous to your well-being. If you never had a dog, the compelling, charismatic human-animal relationship could add much to your happiness. The dog is the great egalitarian. It doesn't care about wealth, beauty or age. All it wants is to be part of the family. The dog has proved its worth as a worker and is proving it nowadays in the dual role of pet and watchdog.

Dogs are also a sport, and it is hard to think of any other sport in which so many men, women and children take part together. A prominent lawyer who shows his dogs once told me, "My work takes me all over the country, and I'm away a great deal. When I'm home I want to be with my wife and youngsters. What other activity could I participate in and still be with my family?"

Whether you intend to play an active role in the sport or to be one of the millions who simply own and enjoy a pet. The *Dog Catalog* will be a help to you. The book sums it up nicely when it says that "the dog is today the all-American pet." The *Dog Catalog* is the all-American dog book for the owner or potential owner. It is fascinating reading and a distinct contribution to a more enjoyable relationship with dogs.

1

In Man, Dogs Met Their Match

HISTORY

History

How the Perfect Couple Got Together

Dogs are not only proverbially man's best friend but probably his oldest in the animal kingdom. Before he knew how to grow crops rather than move from place to place in search of edible plants, before he learned to raise beasts for food rather than hunt them, man had already made the dog a part of his domestic arrangements. Archaeological remains show that for more than ten millennia the two species *Homo sapiens* and *Canis familiaris* have worked and played together in a unique symbiotic relationship.

How did men and dogs first meet? That depends in part upon where the domestic dog came from, a subject upon which the experts are in profound disagreement. One theory is that the progenitor of the dog was another member of the same biological genus, the wolf or *Canis lupis*. Wolves look and act a good deal like today's dogs, but so do other members of the genus, the jackal and the dingo, or "wild dog." Dog fossils unearthed in several parts of the world have resembled either wolves, jackals or dingoes, which may mean that early man, beginning with various animals in various places, produced domestic breeds that shared a genetic inheritance from all three. Evidence of the wolf connection comes not only from the remote past; Eskimos have occasionally bred their dogs back to wolves to add vigor to the strain.

If the wolf is at least part-predecessor of the dog, some drastic physical modifications have

Part of a Greek vase. Archaeological evidence suggests that the Greeks found dogs indispensable for hunting.

A pack of wild Cape Hunting Dogs. Dogs have adjusted to following human pack leaders in the field and elsewhere.

obviously resulted from domestication and interbreeding. Most dogs are smaller in stature and have shorter legs than some of their wild ancestors, but such differences are common in all animals that have made the transition from nature to nurture by man.

The animals that dogs evolved from were not always friendly, because they initially competed with man for the same quarry. But the competitors eventually noticed that they shared similar hunting techniques—tracking their prey in packs under a leader—and each realized that there was something to gain by cooperation with the other. The proto-dog's first sign of intelligence—and the one that endeared him forever to flattered humanity—was to recognize that his two-legged rival was even more intelligent and therefore able to provide enough food for both if he simply tagged along. The dog thus more or less domesticated himself, following behind the hunters and eating the leftover bits of the prey, a rather useful cleanup service in the days before twice-weekly sanitation pickups. The humans also noticed, possibly from the times when barking packs accidentally chased game into their waiting spears, that dogs could be assets in the field.

It is also likely that man's association with

The Testimony of Linear B

When the strange writing known as Linear B, baked on clay tablets, was deciphered 25 years ago, the inscriptions told us much about what life was like in Greece of the Bronze Age, the era of the Homeric heroes. Among the bits of information gleaned was a direct confirmation that the Greeks kept dogs. For the tablets mention hunters, and the term for them in that ancient form of the Greek language is "dog leaders." Evidently the Greeks could not even conceive of hunting without the assistance of these animals.

dogs began partly as a playful relationship. The person who falls in love with a puppy today is no different than a Stone Age hunter coming across a floppy wolf cub and taking it home as a pet. When such home-raised wolves began mating with each other, domestic breeds arose. (The practice of snatching wolf cubs from their mothers obviously was the inspiration, by inversion, for the ancient Roman legend about two human babies, Romulus and Remus, who were suckled by a she-wolf.)

It is a tribute to the canines' ability and lovability that man seems not to have viewed them, for the most part, as a source of food, the way he views cows, pigs, sheep, goats and even at times his faithful horse. Fortunately for dogs, people have desired from them affection and work rather than protein and carbohydrates. There are, of course, exceptions. Excavations of a village in Germany from the first millenium B.C. have uncovered dog bones bearing knife marks, indicating that the ancient Celts were given to using dogs for meals as well as mascots. The Aztecs of Mexico and Incas of South America kept toy breeds for religious sacrifices, and the Maoris of New Zealand relished the dog as a sacrificial dish. They served it to the English explorer Captain Cook in 1769; the Captain evidently thought he was having lamb. (The Maoris may have served it with mint sauce.)

An Aztec statue. The Aztecs and Incas valued the dog's metaphysical worth as a sacrificial victim.

Captain Cook is greeted by the Maoris. They honored him with a local delicacy, a dish of dog.

In modern times, dogs have been raised as a source of food in China, where a breed, aptly named the Chow Chow, is considered a delicacy. The Chinese have dog farms, dog butchers and dog restaurants and consider those with black coats to be more nutritious and to have better fat for frying. Dogs have also been bred for fur—for hats, gloves and boots—and to provide hair that is made into clothing. Samoyed sweaters, for example, are often sported, and Sherpa Tenzing, of the team that first scaled Mount Everest, is said to have worn clothes woven from fine Lhasa Apso hair—obviously by a patient weaver.

Taking on Tasks

But apart from these exceptions, the dog's main utilitarian role has been to help with economic pursuits. When agriculture developed and hunting ceased as a way of life, dogs guarded homes, villages, crops and herds. Specialized breeds met specialized needs. Large, powerful dogs of the Mastiff variety were bred as watchdogs and often equipped with spiked collars to protect them from marauding animals. Hunting was now a sport, and breeds were perfected to track large game, such as tigers, by scent or to hunt fast game by sight, as the Greyhound does. Breeds like the Great Pyrenees dog were developed to tend flocks of sheep as they grazed on the hillsides.

Dogs were also useful for another of man's pursuits: warfare. In the pre-Christian era, battalions of dogs were unleashed by Celtic, Roman and Persian armies to attack and disconcert the enemy's front line. That tactic is recalled by the famous line spoken in Shakespeare's *Julius Caesar* by Mark Antony: "Cry 'havoc!' and let slip the dogs of war" (Act 3, Scene 1). Julius Caesar's archenemies, the Gauls, even equipped their dogs with armor and weapons: a broad collar studded with knives. Sent against cavalry, the dogs would lacerate the horses' legs.

ILLUSTRATION BY DEBBIE HALL

The advent of urban living created a demand for household pets suitable for cramped quarters. Egyptians, Greeks and Romans favored toy breeds, such as the Maltese, and other miniatures were developed in China and Tibet. Inscriptions left by their masters indicate that they were held in as high regard as modern man's pets.

In the days of the ancient Hebrews, the dog had a rather unsavory reputation, largely because cities of the Holy Land and other parts of the Middle East were plagued by so-called "pariah" dogs, wild or semi-wild creatures that

"If you pick up a starving dog and make him prosperous, he will not bite you. This is the principal difference between a dog and man."

—MARK TWAIN *in* **Pudd'nhead Wilson (1894)**

scavenged in the streets. References to them are common in the Bible, as when it is said in 1 Kings 14:11 that "those . . . who die in the city shall be food for the dogs." The abhorrence of the scavengers may have been related to a tapeworm that they carried and spread to humans and other animals, but, for whatever reason, the pariah scourge helped make "dog" an epithet of contempt. In another part of the Book of Kings, one Hazael denigrates himself by saying, "But I am a dog, a mere nobody." Ever since then the term has been used for a disagreeable person,

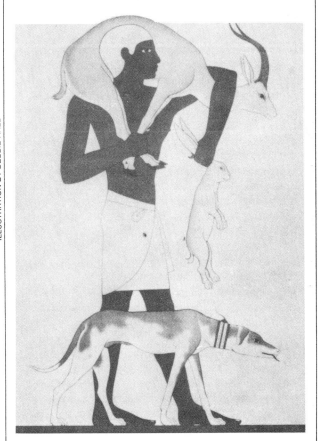

An Egyptian hunter. Hunters such as Salukis and Greyhounds were popular in Egypt.

Piecing Together the Hard Evidence From the Past

The oldest known fossil of a domesticated dog—merely a jawbone with some teeth—is about 14,000 years old, the remains of the canine companion of a group of Stone Age cave dwellers in what is now Iraq. The fossil's antiquity was not determined until many years after it was dug up in the 1950s, because archaeologists, who found it only two feet under the cave floor, thought it might merely have been a modern dog. Researchers at the British Museum in London finally solved the puzzle in 1974 with a classic piece of scientific detective work. They knew that buried bones tend to accumulate each year a slight but predictable amount of the element fluorine from ground water. The fluorine in the jawbone was measured. The test produced an estimate of 14,000 years, which was the same estimate that the archaeologists had made of the time since the cave was first inhabited.

Until the Iraqi fossil was dated with certainty, the oldest dog remains were thought to be 11,000-year-old bones found in a place called Jaguar Cave in Idaho. The Idaho fossil is now classed as a relative newcomer, but it is still the relic of the oldest dog in America, probably a descendant of those that crossed the land bridge from Asia with the earliest immigrants.

Both fossils provide valuable evidence about a crucial point in the history of the man-dog relationship. Neither the cave dwellers in Idaho nor those in Iraq were herders by trade; rather, they hunted. So dogs obviously established their enduring ties with man at least partly because of their usefulness in tracking and killing game.

A complete fossilized dog skeleton was discovered in the excavation of a neolithic camp at Windmill Hill in England. It is probably no older than 3,000 years but is remarkably well preserved and shows signs of having been well fed and cared for—obviously the remains of a valued animal. From the skeleton, researchers have deduced that this variety of domesticated dog had good speed and stamina and a well-developed scenting ability. Possibly, it was the forerunner of the Pointer types of today.

however unfair it is to the species as a whole.

Elsewhere in the ancient Middle East, dogs seemed to have been held in much higher regard. During the height of the Assyrian Empire, in the seventh century B.C., dogs were portrayed on palace friezes in military and hunting scenes; servants are shown holding huge, leashed Mastiff-like animals and carrying hunting nets. The Hittites, who lived in what is now Turkey, buried dogs in the royal tombs, and in Egypt dogs were so venerated that they were often mummified and interred in special canine cemeteries. Egyp-

An Egyptian god. Like god-kings Egyptian dogs were often mummified and buried in tombs.

tian tombs and papyruses suggest that several breeds were common, including versions of the Pointer, Basenji, Greyhound and Saluki.

Dogs were so important to the classical Greeks that they figure prominently, and by name, in several legendary and mythological tales. When Odysseus returns after ten years from the Trojan War, his faithful dog, Argus, recognizes him immediately, although his beggar's disguise deceives even his wife. The Greeks believed that a huge dog, Cerberus, stood guard over the gates of Hades.

Native species that resemble domesticated dogs still exist in many parts of the world. Clockwise from the upper left are the Siberian Wild Dog, the Malay Wild Dog, the Indian Wild Dog and the Dingo of Australia.

The Canine's Feral First Cousins

The English aristocracy has followed dogs to the hunt since the Middle Ages.

Playing to the Crowd

One of the benefits of the Pax Romana was that representatives of virtually every breed of dog from various parts of the empire collected in the capital. Dogs naturally joined the other combatants in the arena, beginning the gruesome history of dog fighting as a spectator sport. Romans classified dogs broadly according to their use. Two of the groups were the *Canes nares sagaces* (literally "dogs with keen noses") or the scent hunters and *Canes pedibus celeres* (literally "dogs with fast feet") or the sight hunters.

From the Middle Ages onward, hunting was such a widespread activity that myriad breeds were developed to suit the quarry and the methods of hunting. It was by no means totally an aristocratic hobby; peasants hunted to kill destructive vermin and predators. They used Terriers of various sorts, for example, to kill mice and rats infesting farm buildings and to catch badgers, otters and foxes. Fierce hounds were produced for hunting wolves, bears and boars.

In open country, fleet-footed dogs like Grey-

The Dominican friars in the Middle Ages were sometimes called in Latin **domini canes,** *"the hounds of the Lord," a punning reference to their enthusiastic preaching against heresy.*

hounds were used to pursue the game; in wooded or bushy terrain, hounds tracked game which, when flushed, would be killed by the hunter's trained hawk or driven into nets. In the bogs of countries like England, Spaniels at home in marshland were invaluable. When the hunter acquired more technologically advanced equipment, that is, when firearms replaced the bow and the spear, new types of dogs were required: Pointers and Setters that could target the game for the shooter; Springers that could roust them from their camouflaged havens; Retrievers that could swim in lakes and rivers to recover wounded ducks and geese. Extremely specialized breeds arose; the "Cocker" was a Spaniel especially adept at flushing woodcock from thickets.

At some point, however, hunting was done less for food or to eliminate destructive animals than for the excitement. Broad sections of the countryside were cleared to make "chases" for hunting dogs. The memory of such a clearing operation is preserved in the name of a large stretch of open land in Southern England: Cannock Chase. Fox hunting became a ritual; men and women in more or less formal attire rode on horseback after a pack of hounds, controlled by blasts of a horn.

A Royal Passion

Because of their usefulness in hunting, well-bred dogs became a possession prized by noblemen of all ranks. Ruddy-cheeked English squires slumbered before the hearth at their country seats, surrounded by their hunting packs, and even kings kept them around the table to dispose of bones casually discarded by the diners. Dogs acquired a diplomatic role as the gift for the king who had everything. In 1603 the Holy Roman Emperor, Rudolf II, received a dozen dogs as a gift from Maximilian, the Duke of Bavaria, to console the monarch for having been refused as a husband by the duke's daughter. Apparently, Rudolf was appeased. He wrote, "These great animals are my joy and comfort. My admiration for them is stronger and bigger than my understanding of marriage." The emperor was so enamored of the dogs, in fact, that he organized the first known field trial in Central Europe: 480 dogs, some from as far away as Spain, competed for eight days on the grounds of his castle in Prague.

Dogs were considered so indispensable that even the first European settlers in America would not think of braving the wilderness without them. On the passenger list of the Mayflower were a Mastiff and a "Spannel" when the ship sailed from Plymouth. The Marquis de Lafay-

Dogs can claim American stock as pure as any Pilgrim's. Two sailed from Plymouth on the Mayflower.

ILLUSTRATION BY KIMBLE P. MEAD

Prince William and the Spaniel

One occasion when dogs changed the course of history was in 1572, during the Dutch war of independence against Spain. The Spanish launched a surprise nighttime attack against the Dutch leader, Prince William of Orange. The prince and his men were still asleep in their tents as the Spaniards broke into their camp. Alarmed by the noise, the prince's dog, a Spaniel, began scratching and crying. Finally it leaped upon his face, waking him up and enabling him to make his escape. William went on to found the royal house that has reigned over an independent Netherlands ever since. Of this incident, the historian John Lothrop Motley wrote in *Rise of the Dutch Republic*:

But for the little dog's watchfulness, William of Orange, upon whose shoulders the whole weight of his country's fortunes depended, would have been led within a week to an ignominious death. To his dying day the Prince ever afterwards kept a spaniel of the same race in his bedchamber. In the statues of the Prince a little dog is frequently sculpted at his feet.

ette not only helped the fledgling nation by commanding armies but also by importing dogs. He sent George Washington seven Foxhounds from Europe and dispatched to America the first pair of Great Pyrenees ever seen in this country.

Dogs went west with the pioneers and became part of the national culture. The dog is today the all-American household pet, a sport, a hobby, the playmate of childhood, the companion of old age, the farmer's helper, the hunter's assistant, the guardian of the home and the shop, the hero of a thousand tales. About 10 million purebred dogs are registered in the United States and there are an estimated 30 million other dogs whose lineage has not been deemed worthy of recording but who nevertheless testify to our attachment to canines.

Benjamin Franklin's Secret Weapon

The fertile, inventive mind of Benjamin Franklin foresaw a role for dogs in settling the American colonies. In 1755, when Franklin was planning the protection of Pennsylvania from Indian raids, he gave these detailed instructions in a letter:

Dogs should be used against the Indians. They should be large, strong and fierce; and every dog led in a slip string, to prevent their tiring themselves by running out and in and discovering (i.e., giving away) their party by barking at squirrels, etc. Only when the party come near thick woods and suspicious places they should turn out a dog or two to search them. In case of meeting a party of the enemy, the dogs are all then to be turned loose and set on.

Franklin's idea was later taken up by John Penn, the Lt. Governor of Pennsylvania, who wrote to the paymaster of the colony's militia:

You will acquaint the Captains that every soldier will be allowed three Shillings per month who brings with him a strong Dog that shall be judged proper to be employed in discovering and pursuing the Savages.

However, these proposals were evidently not taken very seriously. A member of the Pennsylvania's Supreme Executive Council complained in 1779:

I have sustained some ridicule for a Scheme which I have long recommended, Vis., that of hunting the Scalping Parties with Horsemen and Dogs.

It was not until much later in the country's history, when the enemy was no longer Indians but the Axis Powers of World War II, that dogs were put to military use on a large scale.

Kings of the Track

The greats of dog racing also have their pantheons. Near the headquarters of the National Greyhound Association in Abilene, Kansas, there is a Greyhound Hall of Fame. Opened in 1973, it enshrines the memory, among others, of Flashy Sir, who set track records between 1944 and 1947, and earned $50,000 in prize money.

At the Natural History Museum in London, Mick the Miller, one of the outstanding British Greyhounds, stands poised but, alas, stuffed. Even more illustrious is the memory of Master McGrath, who was only beaten once in his racing career, from 1867 to 1873, and who won the Waterloo Cup three times. There is even a legend of Master McGrath: as a puppy he was saved by a nobleman from being drowned by a drunken tenant farmer. The dog's success was said to have been a handsome reward to his master for this kindness.

2

The Animal Kingdom Has a Working Class

WHAT DOGS DO

What Dogs Do

From Each According to His Breed

Some dogs, at least, have always earned their keep. They have paid for their nurture by hunting, by herding, by guarding, by pulling sleds and wagons. Those are traditional canine roles, but man is constantly finding unusual ways to utilize the particular combination of aptitudes that the dog possesses.

The Detectives

Dogs are natural detectives. Possessed of keen scenting powers, they can ferret out cattle and sheep rustlers, track down escaped convicts and lost children, and flush out burglars. Adapting themselves to the law enforcement needs of the 1970s, they have also become adept at combating such modern crimes as drug smuggling and terrorist bombing.

Dogs are especially good at locating narcotics because the resins in marijuana, cocaine and heroin have, for them, an unforgettable smell. In the early years of the decade, when canine drug squads were being formed, the police feared that the dogs might themselves become addicts from perpetually sniffing narcotic substances, especially during training. Dogs are apparently affected by a dose of cocaine, because the "nose candy," as its aficionados call it, effectively anesthetizes the dog's sense of smell. But blood and urine tests of police dogs showed no signs of addiction despite the steady inhalation of drugs.

In training, the dogs are taught to respond to the command to "Find it" no matter where the drug is hidden physically—floating in gas tanks and sealed in engine air filters, sewn into clothes linings or stuffed up chimneys. They are also taught to ignore the dozens of other scents with which drug dealers try to jam the dog's nose radar: perfume, spices, tobacco smoke, incense and frying onions—even the smells of another dog. Police dogs have been known to find a stash tightly wrapped in mothballs, surely the most

In the early 1970s, when hijackings and bombings became weapons of choice for terrorists, Lucky IV, left, and Satan were prize pupils in a pilot bomb detection program sponsored by the Federal Government. Canine sleuths depend on their noses for clues, but it is desire for master's approval that motivates them to find contraband.

Peerless trackers, Bloodhounds have followed criminal trails for centuries. Even Holmes occasionally used a Bloodhound.

powerful olfactory camouflage.

When they graduate, dogs not only accompany officers on busts but regularly patrol parcel rooms in post offices and the baggage rooms at airports. The same premises may also be patrolled by their canine colleagues, the bomb sniffers. It is the smell of sulphur, the dominant ingredient in gunpowder, or the acidic smell of nitroglycerin, which is made with nitric acid, that attracts them.

Why do dogs take so naturally to tracking scents that are foreign to them? The answer is that the dog is doing it for the approval he gets from his handler, not because of any intrinsic interest in the material he is hunting. Some trainers, in fact, believe in giving dogs a double motivation for a thorough search. In training, the "suspect" also rewards the dog when it finds contraband on him. The dog thus gets the im-

"I like a bit of mongrel myself, whether it's a man or a dog; they're best for every day."

—*GEORGE BERNARD SHAW in* **Misalliance (1914)**

A Hero's Reward

The equivalent, for dogs, of the Congressional Medal of Honor is the Ken-L Ration gold medal, presented annually since 1954 to "America's Dog Hero of the Year" by the Quaker Oats Company (the medal is named after the dog food produced by the company). The selection process is rigorous and open only to amateur heroes; no professionally trained dogs, such as police canines, are considered. The first step is to be awarded a bronze medal by a local selection committee, which verifies the heroic deed. The second step, for the bronze medal winner, is to be selected by a three-judge panel as America's Dog Hero from among the approximately 70 medalists.

Besides the gold medal and a year's supply of dog food, America's Dog Hero receives a specially tailored blanket and a gold-plated leash and collar. The owner gets a $1,000 bond and a chance to escort the winner to a unique type of award banquet: everyone eats but the guest of honor.

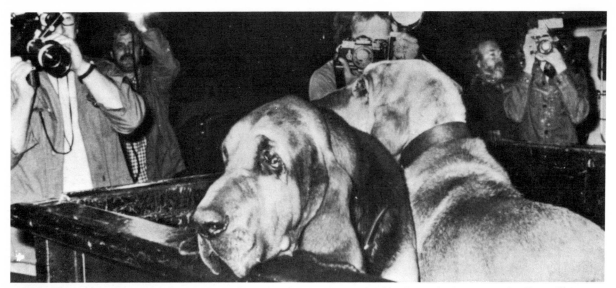

Though more sophisticated search techniques have relegated Bloodhound chases to the Late Show, these two helped capture James Earl Ray (opposite page) in the Tennessee hills a few days after his dramatic escape.

Artillery Spotting by the Nose

France employed a great number of dogs in World War I and put them to some unusual uses. Here is an account of how Sergeant Paul Mégnin, who was to become chief of the French Army's canine service, invented an ingenious method of finding enemy targets—and convincing a skeptical captain:

One afternoon about the time when dogs were being introduced in the army, Sergeant Mégnin and an assistant appeared in the front line trenches with Za and Helda, two Alsatian sheep dogs trained to sentry duty. They had come to offer the services of the quartet for night work at the front, but the Captain to whom the matter was referred was merely amused. Mégnin politely pressed his offer, and at last the Captain said, "Well, there's a Boche outpost somewhere out there, which we haven't been able to find; if your dogs can discover it for us, then I'm for sentry dogs."

Mégnin bowed. "If the outpost is within 250 meters," he said, "we shall probably find it. If the men on duty there move or are relieved during the night, my dogs will hear them and tell me where they are."

As soon as it was dark Mégnin took up a position in the trench, with Helda lying on the edge of it. One hundred and fifty meters to his left his assistant, a sergeant of the 22nd Chasseurs and an expert dog-trainer, occupied a similar position with Za. They had not been watching for more than ten minutes when Helda's ears went forward, she turned her head slightly and began to growl. Her master tried gently to calm her, but her attention was firmly fixed on something he could neither see nor hear. So he very carefully marked the point at which he stood and the exact direction of the dog's nose from that point. A minute later he learned from his assistant that Za also had growled, and that of course the sergeant had marked the direction of her nose. The Captain was awakened and Mégnin indicated the lines along which the dogs had pointed.

"Where those lines meet," said he, "you will probably find what you are looking for."

"We'll see," said the Captain, and mounting an observation post, he ordered a starshell sent up above the point which Mégnin referred to. There, sure enough, was the German outpost he wanted, and a French battery did its duty.

—Ernest Harold Baynes,
Animal Heroes of the Great War, 1925

pression that he is doing the suspect as well as the officer a favor by being diligent.

The most ancient of the dog detectives, of course, is the Bloodhound, whose astounding scenting powers were remarked upon even by classical writers. They were first used for hunting but later, especially in the United States, were put to work following the trail of fugitives. Bloodhounds tracked down runaway slaves before emancipation and criminals afterward.

Because of advances in law enforcement technology, including radio communications and helicopters, the use of Bloodhounds has declined; many persons no doubt consider them a relic of 1930s cops-and-robbers films. But in the most notorious prison break of recent years, the 1977 escape of James Earl Ray, the convicted killer of Martin Luther King Jr., it was the old standby, a pack of Bloodhounds that found the escapee a few days later in the East Tennessee hills. Moreover, some Bloodhound owners have opened up traveling missing-persons services, flying around the country to track lost or kidnapped people.

Stories of Bloodhounds' prowess are legion. The dogs have been known to follow trails more than four days old and to track their quarry more than 100 miles. Their noses are considered so reliable that identification of a culprit by a Bloodhound has often been accepted as evidence in court.

Because of the fear that "Bloodhounds of the law" inspired in fugitives, the animals have acquired a rather chilling reputation as heartless pursuers. "Coldblood hounds" would be a name more expressive of their image. But behind that solemn visage is a rather gentle, shy animal who tracks for the sport of it, not because it lusts for the capture. The Bloodhound may be an assiduous detective, but once the quarry is found, it is more likely to be licking his face than helping the two-legged members of the police force put the cuffs on.

The Rescuers

High in the Swiss Alps, a climber hears a

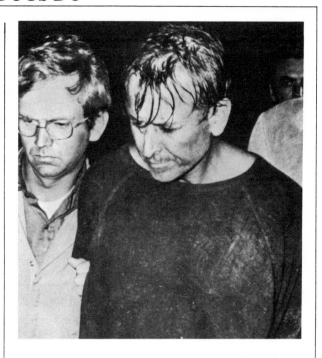

rumble echoing from the mountainsides. He turns to see a wall of tumbling snow just as it cascades over him, trapping him in a tiny air pocket just big enough to breathe—for a while. Hours go by; the air is quickly being exhausted. At last there is a scratching sound outside. It is a dog searching through the snow. The animal begins to dig, and soon a shaft of light and air breaks through.

To the victim, saved from imminent suffocation, the dog is a hero, but it is all in a day's work for the avalanche dog, trained in the art of detecting and excavating trapped persons. The pioneers in that work were the St. Bernards, who patrolled the Alpine passes for centuries, but in modern Switzerland the army rescue service has found that other dogs, particularly German Shepherds, can develop the discipline necessary for the job.

A dog begins training by locating its master, deliberately hidden in the snow (claustrophobia is an obvious disqualification for the trainer). Eventually, the dog understands that its responsibility extends to any buried person. Some of the dogs became so expert that, upon locating the spot where someone is buried, they can signal to their handler whether the person is alive or dead.

The Myth of the St. Bernard

The St. Bernard out in search of snowbound travelers with a keg of brandy tucked under his chin is a stock character in fictional tales of rescue. But that portrayal gives a misleading impression of how these reliable dogs performed their rescue missions. The St. Bernards did, indeed, recover many persons from the snow. For more than 300 years they were kept by the monks who ran a "hospice" or inn in the Great St. Bernard Pass between France and Italy. But they did not rely on spirits to revive frozen victims. They patrolled in packs after storms, and when they found a fallen person, two dogs would lie down to warm him with their bodies and bring him to consciousness by lapping at his face. Meanwhile, another member of the pack would go for human help.

The dogs were also said to have another mountaineer's virtue: a sixth sense that told them when an avalanche was imminent. There have been accounts of St. Bernards who uncannily moved themselves just before an avalanche descended on the place where they had been standing.

The St. Bernard's hulking body was obviously an asset in the snowy passes, but it also had its disadvantages, as the story of Barry demonstrates. Barry, who lived at the hospice between 1810 and 1814, is remembered as the greatest of the St. Bernards, having saved 40 persons. According to legend he met his end when the forty-first mistook him for a bear. Some say, however, that he died peacefully, of old age. In either case. his exploits practically changed the name of the breed, for in many parts of Switzerland St. Bernards became known as "Barry Hounds."

Rescue dogs are specialized; an animal accustomed to snowy hillsides would not do well at saving drowning persons. For water rescue, the unchallenged expert is the Newfoundland, a strong swimmer even in ocean waves. (Appropriately, when the St. Bernard strain began losing its vigor in the 19th century, it was bred to its aquatic counterpart, the Newfoundland. From that cross emerged the first long-haired St. Bernards.) The "Newf," as it is fondly called, has webbed feet and does a breast stroke, moving through the water more like a seal than a dog.

The breed made a name for itself in many ocean disasters—Napolean was supposedly saved by one—including a 1919 episode in which a Newfoundland rescued 92 passengers aboard a foundering ship by carrying a rope through water too rough for life boats. The rope was used to rig a breeches buoy.

Today, many Newfoundland owners do not leave their dog's performance in an emergency to chance. The dog is often given intensive training similar to that of a professional lifeguard. (In France, they work as lifeguards' assistants on the beaches). Newfoundland clubs offer life-saving certificates divided into junior and senior categories, much like the qualifications awarded to human lifesavers by the Red Cross. To win a junior certificate, the dog must demonstrate at a trial that it can retrieve objects from the water, tow a boat for 50 feet, and deliver a line across 75 feet of water. (The water-rescue dog needs strong teeth as well as a good swimming stroke). For the senior certificate, the acid test is when the handler takes the dog out in a boat and falls overboard. The Newfoundland must jump into the water and drag the trainer ashore.

Sailors in the late 19th century referred to the heavy sea swell that preceded a gale as **the dog before its master.**

Despite the trend toward professionalism, however, it is the untrained dog, the ordinary pet that rises to the occasion in an emergency, which attracts the most admiration. The hero dog is the one that rescues its master, through alertness, diligence, courage and loyalty—often with no thought of its own comfort or safety. Take the case of Zorro, a German Shepherd. In November, 1975, he and his owner, Mark A. Cooper of Orangevale, California, were on a backpacking trip in the Sierra Nevada. Cooper lost his balance and fell 85 feet into a creek, where he lost consciousness.

The next thing he knew, he was being dragged out of the water up a steep, rock-slab bank by the dog. Cooper kept sliding back into the water, but each time Zorro would pull him up again, finally laying across his legs to pin Cooper down. While Cooper's companions went for help, the dog laid next to him, keeping him warm. He was flown out of the wilderness by helicopter the next day, but in the confusion the dog got left behind.

Radio and television appeals brought dozens of dog lovers out to look for Zorro. He was found the following day—starving but still guarding his master's pack. The searchers had to use a sandwich to win the hungry dog's confidence.

Because of his steadfastness, however, Zorro's food problems would be over for some time to come. Ken-L Ration chose him as the "dog hero of the year" and awarded him, in addition to a gold medal, 12 months' supply of dog food.

The Racers

Dogs, like horses, have been used for centuries to satisfy the human craving for competition in speed. The obvious choice for the sport of racing was the Greyhound, whose only method of obtaining food in his native habitat, the flat, open country of the Middle East, was to run its quarry to the ground. Scenting abilities were sacrificed to speed, because the game was always in plain

Zorro's heroism was epic in scale; his reward, gold medal and all, was well earned.

A muzzled Greyhound. Sight hunters who rely on blazing speed, Greyhounds are ideal for competition racing.

Disgust at an animal's dismemberment for sport hastened the introduction, at this London race, of mechanical lures.

view; the Greyhound had only to catch it. Its success at sight hunting was celebrated as early as 2,000 years ago by the Roman poet Ovid:

The impatient greyhound slipped from far
Bounds o'er the glade to course the fearful
hare

The sport known as coursing resembles the Greyhound's natural hunting. A rabbit is released and given a headstart over two or more Greyhounds. The first Greyhound to catch the rabbit is the winner. Queen Elizabeth I is said to have ordered rules drawn up for the sport in the 16th century. By 1776 an organized coursing club had been established, and in 1836 the first Waterloo Cup Competition, the premier event of the coursing world, was held.

As a sport coursing has a number of drawbacks, particularly for the rabbit. Revulsion at having the furry animal torn to pieces just to prove that one dog is faster than another led to track racing, using mechanical lures which, to

the Greyhounds at least, resemble rabbits. The oval Greyhound tracks also made it practical for thousands of persons to watch the events—and to bet money. More than a hundred tracks had been opened in the United States by the 1920s, but the sport is even more popular in Britain and Australia, where the dogs run distances of up to 1,000 yards for sizable stakes.

There is another variation of the sport, called "rag racing," which uses Whippets. Rather than chasing a lure, the dog runs to the finish line, where his owner stands, waving a towel furiously to spur him on. (At one time a second person was at the starting line to ensure that the dog got off to a good beginning by throwing it forward at the signal.)

Another variation is the lure field trial, organized by clubs that are members of the American Sighthound Field Association, which was founded in 1972. Many breeds of sight-hunting dogs have competed, including Greyhounds,

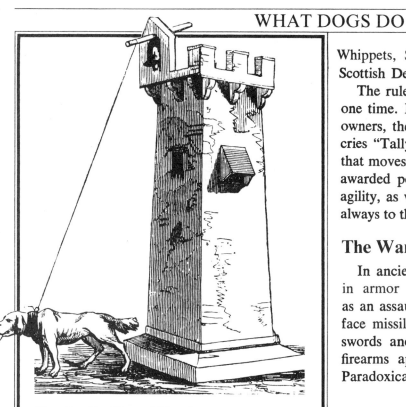

Early Police Work

The use of Bloodhounds for law enforcement work goes back many centuries. In the 1600s, the border country between England and Scotland was disturbed by bands of cattle rustlers called "moss troopers," who would disappear into the mossy swamplands with their plunder. To track down these marauders, the king ordered that "slough-dogs" ("slough" is an archaic term for a swamp), a variety of Bloodhound, be kept by the local authorities, who were supposed to pursue the culprits "by hound and horn." Here is one such royal order for the creation of a Bloodhound patrol:

September 29, 1616.—Sir Wilfride Lawson and Sir William Hutton, Knights, two of His Majesty's Commissioners for the government of the middle shires of Great Britain, to John Musgrave, the Provost-Marshall, and the rest of His Majesty's garrison (of Carlisle), send salutations. Whereas upon due consideration of the increase of stealths daily growing both in deed and report among you on the borders, we formally concluded and agreed, that for reformation therefore watches should be set, and slough-dogs provided and kept, according to the contents of His Majesty's directions to us in that behalf prescribed.

Whippets, Salukis, Borzois, Irish Wolfhounds, Scottish Deerhounds and Afghan Hounds.

The rules are simple. Three dogs compete at one time. Brought to the starting line by their owners, they are released when the huntmaster cries "Tally Ho!" and chase a mechanical lure that moves at 35 to 50 miles an hour. Dogs are awarded points based on their enthusiasm and agility, as well as speed, so that the race is not always to the swift.

The Warriors

In ancient times dogs, sometimes accoutered in armor like the other soldiers, were used as an assault weapon, a kind of surface-to-surface missile. They were quite effective against swords and spears but became obsolete when firearms appeared in the later Middle Ages. Paradoxically, it was in the First World War,

Canine combatants in World War I numbered over 75,000. They served as sentries, messengers, freight haulers and rescuers.

Thin Air May Be Filled With Clues

Bloodhounds are the recognized experts at following a trail, but often someone will become so lost in the wilderness that there is no way of determining where the trail begins. For such situations, the American Rescue Dog Association, headquartered in Seattle, has been training German Shepherds as "air scenters" to work with search teams.

The handlers are all nonprofessionals pledged to respond like volunteer firemen to emergency calls. The basic technique is to determine the geographical area in which the lost person is most likely to be found. The area is then divided up into sections, and each is searched by a man-and-dog unit that can cover large stretches of ground. (The dog has been taught to note the airborne scents of persons as much as two miles away.) When a unit, equipped with a portable radio, has "cleared" its section, it moves to the next one, assuring a systematic search.

Perfecting the necessary teamwork between man and dog requires about 10 hours a week for about a year. Because searches are often so gruelling, the chief prerequisites for air scenting dogs, assuming they have a good nose, are endurance and an extra-long span of concentration. It also requires a certain indefinable quality that the searchers refer to as "heart" and that is only apparent when the pressure is on.

the conflict that brought such technological advances as tanks, fighter planes and poison gas, that military strategists returned to the dog. But this time the animal was used for reconnaissance rather than attacking the enemy's front. Armies on both sides found that the dog's superior powers of scent, sight and hearing could be used to advantage in the trenches, where distinguishing friend from foe in the darkness was critical.

More than 75,000 dogs were used by the belligerents, 30,000 by the German Army alone. But the dogs did more than mere sentry work. The French used sled dogs imported from Alaska to haul ammunition and supplies across the Vosges Mountains; the Italians sent St. Bernards on mountain rescue missions, and the British and the Belgians used canine messengers.

The United States Army lacked a canine branch in World War I, but it closed the dog gap in the next world conflict, in part because dog fanciers were able to persuade the military how useful the animals could be. The famed K-9 Corps was formed and supported with much the same volunteer enthusiasm that was poured into bond sales and scrap metal drives. A private organization called Dogs for Defense was formed to receive dogs (and monetary contributions), train them and deliver them to the armed forces at no cost to the government. The United States was handicapped by having few native working dogs, like the German Shepherd, that could easily be converted to war work, but it did have a number of obedience training schools, and these changed their curriculums to include military commands.

About 25,000 dogs saw service in the North African, Italian, French and Pacific Campaigns, and in guarding the home shores and war plants. The dogs served as "point men" on patrols and

*"A dog starv'd at his master's gate
Predicts the ruin of the state"*

—WILLIAM BLAKE (1757-1827)

The Case of the Crowded Lifeboat

In most rescue stories involving dogs, the animal is a hero who saves human life. But there is one bizarre tale of shipwreck and rescue in which the dog, if not clearly the villain of the piece, may have been at least indirectly responsible for the loss of human life. The story began when Cyril E. LaBrecque took his schooner on a voyage from Connecticut to Florida in 1974. Encountering a January storm off the New Jersey coast, the craft broke up, and LaBrecque gave the order to abandon ship. LaBrecque, his wife and another crewman found themselves in an 11-foot rowboat with Hap, the captain's Labrador Retriever. No one is quite sure how he got into the boat, to which three other crewman were clinging in numbing, 43-degree water.

After 10 hours, two of the crewman in the water died of exposure. When the others were rescued by a passing freighter and brought ashore, the Federal prosecutor charged LaBrecque with involuntary manslaughter for, among other things, failing to throw the dog overboard to make room in the boat for the dying crewmen. The implication was that the captain thought more of the dog than of the men's lives.

At the trial, the rowboat was brought into court, and the United States Attorney stretched himself out in the stern to show the jury how much room had been taken up by the dog. But LaBrecque contended that trying to jettison the 80-pound animal could have capsized the boat, which was being tossed about by 10-feet-high waves. The captain's story was corroborated by the first mate, one of those who had been in the water.

After five hours of deliberation, the jury acquitted LaBrecque.

---

pulled rescue sleds in the Arctic (one sled team found eight planes that had crashed in Greenland).

A German Shepherd became the official mascot of the Army, a Doberman of the Marines. One famous dog, Chips, assigned to the Third Infantry Division, was credited with routing a machine-gun crew in Sicily. When President Roosevelt and Prime Minister Churchill met in January, 1943, Chips was on sentry duty.

The Guinea Pigs

Although in many fields of activity the dog has been the faithful assistant of man, in one pursuit, scientific research, the dog is frequently man's victim. By one estimate, more than 500,000 are used annually as experimental animals in the laboratory. They are far behind rodents (45 million annually), but they have taken part in some of the most significant psychological, medical and aeronautical research. The dogs' popularity among experimenters evidently stems from the fact that they are intelligent, relatively easy to acquire (cheaper than monkeys, for example) and physiologically close enough to humans to enable researchers to draw reasonable conclusions about how people would fare under the same treatment.

Dog research goes back at least to the turn of the century. Pavlov used them in the famous experiments that established basic behavioral principles. Diabetic dogs were used to test insulin in the 1920s. The early heart transplant operations—in which the doctors learned to

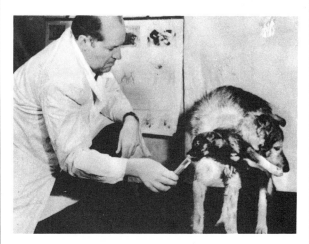

A dog with a second head grafted on is fed by a Soviet scientist.

Laika, The Space Traveler

Typical of countless other situations in which man faced the unknown, he sent his trusty dog ahead of him before venturing into space. The date was November, 1957, the threshold of the Space Age. Rockets were capable of putting a person into orbit in a satellite, but no one was quite sure how organisms designed for terrestrial life would function in a zero-gravity environment.

To gain precise information, the Soviet Union launched a satellite carrying a female dog named Laika. Her reactions were monitored by television and through wires attached to her body. Unfortunately, in those primitive days, the state of the art of space flight was such that it was impossible to bring her back to earth. So Laika was killed, painlessly, by remote control. But from Laika's flight, scientists learned enough to bring later space dogs—and ultimately astronauts—back alive.

overcome the rejection of the implanted organ by the body's immunological system—were performed on dogs, many of whom surprised the experimenter by living for years. Dogs were pioneers in space, preceding man by several years and proving to him that it was possible to function under the conditions—extreme gravitational pressure followed by weightlessness—of space travel.

Of course, since dogs are more popular than rats as pets, experimenting on them often seems cruel—especially if the animal is likely to suffer. Beagle lovers especially have been horrified to find their favorite breed also favored by the experimenters. Beagles have been used to test the effects of radioactive substances, X-rays and pesticides. In one Federal Food and Drug Administration experiment a group of Beagles were fed large amounts of methoxychlor, a pesticide; in two months, many of the dogs began behaving abnormally. Antivivisectionists and others condemn such experiments on the ground that no human could possibly ingest as much insecticide as the dogs did, so the Beagles died to produce meaningless test data. Such experiments, it is said, are nothing but "speciesism," the result of scientists' insensitivity toward "nonhuman animals" and a denial of the basic affinity among all living creatures.

Abhorrence of dog experiments is not confined to crusaders for "animal liberation." In 1973, when it became known that the United States military was planning to use 600 Beagles to test poison gases, letters of condemnation began flooding Washington. The House Armed Services Committee reportedly received more letters than on any topic since President Truman fired General MacArthur.

Many scientific organizations have laid down guidelines for research to minimize animal suffering, and in some places experimentation is regulated by law. But often these restrictions do not apply to commercial testing of products like soap and cosmetics and food additives. Moreover, supplying dogs and other laboratory animals has become a booming industry, much like the breeding of pets and show dogs.

Dr. Pavlov's Laboratory

The term "Pavlovian," to describe an automatic response, entered the English language as a result of the dog experiments conducted by Ivan P. Pavlov (1849-1936), a Russian physician and winner of the Nobel Prize. Pavlov was trying to discover the physiological mechanisms that determined behavior in dogs and other "higher animals," including man. Here is his description of his research:

The experiment proceeds in this way: We take, for example, a sound, no matter what, which has no relation to the salivary glands. The sound acts on the dog, and he at the same time is fed....After several repetitions of such a procedure the sound itself without... food... will stimulate the salivary glands. There are altogether four or five, perhaps six conditions under which, in every dog, any stimulus, any agent of the external world inevitably becomes a stimulator of the salivary glands....
Thus, you see, that it is necessary to recognize the existence of two kinds of reflexes ....The congenital, generic, constant, stereotyped one we term unconditioned; the other, because it depends upon a multitude of conditions and constantly fluctuates in correspondence with many circumstances, we called conditioned....

Pavlov, some of whose experiments involved surgery, was noted for the humane treatment he gave his dogs. He designed special operating rooms, used the same anesthetic and antiseptic procedure employed in human surgery and gave the animals post-operative nursing care.

Although he believed the dogs should be treated humanely, Pavlov was convinced of the necessity of animal experiments. In an article on vivisection in the Encyclopedia of Medical Science, published in Russia in 1893, he offered this rationale:

In spite of our measures inspired by the feelings of mercy and pity, there are, nevertheless, painful and violent deaths of animals. Is there justification for this? The human mind has no other means of becoming acquainted with the laws of the organic world except by experiments and observations on living animals....If we continue to permit the hunting of animals, i.e., their suffering and death for our own recreation; if we slaughter them for our food; if we consent to the torture and killing of thousands of even our fellow-men in wars: then how can we object to the sacrifice of a few animals on the altar of the supreme aspiration of man for knowledge in the service of a high ideal, the ideal of attaining to truth!

3

As Models, Dogs Have Their Virtues

THE ARTS

The Arts

A Symbol for All Seasons

Whether a supporting character or the central figure, the dog in literature usually symbolizes virtues that are too often lacking in humans. As the chosen metaphorical animal, the dog exemplifies love, devotion, fidelity, dependability, courage, initiative, intelligence and judgment. By endowing the fictional canine with these qualities, authors have faulted humanity for failing to live up to the high standards set by its pet.

The classic example is the fidelity of Argus in Homer's *Odyssey*. Two decades old, sick and abandoned, Argus nevertheless recognizes the voice and the footsteps of a former master, although Odysseus, who is disguised as a beggar, is unrecognizable to everyone else when he returns to Ithaca:

> *Thus, near the gates conferring as*
> *   they drew,*
> *Argus, the dog, his ancient master knew;*
> *He, not unconscious of the voice and tread,*
> *Lifts to the sound his ear, and rears*
> *   his head*
> *   *   *
> *He knew his lord—he knew, and*
> *   strove to meet,*
> *In vain he strove to crawl, and kiss his feet;*
> *Yet (all he could) his tail, his ears,*
> *   his eyes,*

> *Salute his master and confess his joys.*
> *Soft pity touch'd the mighty*
> *   master's soul,*
> *Adown his cheek a tear unbidden stole.*
> *   *   *
> *The dog whom Fate had granted to behold*
> *His lord, when twenty tedious years*
> *   had roll'd,*
> *Takes a last look, and, having seen*
> *   him, dies;*
> *So closed forever faithful Argus' eyes.*
>
> *(Pope Translation)*

From Argus it is but a short step, albeit through about 2,000 years, to Lassie, the Yorkshire Collie who makes her own odyssey to find her master (the original short story has blossomed into an entertainment industry), or that other Collie, Lad, one of the noble creatures at Albert Payson Terhune's home in Sunnybank,

The Pathfinders

A Pointer once pointed my way,
But did not turn out quite so pleasant,
    Each hour I'd stop
    At a poulterer's shop
To point at a very high pheasant.

*   *   *

A Poodle once towed me along,
But always we came to one harbour,
    To keep his curls smart,
    And shave his hind part,
He constantly called on a barber.

*   *   *

A Mongrel I tried, and he did,
As far as the profit and lossing;
    Except that the kind
    Endangers the blind,
The breed is so fond of a crossing.

*   *   *

My profits have gone to the dogs,
My trade has been such a deceiver,
    I fear that my aim
    Is a mere losing game—
Unless I can find a Retriever.

> — "Lament of a Poor Blind"
> by Thomas Hood (1835-1874)

Francis Bacon, Dog. (1952).
Oil on canvas, 6′ 6¼″ x 54¼″.
Collection, The Museum of Modern Art, New York. William A. M. Burden

Old Yeller saved master Tommy Kirk's life but, the threat of rabies forced pop Fess Parker to bring the movie to a sad conclusion.

© WALT DISNEY PRODUCTIONS

New Jersey. Lad, a character in the long series of books that Terhune wrote, "had a heart that did did not know the meaning of fear or of disloyalty or of meanness."

There are also fictional dogs who drag children from burning buildings, save people from wolves, prevent drownings or simply love unstintingly. Often, the dog's reward is ingratitude. After saving his master from a rabid wolf, the title character of Fred Gipson's novel *Old Yeller* is executed as a potential rabies carrier. In Mark Twain's short story, "A Dog's Tale," a dog who rescued its master's infant from a fire has its puppy destroyed by the master in a laboratory experiment. The servant who buries the puppy pats the dog's head tearfully and remarks, "Poor little doggie, you saved *his* child."

Dogs also are evocative symbols of the lost purity of childhood in literary reminiscences. A dog named Rex recalls for the novelist D.H. Lawrence his youth in England:

When we came home from school we would see him standing at the end of the entry, cocking his head wistfully at the open country in front of him, and meditating whether to be off or not: a white, inquiring little figure, with green savage freedom in front of him.

Another dog is intimately involved with the upbringing of the American essayist E.B. White:

I've never dared get another collie for fear the comparison would be too uncomfortable. I can still see my first dog in all the moods and situations that memory has filed him away in, but I think of him oftenest as he used to be right after breakfast on the back porch, listlessly eating up a dish of petrified oatmeal rather than hurt my feelings. For six years he met me at the same place after school and convoyed me home—a service he thought up himself. A boy doesn't forget that sort of association.

The death of a dog frequently provokes feelings of unworthiness, of having unpaid debts. In the 17th century, the poet Robert Herrick wrote:

Bionics for Quadrupeds

Television has added to the pantheon of fictional dog heroes a character who, appropriately enough for the 1970s, is a triumph of technology. Max, the Bionic Dog, has state-of-the-art circuitry that allows his leaps and bounds to match those of the Bionic Woman. A German Shepherd, Max is strong enough to smash down doors that others might have adroitly opened, unclamp bear traps with his teeth and bite rifle muzzles in two. But his mental condition does not equal his physical fitness. Shorts in the wiring sometimes cause him to turn on his mistress, and he was traumatized in puppyhood by the experience of being caged in a burning building. At the end of his debut, in fact, after having temporarily supressed his fear of flames to save the protagonist from certain death, his reward is an appointment with a psychiatrist.

Now thou are dead, no eye shall ever see
For shape and service, Spaniell like to thee
This shall my love doe, give thy sad death one
Teare, that deserves of me a million

Despite his long association with man, the dog represents indomitable, pristine nature, uncorrupted by civilization. The exemplar of this fictional type is Buck, the hero of Jack

A Test of Strength

The crowd fell silent; only could be heard the voices of the gamblers vainly offering two to one. Everybody acknowledged Buck a magnificent amimal, but twenty fifty-pound sacks of flour bulked too large in their eyes for them to loosen their pouch-strings.

Thornton knelt down by Buck's side. He took his head in his two hands and rested cheek on cheek. He did not playfully shake him, as was his wont, or murmur soft love curses; but he whispered in his ear. "As you love me, Buck. As you love me," was what he whispered. Buck whined with suppressed eagerness.

The crowd was watching curiously. The affair was growing mysterious. It seemed like a conjuration. As Thornton got to his feet, Buck seized his mittened hand between his jaws, pressing in with his teeth and releasing slowly, half-reluctantly. It was the answer, in terms, not of speech, but of love. Thornton stepped well back.

"Now, Buck," he said.

Buck tightened the traces, then slacked them for a matter of several inches. It was the way he had learned.

"Gee!" Thornton's voice rang out, sharp in the tense silence.

Buck swung to the right, ending the movement in a plunge that took up the slack and with a sudden jerk arrested his one hundred and fifty pounds. The load quivered, and from under the runners arose a crisp crackling.

"Haw!" Thornton commanded.

Buck duplicated the manoeuvre, this time to the left. The crackling turned into a snapping, the sled pivoting and the runners slipping and grating several inches to the side. The sled was broken out. Men were holding their breaths, intensely unconscious of the fact.

"Now MUSH!"

Thornton's command cracked out like a pistol-shot. Buck threw himself forward, tightening the traces with a jarring lunge. His whole body was gathered compactly together in the tremendous effort, the muscles writhing and knotting like live things under the silky fur. His great chest was low to the ground, his head forward and down, while his feet were flying like mad, the claws scarring the hard-packed snow in parallel grooves. The sled swayed and trembled, half-started forward. One of his feet slipped, and one man groaned aloud. Then the sled lurched ahead in what appeared a rapid succession of jerks, though it never really came to a dead stop again . . . half an inch . . . an inch . . . two inches . . . The jerks perceptibly diminished; as the sled gained momentum, he caught them up, till it was moving steadily along.

Men gasped and began to breathe again, unaware that for a moment they had ceased to breathe. Thornton was running behind, encouraging Buck with short, cheery words. The distance had been measured off, and as he neared the pile of firewood which marked the end of the hundred yards, a cheer began to grow and grow, which burst into a roar as he passed the firewood and halted at command. Every man was tearing himself loose, even Matthewson. Hats and mittens were flying in the air. Men were shaking hands, it did not matter with whom, and bubbling over in a general incoherent babel.

But Thornton fell on his knees beside Buck. Head was against head, and he was shaking him back and forth. Those who hurried up heard him cursing Buck, and he cursed him long and fervently, and softly and lovingly.

— *The Call of the Wild* by Jack London

London's *The Call of the Wild,* who returns to nature to be free, as the leader of a wolf pack, after having been sold into sled dog servitude. No doubt the enduring popularity of the novel, published in 1903, reflects the supressed yearning of generations of human sled pullers to slip out of the harness.

But not all writers have seen the dog in ro-

Another television favorite was Sergeant Preston of the Yukon, whose only friend in a pinch was his trusty Husky, Yukon King.

As in the Mark Twain story, dogs often narrate their own tales, providing a sarcastic but understanding view of human foibles as seen from the lower end of the leash. O. Henry's "Memoirs of a Yellow Dog" are self-told:

I was born a yellow pup; date, locality, pedigree, and weight unknown. The first thing I can recollect, an old woman had me in a basket at Broadway and Twenty-third trying to sell me to a fat lady. Old Mother Hubbard was boosting me to beat the band as a genuine Pomeranian-Hambletonian-Red-Irish-Cochin-Stoke-Pogis fox terrier.

The foibles of dogs themselves have been a rich literary vein. The humorist James Thurber mined it for stories like the one he told of Muggs the Airedale, "The Dog That Bit People." Muggs, an incorrigible biter who had to be chased into the house by means of an artificial thunder machine, finally died:

Mother wanted to bury him in the family lot under a marble stone with some such inscription as "Flights of angels sing thee to thy rest" but we persuaded her it was against the law. In the end we just put up a smooth board above his grave along a lonely road. On the board I wrote with an indelible pencil "Cave Canem." Mother was quite pleased with the simple classic dignity of the old Latin epitaph.

mantic or nostalgic terms. The 17th century French fable writer La Fontaine satirized complacency by contrasting a smug dog with a feral wolf.

The hungry wolf meets the well-fed dog and, seeing the nutritional advantages, decides he would like to be a pet also. But he notices a mark around the dog's neck and is told that it was made by the collar of the dog's chain.

"Your chain?" exclaimed the wolf, "then you're not free
To come and go?" "Not always—but no matter."
"Indeed? It wouldn't do for me,"
Replied the starveling. "You may be fatter,
But I prefer my own sweet will
To all the riches of your platter."
Therewith he ran: I guess he's running still.

Imitator of Adriaen Brouwer, Old Woman with a Dog
Oil on wood
The Metropolitan Museum of Art, Bequest of Michael Friedsam, 1931. The Friedsam Collection.

If dogs die even in the humorous stories, it is no wonder that so many dog tales end with the creature's demise. Death is the most emphatic way of making humans feel ashamed of being unworthy of their dogs, although as a literary device it has tended to make the dog story the quintessential tearjerker. The difference, however, is that when tears are shed for dogs they are usually real.

Mythology and Folklore

The symbolic uses of dogs have also been exploited by mythology and folklore, perhaps because canines were the most intimately known representatives of the animal kingdom. In ancient Egyptian mythology a dog-headed god, Anubis, guards the home of the dead, just as real dogs guard the homes of the living. Similarly, in Norse mythology a hero, as pictured on a medieval Swedish stone carving, enters Valhalla on his horse, preceded by his dog. There is also a legend that the Swedes, to impress the fact of their overlordship upon the Danes in the early Middle Ages, imposed a dog upon them as king. The dog, named Rakkae, reigned until one day, becoming ex-

Detail from Le Cardinal
Velasquez

Noble Beasts

Among the gules, frets, pales and flaunches of heraldic emblems the dog is not as common as the imaginary griffin, but dogs nevertheless have graced many coats of arms. English sovereigns up to the time of Elizabeth I used Greyhounds, among other animals, as "supporters," the beasts that appear to be holding up the central design of the shield. They were later replaced by the lion and unicorn, the beasts that still adorn the royal insignia.

Hunting dogs were also on the arms of noble families. Since Greyhounds were sometimes called "leverers," they were appropriated as a punning symbol by the Mauleverer family. The Talbots of Cumberland emblazoned the Talbot Hound on their armorial bearings.

The positions of heraldic dogs, like lions, would be officially described as *couchant* (lying down), *coursant* (running) or *rampant* (with forepaws raised.) There is apparently no official term for barking.

Medieval aristocrats admired dogs so much that they also included them on effigies as a chivalric motif. The tomb of Sir Roger de Trumpington in Cambridgeshire, England, is covered by a full-length portrait of that 13th century veteran of the Crusades engraved in brass. At his feet, clothed in chain mail booties, crouches a small dog of indeterminate type, flicking its rather elongated tail and gazing up at the knight reverentially.

The Start of the Hunt — from The Hunt of the Unicorn Tapestry,
The Metropolitan Museum of Art,
Gift of John D. Rockefeller, Jr., 1937

Alex Colville, Dog with Bone. 1961.
Serigraph. Sheet: 29⅞ x 25 1/16″.
Collection, The Museum of Modern Art, New York. Gift of Graham Colville.

cited, he jumped from the table to the floor of the banqueting hall. There, in the words of historian Gwyn Jones, "hounds of lower degree but taller stature tore him to Hell."

Dogs perform for anthropomorphic deities the same tasks they perform for mortals. They serve as the gods' messengers, hunting companions and sentries. An oracle told the Greeks to build a shrine to Heracles on the spot where a dog left a piece of meat snatched from a sacrificial altar; the dog was considered to be communicating the divine preference in building sites. The Roman Lares, guardians of the household, are pictured with dogs at their feet.

But there are also deities who have dogs with no visible function; even gods, apparently, need pets. Marduk, the main object of ancient Babylonian worship, kept four dogs. The Micmac Indians of the Canadian maritime

I am his Highness' dog at Kew
Pray tell me, sir, whose dog are you?

—Couplet on the collar of the Prince of Wales' dog, by Alexander Pope (1688-1744)

provinces have preserved a myth about a giant who went about remaking the landscape with dogs tagging along. The large rocks on the Nova Scotia coastline are said to be the petrified mascots of the giant, mourning their master.

Present at the Creation

Dogs loom large in mythological accounts of the origin of the world. In Persian mythology, a dog helps the hero Mithra kill the primeval

Peter Paul Rubens, (1577-1640)
Wolf and fox hunt
The Metropolitan Museum of Art, John Stewart Kennedy Fund, 1910.

The Lassie Cult

The performing arts are probably the only artistic medium in which the dog has been a participant as well as a subject. Canine circus performers have been known for centuries, but the advent of the film and television has made it possible for dogs to be entertainment personalities in their own right. Rin-Tin-Tin was the first of the dog idols, but there is no rival in stardom to the line of Collies collectively known as "Lassie."

The Lassie character began with Eric

Eric Knight with a Lassie prototype.

Knight's 1938 short story, later expanded into a best-selling book. The book became a movie in 1943, *Lassie Come Home,* in which the Collie made its debut. The film was so successful that five sequels were made. A radio show (in which Lassie pronounced in favor of Red Heart dog food) followed and, beginning in 1953, a popular television series.

Lassie's career is a tribute to masterful deceptions perpetrated on willing audiences. All the Collies that have played the part have been female impersonators; male dogs were considered necessary because they are bigger and less timid. Audiences seem not to have noticed nor cared when one generation quietly succeeded another, so long as a Collie with a white blaze on its face appeared on the screen. (White female Collies were used for breeding to assure a supply of heirs with that trait.)

Lassie's admirers also did not mind that the well-known feats of derring-do (jumping through windows, crawling under gunfire, unlatching doors) were less than they seemed. When Lassie stood up against a door, ostensibly looking for a way out, she was watching her trainer, Rudd Weatherwax, dangle a rag from a catwalk, and when she gave a devoted look she was really fixing her stare on Weatherwax's pocket, which held a dog biscuit.

The audiences always thought more of Lassie than of the dog's co-stars. Scriptwriters would find convenient pretexts, like having Lassie's screen family move to Australia, for bringing in a new set of human backdrops. They also endowed the co-stars with sub-human intelligence for Lassie's benefit. Cloris Leachman, who played the mother in one family, has recalled that "they had to find reasons for us to be morons so the dog could outsmart us."

The only moment of genuine drama in Lassie's life was when a Collie named Pal auditioned for the original part in the first movie. The director eliminated him for poor looks but later called on Weatherwax for stunt swimming shots during a flood. On the theory that all wet Collies look alike, the director intended to work the footage into the film after the star had been chosen. But Pal put on a stunning performance, pretending to emerge from the water too exhausted to even shake off and dropping down in front of the camera with his head between his paws, his eyes closed. Pal got the part and held it until the television series, when his son took over.

Although producers, directors and trainers have all cashed in on the millions of dollars earned by Lassie, its creator, Knight, received a relative pittance. He sold the film rights to MGM in 1941 for $10,000 and received nothing more.

THE ADVENTURES OF RIN-TIN-TIN

Television watchers joined the legions of Riny's movie admirers and watched Riny and master Rusty survive weekly bouts with western villains and Army regulations.

Of Two Natures

Shining black in the shining light,
    Inky black in the golden sun,
Graceful as the swallow's flight,
    Light as swallow, wingèd one,
Swift as driven hurricane—
    Double-sinewed stretch and spring,
Muffled thud of flying feet,
    See the black dog galloping,
    Hear his wild foot-beat.

See him lie when the day is dead,
    Black curves curled on the boarded floor.
Sleepy eyes, my sleepy-head—
    Eyes that were aflame before.
Gentle now, they burn no more;
    Gentle now and softly warm,
With the fire that made them bright
    Hidden—as when after storm
    Softly falls the night.

God of speed, who makes the fire—
    God of Peace, who lulls the same—
God who gives the fierce desire,
    Lust for blood as fierce as flame—
God who stands in Pity's name—
    Many may ye be or less,
Ye who rule the earth and sun:
    Gods of strength and gentleness,
    Ye are ever one.

"To a Black Greyhound"
by Julian Grenfell (1888-1915)

bull from which sprang the vegetation and the wildlife of the earth. On the island of Luzon in the Philippines, the appearance of mountains and valleys in the formerly flat earth is explained in this way: the gods were hunting but found it difficult to hear their dogs as they spread out after the game, so the deities created mountains to echo the barking. The Aztecs of Mexico believed that the present cosmic cycle of human life was created by a dog, Xolotl, who traveled to the underworld to fetch the bones of those who had lived in previous cycles. On the return journey, Xolotl, pursued by the angry god of death, accidentally dropped the bones, which shattered into many pieces. The incident explains the proliferation of cultures on earth, for from each of the pieces sprang a different tribe.

The Legend of Gelert

Perhaps the saddest dog legend is the story of Gelert, the Wolfhound that belonged to the Welsh Prince Llewellyn in the 13th century. Upon returning home one day, the prince met the dog coming out of the house, its face and coat matted with blood. Running inside, Llewellyn saw his baby son's cradle overturned in a pool of gore. Thinking that the dog had attacked and eaten the child, the prince drew his sword and ran Gelert through. Then, remorsefully, he realized what had happened. He saw the body of a dead wolf and heard the infant crying beneath the cradle. Gelert had killed the wolf to protect the baby. Today thousands of tourists each year visit a village in North Wales called Beddgelert (Gelert's grave), where a stone marks the supposed burial place.

Although it is a stirring tale of injustice to a faithful dog, the legend's authenticity has been questioned by some folklore specialists, who contend that it was invented by an 18th-century balladeer and that the village was in fact named after a St. Kelert. In any event, the legend has been seen as the source of a Welsh expression that no one repents as deeply as someone who has killed his dog.

Dogs are also credited by the mythmakers with having provided man with many of his essential foods, tools and skills. In Chinese lore, a dog discovered the main staple, rice. The dog, emerging from the wreckage of a great flood, carried rice seeds stuck to its tail, saving the survivors from starvation. From the myth arose the custom of giving some rice to the family dog at the beginning of each meal as a token of gratitude. In a number of African and American Indian tribes, the dog is regarded as the provider of fire and the bow and arrow. (The fire-giving Greek god Hephaestus, later known as Vulcan, is sometimes depicted with dogs around his brazier.)

The origin of the dog itself is explained in many American native myths. Often the dog

I'd Walk a Mile for an Alpo

Canine performers have made a profession out of selling the food they eat. Like tennis and basketball stars, the dogs on television commercials endorse the flavor, body and aroma of the brand that retains their services. The main qualification is an ability to stimulate intense desire for the sponsor's recipe and utter disdain for the competitors', a trick that is not beyond the trainer's art. But at times dog actors on live commercials have forgotten their lines, failing to show even the faintest glimmer of hunger in the presence of Mighty Morsels. Once faced with such an emergency, Johnny Carson bit the bullet, so to speak. He got down on all fours to demonstrate to the dog the tantalizing appeal of the bowl of food.

Rufino Tamayo, Animals. 1941.
Oil on canvas, 30⅛ x 40".
Collection, The Museum of Modern Art, New York. Inter-American Fund.

Mme Charpentier and her Children, Pierre Auguste Renoir. The Metropolitan Museum of Art, Wolfe Fund, 1907.

The Power of Speech

My father was a St. Bernard, my mother was a Collie, but I am a Presbyterian. This is what my mother told me; I do not know these nice distinctions myself. To me they are only fine large words meaning nothing. My mother had a fondness for such; she liked to say them, and see other dogs look surprised and envious, as wondering how she got so much education. But, indeed, it was not real education; it was only show: she got the words by listening in the dining-room and drawing-room when there was company, and by going with the children to Sunday-school and listening there; and whenever she heard a large word she said it over to herself many times, and so was able to keep it until there was a dogmatic gathering in the neighborhood, then she would get it off, and surprise and distress them all, from pocket-pup to mastiff, which rewarded her for all her trouble. If there was a stranger he was nearly sure to be suspicious, and when he got his breath again he would ask her what it meant. And she always told him. He was never expecting this, but thought he would catch her; so when she told him, he was the one that looked ashamed, whereas he had thought it was going to be she. The others were always waiting for this, and glad of it and proud of her, for they knew what was going to happen, because they had had experience.

When she told the meaning of a big word they were all so taken up with admiration that it never occurred to any dog to doubt if it was the right one; and that was natural, because, for one thing, she answered up so promptly that it seemed like a dictionary speaking, and for another thing, where could they find out whether it was right or not? for she was the only cultivated dog there was.

— "A Dog's Tale" by Mark Twain

57

ONE HUNDRED AND ONE DALMATIANS

LADY AND THE TRAMP

Drawing Inspiration

Cartoons, both still and animated, make good use of dogs as foils for satirizing the human condition. The meditations of the Beagle-ish Snoopy in ''Peanuts,'' the mis-alliance of *The Lady and the Tramp* and the adventures of the uncanny canine Pluto and his animal masters gently spoof the pretensions of the higher orders.

Some, like Pluto, have had enormous fol-lowings for generations. A central question to his fans is what kind of dog is he. He has the ears of a Bloodhound, the tail of an Irish Water Spaniel and the nose shape of Rudolph the Red-Nosed Reindeer. His feet (usually crossed fore and aft) seem to have been transplanted from an elephant, and his neck —12 sizes too small for his collar — from an ostrich. Pluto, clearly, was manu-factured under cartoonist's license.

was sent by the gods or by a friendly giant as a helpmate. The Crow Indians, nomads of the Great Plains, believed that the Creator gave them dogs to help carry their possessions about. The Eskimos tell a story of the dog's arrival that resembles the tale of Adam's rib. The dog, the story goes, was made from human fingernails.

Myths often assert that the dog was first created in unsatisfactory form and then perfected in a later model. In legends of the Tlingit Indians of the Pacific Northwest, the raven who created their culture designed an upright dog after making man and the sun, but the animal proved to be too smart for its own good. So the raven made the dog get down on four legs and accept a humble role. Traditional tales

Bullet, like Roy Rogers' horse Trigger, was stuffed and displayed after his death.

The Mistress

From a pedigreed yellow pup I grew up to be an anonymous yellow cur looking like a cross between an Angora cat and a box of lemons. But my mistress never tumbled. She thought that the two primeval pups that Noah chased into the ark were but a collateral branch of my ancestors. It took two policemen to keep her from entering me at the Madison Square Garden for the Siberian bloodhound prize.

I'll tell you about that flat. The house was the ordinary thing in New York, paved with Parian marble in the entrance hall and cobblestones above the first floor. Our flat was three fl—well, not flights—climbs up. My mistress rented it unfurnished, and put in the regular things — 1903 antique upholstered parlour set, oil chromo of geishas in a Harlem tea house, rubber plant and husband.

By Sirius! there was a biped I felt sorry for. He was a little man with sandy hair and whiskers a good deal like mine. Henpecked? —well, toucans and flamingoes and pelicans all had their bills in him. He wiped the dishes and listened to my mistress tell about the cheap, ragged things the lady with the squirrel-skin coat on the second floor hung out on her line to dry. And every evening while she was getting supper she made him take me out on the end of a string for a walk.

If men knew how women pass the time when they are alone they'd never marry. Laura Jean Libbey, peanut brittle, a little almond cream on the neck muscles, dishes unwashed, half an hour's talk with the iceman, reading a package of old letters, a couple of pickles and two bottles of malt extract, one hour peeking through a hole in the window shade into the flat across the air-shaft—that's about all there is to it. Twenty minutes before time for him to come home from work she straightens up the house, fixes her rat so it won't show, and gets out a lot of sewing for a ten-minute bluff.

I led a dog's life in that flat. 'Most all day I lay there in my corner watching that fat woman kill time. I slept sometimes and had pipe dreams about being out chasing cats into basements and growling at old ladies with black mittens, as a dog was intended to do. Then she would pounce upon me with a lot of that drivelling poodle palaver and kiss me on the nose—but what could I do? A dog can't chew cloves.

—"Memoirs of a Yellow Dog" by O. Henry

How Barge Was Led Astray

The dog has seldom been successful in pulling Man up to its level of sagacity, but Man has frequently dragged the dog down to his. He has instructed it in sloth, gluttony, pride, and envy; he has made it, in some instances, neurotic; he has even taught it to drink. There once lived in Columbus, Ohio, on Franklin Avenue, a dog named Barge. He was an average kind of dog, medium in size and weight, ordinary in markings. His master and mistress and their two children made up a respectable middle-class family. Some of the young men in the neighborhood, however, pool-shooting, motorcycle-riding bravos, lured Barge into a saloon one day and set before him a saucer of beer. He lapped it up and liked it. From there it was but an easy step to whisky.

Barge was terribly funny, the boys thought, when he got stiff. He would bump into things, hiccup, grin foolishly, and even raise his muzzle on high in what passed for *Sweet Adeline.* Barge's coat became shabby, his gait uncertain, and his eyes misty. He took to staying out on the town all night, raising hell. His duties as watchdog in the home of his owners were completely neglected. One night, when Barge was off on one of his protracted bats, burglars broke in and made off with his mistress' best silver and cut glass.

Barge, staggering home around noon of the next day, sniffed disaster when he was still a block away. His owners were waiting for him, grimly on the front porch. They had not straightened up after the burglars. The sideboard drawers were pulled out, the floor littered with napkins and napkin rings. Barge's ears, chops, and tail fell as he was led sternly into the house to behold the result of his wicked way of life. He took one long, sad look around, and the cloudiness cleared from his head. He realized that he was not only a ne'er-do-well, but a wrongo. One must guard the house at night, warn the family of fire, pull drowning infants out of the lake. These were the sacred trusts, the inviolable laws. Man had dragged Barge very far down, but there was still a spark of doghood left in him. He ran quickly and quietly upstairs, jumped out of an open window, and killed himself. This is a true and solemn legend of Franklin Avenue.

—Introduction by James Thurber to *The Fireside Book of Dog Stories*

A Cairn Terrier named Toto followed Judy Garland down the yellow brick road in "The Wizard of Oz."

Paul Gauguin, Still Life with Three Puppies. 1888.
Oil on wood, 36⅛″ x 24⅝″.
Collection, The Museum of Modern Art, New York. Mrs. Simon Guggenheim Fund.

of the Gullah Blacks of the Sea Islands of South Carolina and Georgia say that God made all the other animals first and then the dog to control them. Unfortunately, God forgot to give the dog a mouth, but he soon compensated for his omission by carving out a large one, filled with big teeth.

The Nyanga peoples of central Africa have a legend that explains why their traditional dog, the Basenji, does not bark. The ancestor of the Basenji, an animal named Rukuba, was so clever that it could talk. Plans were thus made to use him as a messenger. To avoid being sent on tiresome errands, Rukuba resolved to give up speaking, and his descendants have kept to his decision.

The Visual Arts

In the visual arts, the dog in general has long been a votive symbol, appearing on pottery, mosaics and sculpture, but canines recognizable as individuals began appearing only in the later Middle Ages and Renaissance. Even then, painters of sacred scenes were reluctant to disturb religious sensibilities by depicting the dog as anything more than a peripheral object, usually with a blank expression. Still, artists mischievously managed to sneak an occasional dog of genuine character into their works, as Rubens did when he painted his Spaniel into his famous work "Raising of the Cross," which hangs in the cathedral at Antwerp.

Pieter Brueghel, Hunters in the Snow.

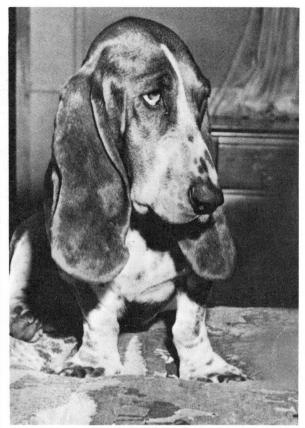

Cleo, a Basset Hound, starred in the television series "The People's Choice."

Docking the Tail

He must be docked. His floating puppy-tail must be docked short. This time my father was the enemy. My mother agreed with us that it was an unnecessary cruelty. But my father was adamant. "The dog'll look a fool all his life, if he's not docked." And there was no getting away from it. To add to the horror, poor Rex's tail must be *bitten* off. Why bitten? we asked aghast. We were assured that biting was the only way. A man would take the little tail and just nip it through with his teeth at a certain point. My father lifted his lips and bared his incisors, to suit the description. We shuddered. But we were in the hands of fate.

Rex was carried away, and a man called Rowbotham bit off the superfluity of his tail in the Nags Head, for a quart of best and bitter. We lamented our poor diminished puppy, but agreed to find him more manly and *comme il faut*. We should always have been ashamed of his little whip of a tail, if it had not been shortened. My father said it had made a man out of him.

— "Rex" by D. H. Lawrence

Asta was an equal partner in the somewhat dissolute lifestyle enjoyed by William Powell and Myrna Loy in the Thin Man movies.

Members of the Our Gang cast were precocious, and Pete fit right in with the rest of the crowd.

This painting by Francis Barraud was originally the trademark of Gramophone Company Limited, later R.C.A. It has been reproduced on millions of record labels.

The Homecoming

Ah, a thousand miles of tor and brae, of shire and moor, of path and road and plowland, of river and stream and burn and brook and beck, of snow and rain and fog and sun, is a long way, even for a human being. But it would seem too far—much, much too far—for any dog to travel blindly and win through.

And yet—and yet—who shall say why, when so many weeks had passed that hope against hope was dying, a boy coming out of school, out of the cloakroom that always smelled of damp wool drying, across the concrete play yard with the black, waxed slides, should turn his eyes to a spot by the school gate from force of five years of habit, and see there a dog? Not a dog, this one, that lifted glad ears above a proud, slim head with its black-and-gold mask; but a dog that lay weakly, trying to lift a head that would no longer lift, trying to wag a tail that was torn and blotched and matted with dirt and burs, and managing to do nothing much except to whine in a weak, happy, crying way as a boy on his knees threw arms about it, and hands touched it that had not touched it for many a day.

Then who shall picture the urgency of a boy, running, awkwardly, with a great dog in his arms, running through the village, past the empty mill, past the Labor Exchange, where the men looked up from their deep ponderings on life and the dole? Or who shall describe the high tones of a voice — a boy's voice, calling as he runs up a path: "Mother! Oh, mother! Lassie's come home! Lassie's come home!"

—"Lassie Come-Home" by Eric Knight

When secular subjects came into vogue, kings and noblemen often chose to have themselves painted in the company of large hunting dogs or their hearth pets. Illustrated treatises on venery and falconry, painted on canvas or woven into tapestries, pictured hunting dogs at work. Dogs appeared prominently in 18th-century portraits, such as Gainsborough's, but they were still essentially props for human subjects.

Portraiture of the dog itself did not flourish until the 19th century, probably under the influence of Romanticism. The French artist Alexandre Decamp's picture of Basset Hounds resting from the hunt shows the results of careful observation of canine character. The British artist Sir Edwin Landseer depicted a noble black-and-white Newfoundland (ultimately named the Landseer type in his honor) that he described as a "distinguished member of the human society." Artistic celebrators of the bucolic life portrayed Collies and other sheepdogs at their tasks, so much more tranquil that the boar-chase scenes of past centuries. Even Toulouse-Lautrec did naturalistic studies of urban wildlife, the stray dogs of Paris. In the 20th century, Picasso introduced dogs into abstract art, and they narrowly missed artistic immortality among modern painters when Andy Warhol chose a soup can instead of a dog food can.

I am quite sure he thinks that I am God—
Since he is God on whom each one depends
For life and all things that His bounty sends—
My dear old dog, most constant of all friends

—William Croswell Doane (1832-1913)

Alberto Giacometti, Dog.
Bronze (cast 1957), 18" high, 39 x 6⅛" at base.
Collection, The Museum of Modern Art, New York. A. Conger Goodyear Fund.

4

Hard Work May Produce a Strain

BREEDING

Breeding

Cultivating the Family Tree

The high-status dogs have always been the purebreds, probably because of the effort and the ingenuity that has gone into producing them. The "pure" breeds are so called because attempts have been made, over centuries in some cases, to purify the bloodlines, incorporating desirable traits and eliminating the undesirable. What is desirable and what is undesirable often is a matter of caprice, an arbitrary choice from among many physical and mental attributes, Beauty, balance, strength, speed, endurance, powers of sight and smell, intelligence and affectionateness are universals, but some qualities are more important in some breeds than others, especially if there is a job to be done. To a Bloodhound, a keen nose and stamina are more useful occupational skills than speed or sharp vision. Miniature size is obviously more crucial to a lap dog than endurance.

The basic assumption in dogs as in every other creature is that like will beget like. The breeder attempts to control the heredity of a litter by choosing as its parents two animals that have all or most of the characteristics that he wants in the strain. His object is to transmit the desirable qualities. He is often disappointed because the principles of heredity work in inscrutable ways—inscrutable that is to the breeder who has only the dog's appearance to go by. The difficulty is in the way genes—the units of heredity—combine in the offspring. Some traits carried by dogs' genes are dominant, others recessive. Dominant characteristics mask recessive ones so that whether a trait appears in the offspring depends upon the particular combination of genes. For example, in Boxers the brindle coat color gene is dominant and the red is recessive. Therefore, mating brindle Boxers and red Boxers can have these outcomes:

KEY: B is the dominant brindle gene
r is the recessive red gene

Brindle (BB) to Red (rr)

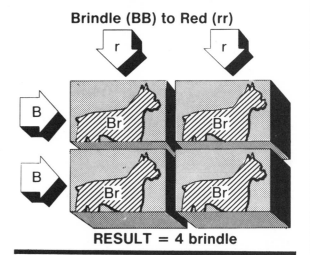

RESULT = 4 brindle

Brindle (Br) to Brindle (Br)

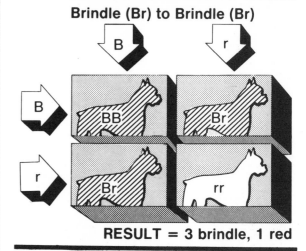

RESULT = 3 brindle, 1 red

Brindle (Br) to Red (rr)

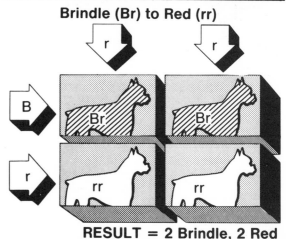

RESULT = 2 Brindle, 2 Red

Dominant and recessive traits vary according to breed—red may be dominant in some dogs—but thankfully the distinguishing characteristics of any breed are usually dominant and the faults recessive. The task of the breeder is to mate the animals in such a way that the bad traits are not only masked in the progeny but do not appear in later generations. An all-white puppy snuggled among the mahogany-red fur of an Irish Setter litter or a Borzoi with an unfashionably curly coat indicate that somewhere along the line a breeder has left a hole in his genetic screening. Despite the best efforts, however, reversions to traits not seen in a century or more have been known to occur.

Systematic breeding requires ruthlessness. Through sucessive generations, puppies with unwanted traits are supposed to be "culled"—a polite word for destroyed—to avoid polluting the gene pool. But many a breeder is reluctant to do so, either because the puppies are valuable commodities, even though flawed, or because they possess that universal puppy defense mechanism: cuteness. A tender breeder will never make a tough line of dogs.

The basic techniques are inbreeding, linebreeding and outcrossing. Inbreeding consists of mating two dogs that are closely related, such

as father and daughter, mother and son, and brother and sister. Linebreeding has the same objectives, to achieve a concentration of the best traits, but it involves mating less closely related dogs, such as cousins, or uncles and nieces or half brothers and sisters. In outcrossing, a dog is mated to one of another strain, often to correct a fault.

Unfortunately, inbreeding and, to a lesser extent, linebreeding, can also have disastrous consequences, because if there are any serious faults in the line, they will be transmitted to the progeny along with the good points. Through the combination of recessive genes, the offspring may exhibit flaws that were hidden in the parents. Weakness, infertility, nervousness and small size are not invariably associated with inbreeding, but they can result from it. Linebreeding is less likely to make those defects appear in the offspring, but it is also less likely to fix the traits that are wanted.

Among the disorders that experts have attributed to "overbreeding" are hip dysplasia, a deformation of the hip that makes walking difficult, in the German Shepherd and some other breeds; unusual aggressiveness in the normally placid, devoted St. Bernard; and hydrocephalic skulls (producing water pressure on the brain) in Chihuahuas, a breed in which domelike heads have been valued.

Toward the Ideal

From time to time probably every dog fancier has dreamed of creating his own breed, perhaps because his ideal dog differs from all those in existence, or perhaps just because it

Three generations of a California Boxer family demonstrate the influence of heredity.

ILLUSTRATION BY DEBBIE HALL

How to Read a Pedigree

A dog's pedigree is its family tree, in a sense, the record of all the matings that produced it. Having a pedigree at all is a point of snob appeal; most humans' ancestry cannot be traced through, say, twelve generations as easily as a dog's can. If all 12 generations (perhaps a quarter-century in time) were listed, the dog would have 8,190 different ancestors, but usually many of the same names reappear generation after generation — sometimes active "producers" more than once in the same generation—making the actual number much less.

The impressive looking certificate that comes with a purebred puppy usually spares the reader this profusion of ancestry by listing only the last three or four generations, obviously, those which have had the most direct effect on the puppy. The number of champions among the "sires" and "dams"

may attract the eye of the casual reader, but the serious breeder knows that star-quality antecedents can be misleading. For breeding purposes, the question is whether an ancestor was able to *transmit* his good points to his offspring. Finding the answer to that question requires patient study. If there is a dog in the line who had a particularly good head, did that head appear in his progeny for several generations afterward, or did his puppies have disappointingly ordinary heads?

Champion studs tend to be famous and valued on a puppy's pedigree certificate more than the "brood bitches," probably because of the biological fact that a male can sire a relatively great number of offspring in a short time, enabling its superior producing abilities to be quickly identified. Meanwhile, the female who is equally good at transmitting desirable traits may not find fame until she is too old for motherhood.

is a challenge. To many of the pioneering 19th century English breeders, the motive was the desire for hunting dogs that combined just the right kinds of physical and mental qualities for particular kinds of game. Creating a new breed can be the labor of a lifetime. It may be necessary to produce 10 generations merely to insure a good start, although dogs have been known to breed true in three.

The most straightforward method of establishing a new breed is to decide what it should look like or behave like and then cross two or more existing breeds which come close to the objective. By persistent mating and elimination of unsuitable puppies, the right features begin to be concentrated in the strain. One of the most elaborately orchestrated new breeds was the Golden Retriever. To get to it, Lord Tweedmouth started with a yellow Wavy-Coated Retriever in the 1860s and crossed it with a Tweed Water Spaniel (now extinct), adding a dash of Irish Setter and Bloodhound to the line later on.

Another method is to keep watch for the appearance of natural mutations in an existing breed. Some of the wirehaired breeds were created that way, as were some with particularly short legs.

A wholly new breed may also be created from an old one by adopting a separate standard and striving to meet it. The history of the Spaniels is a case in point. Before 1600, all of the Spaniels were considered the same breed, although they tended to vary greatly in size. Ultimately each of the sizes developed into a separate breed: the Field Spaniel, the Sussex Spaniel, the English Springer Spaniel, the Clumber Spaniel, the English Toy Spaniel, the American Cocker Spaniel and the English Cocker Spaniel. Even as late as the 1930s, the English and the American Cockers were being indiscriminately bred to each other. Separate lines were not definitely established until a group of determined enthusiasts, the English Cocker Spaniel Club of America, undertook an exhaustive—and no doubt exhausting—search for the "roots" of all

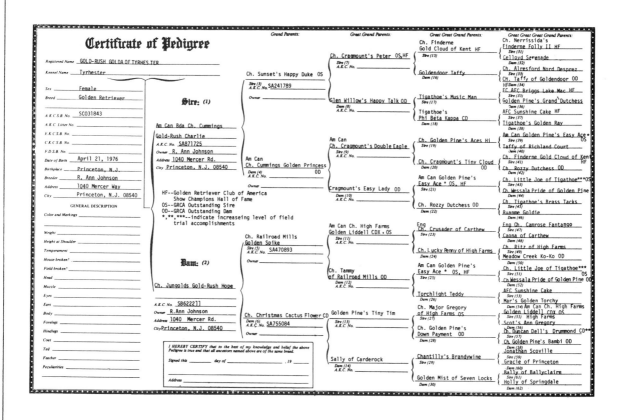

Trends in Breed Popularity

Fluctuations in the popularity of breeds as registered by the AKC, over 31-year period, 1946-1976.

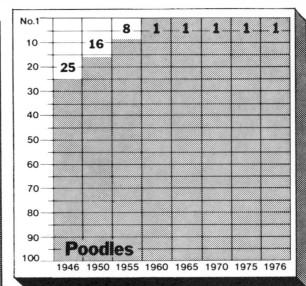

Poodles

1946	1950	1955	1960	1965	1970	1975	1976
25	16	8	1	1	1	1	1

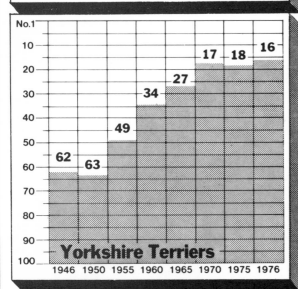

Yorkshire Terriers

1946	1950	1955	1960	1965	1970	1975	1976
62	63	49	34	27	17	18	16

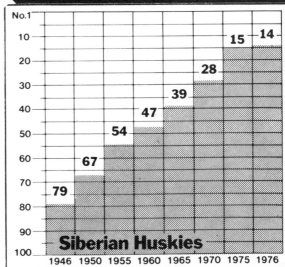

Siberian Huskies

1946	1950	1955	1960	1965	1970	1975	1976
79	67	54	47	39	28	15	14

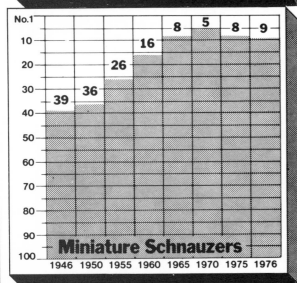

Miniature Schnauzers

1946	1950	1955	1960	1965	1970	1975	1976
39	36	26	16	8	5	8	9

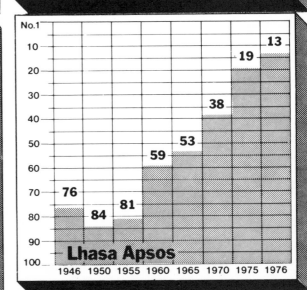

Lhasa Apsos

1946	1950	1955	1960	1965	1970	1975	1976
76	84	81	59	53	38	19	13

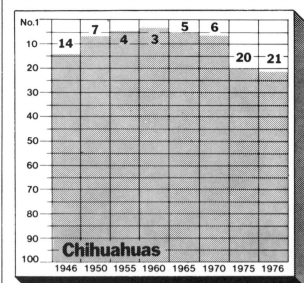

Chihuahuas

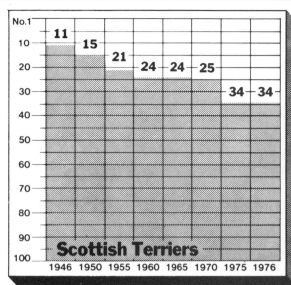

Scottish Terriers

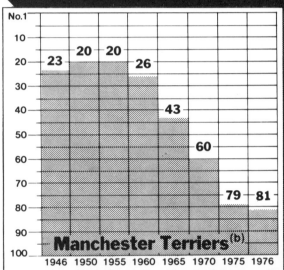

Manchester Terriers (b)

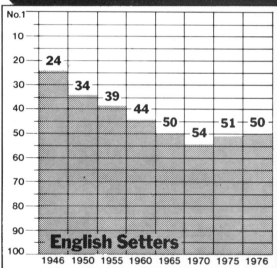

English Setters

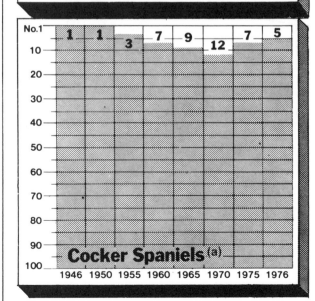

Cocker Spaniels (a)

Explanation of symbols on chart:

(a) The rankings for the Manchester Terrier include both Toys and Standards throughout. Although originally considered separate breeds, the Toys and Standards have been officially regarded as size varieties of the same breed since 1959.

(b) The Cocker Spaniel rankings are only for the American Cocker Spaniel except in the year 1946, when registration figures for English and American Cocker Spaniels were still being kept jointly. In 1947 the English Cocker Spaniel was recognized as a separate breed; its registration figures were kept separately from then on.

the Cockers in England, Canada and the United States, probing back into the 1800s. When the bloodlines were determined, the American Kennel Club, in 1946, rewarded the painstaking research by recognizing the English Cocker Spaniel as a thing apart.

One of the newest breeds is the Swinford Bandog, a strain developed by Dr. John B. Swinford, a Long Island veterinarian. To arrive at the Bandog, he crossed Neapolitan Mastiffs, English Mastiffs and Pit Bull Terriers. (The name Bandog was taken from an old English term for dogs kept chained by day and released as guard dogs at night.) The dogs inherited weight (100 to 140 pounds) and strength from the Mastiff line, and ferocity from the Pit Bull Terriers, which were bred to fight each other to the death in the ring. The Bandog well illustrates the possibilities of breeding for beastliness rather than beauty.

The Rare Breeds

Dog breeding has its share of fadism. German Shepherds, for example, enjoyed a surge of popularity when Germanophobia ended with the World I Armistice. Although they are still No. 2 among purebreds, the unquestioned popularity leader now is the Poodle, which has almost twice the number of AKC registrations. But despite this tendency to cluster around a few favorites of the moment, there are always small bands of owners and breeders passionately devoted to the lesser known dogs, some of them so rare that the chances of passing one in the street are about the same as passing a giraffe. In some cases, strains have been established or resurrected through careful genetic research and patient breeding. Dogs never before seen in this country have also been imported from their native habitats. Here is a guide to unusual canines by Walter R. Fletcher:

JACK RUSSELL TERRIER
Height: About 14 inches
Weight: About 14 pounds

Named after a Devonshire clergyman who is said to have originated the breed, the Jack Rus-

sell Terrier is favored by many huntsmen in England. Besides running with the pack after foxes, it catches rats, rabbits and squirrels. The dog is a variation of the Fox Terrier, having shorter legs than that breed. The color is white with black and brown patches.

PHARAOH HOUND
Height: 21-25 inches
Weight: 35-45 pounds

The Pharaoh Hound is said to have originated in Egypt, where its likeness has been found on sculptures and decorative friezes in temples dating to 4,400 B.C. The dog probably was brought from Egypt by the Phoenicians when they settled on the Mediterranean islands of

Malta and Gozo; it is today the Maltese national dog. The first Pharaohs arrived in the United States in 1967. The dog hunts by both sight and scent and is extremely fast. It blushes when excited or happy, its nose and ears changing from a flesh color to rose. The phenomenon is described in a translation of a letter of the XIX Egyptian Dynasty: "The red,

"Who loves me, let him love my dog also."

ST. BERNARD, 12th century

long-tailed dog goes out into the hills. He makes no delay in hunting. His face glows like a god, who delights in his work." The Pharaoh has clean lines and a long, lean chiselled head. The medium-high set ears are broad at the base and carried erect when alert. The amber-colored eyes blend with the tan to chestnut coat.

NEAPOLITAN MASTIFF
Height: 23-28 inches
Weight: 130-170 pounds

A massive, powerful dog, the Neapolitan made its American debut in 1972, when a pair were imported from Italy. The shiny, short coat is either black, blue, mahogany, tawny or brindle. They have a slow bearlike gait. They are fine guard dogs, generally docile but fearless when it comes to defending their property.

PORTUGUESE WATER DOG
Height: 17-22 inches
Weight: 35-55 pounds

The Water Dog is an ancient breed, long associated with fishermen and the sea. An ex-

The Dog Clubs

Breeding dogs is as much a record-keeping as a reproductive activity. The clerical function is performed by dog clubs, which act as a kind of college of heraldy, registering and tracking bloodlines, as well as the high commission of the sport of purebred dogs. In England, according to the official history of the Kennel Club, "many irregularities—not to say scandals" had arisen in the early days of dog breeding, making it evident that unless some regulatory body were created "breeding must eventually become a pursuit in which no respectable person would care to engage." The desire to prevent misrepresentation led to the compilation of the first Stud Book in 1874, which did for dogs what Debrett's Peerage does for the English aristocracy. The editor of the book, Frank C. S. Pearce, complained of the difficulty of sorting fact from fiction in breeders' accounts of their dogs' ancestry:

By rigidly excluding or pointing out all doubtful pedigrees, I have endeavoured to make it as much a record of fact and truth as possible, and if it be incomplete, I can only say that it must be borne in mind that a dog, unlike a horse, may have

several lots of offspring in the year....

That first volume contained the pedigrees of 4,027 dogs. Its successor in the United States, the Stud Book maintained by the American Kennel Club since the late 19th-century, contains more than 16 million entries and acquires more than a million new ones annually. (Entry No. 1 in Volume No. 1 is an English Setter named Adonis.) Automatic data processing has helped solve the problems encountered by Mr. Pearce; the "book" is now a computerized registry that lists the name of each dog's mother and father and a reference to their individual entries.

The American Kennel Club recognizes 122 breeds, divided into six "groups" customarily listed in this order in the show catalogs: Sporting, Hound, Working, Terrier, Toy and Non-Sporting. Breeds that have few registrations are collected in the Miscellaneous Class. Another organization, the United Kennel Club, receives annually about 300,-000 registrants of 42 breeds. The main difference between the clubs is that the UKC recogizes several breeds of Coonhound, compared to the AKC's one (the Black-and-Tan). Coonhound devotees provide the UKC with almost 50 percent of its registered dogs.

Dog Popularity by Breed

As reported by the American Kennel Club Inc: Dogs Registered January 1, 1976 to December 31, 1976

Breed	Rank	Number		Breed	Rank	Number
Poodles	1	126,799		Basenjis	51	1,674
German Shepherds	2	74,723		Borzois	52	1,658
Doberman Pinschers	3	73,615		Great Pyrenees	53	1,529
Irish Setters	4	54,917		Bichons Frises	54	1,512
Cocker Spaniels	5	46,862		Bloodhounds	55	1,446
Beagles	6	44,156		Irish Wolfhounds	56	1,409
Labrador Retrievers	7	39,929		Rottweilers	57	1,406
Dachshunds	8	38,927		Gordon Setters	58	1,383
Miniature Schnauzers	9	36,816		Schipperkes	59	1,260
Golden Retrievers	10	27,612		Akitas	60	1,213
Collies	11	25,161		Miniature Pinschers	61	1,126
Shetland Sheepdogs	12	23,950		Bouviers des Flandres	62	1,053
Lhasa Apsos	13	21,145		Whippets	63	1,050
Siberian Huskies	14	20,598		German Wirehaired Pointers	64	1,021
Pekingese	15	20,400		Bearded Collies	65	998
Yorkshire Terriers	16	20,392		English Cocker Spaniels	66	942
Brittany Spaniels	17	20,222		Australian Terriers	67	939
Great Danes	18	19,869		Bull Terriers	68	929
St. Bernards	19	17,537		Welsh Terriers	69	888
English Springer Spaniels	20	16,842		Rhodesian Ridgebacks	70	846
Chihuahuas	21	16,478		Mastiffs	71	810
Old English Sheepdogs	22	15,364		Standard Schnauzers	72	785
Pomeranians	23	15,241		Salukis	73	737
Basset Hounds	24	14,997		American Staffordshire Terriers	74	732
German Shorthaired Pointers	25	14,269		Bullmastiffs	75	676
Boxers	26	13,057		Kerry Blue Terriers	76	661
Shih Tzu	27	12,562		Pulik	77	609
Boston Terriers	28	10,806		Giant Schnauzers	78	565
Samoyeds	29	10,147		Belgian Sheepdogs	79	552
Afghan Hounds	30	10,045		Soft-Coated Wheaten Terriers	80	539
Alaskan Malamutes	31	8,324		Manchester Terriers	81	536
Norwegian Elkhounds	32	8,037		Italian Greyhounds	82	506
Dalmatians	33	7,241		Papillons	83	490
Scottish Terriers	34	7,202		Pointers	84	439
Airedale Terriers	35	6,835		Belgian Tervuren	85	430
Pugs	36	6,660		Bedlington Terriers	86	370
Bulldogs	37	6,554		Black and Tan Coonhounds	87	357
Cairn Terriers	38	6,432		Japanese Chin	88	356
Weimaraners	39	6,243		Welsh Corgis (Cardigan)	88	356
Chow Chows	40	6,211		American Water Spaniels	90	302
Maltese	41	6,183		Bernese Mountain Dogs	91	292
West Highland White Terriers	42	6,072		Staffordshire Bull Terriers	92	291
Keeshonden	43	5,871		Norwich Terriers	93	278
Fox Terriers	44	4,673		Irish Terriers	94	273
Silky Terriers	45	2,829		Tibetan Terriers	95	242
Chesapeake Bay Retrievers	46	2,650		Dandie Dinmont Terriers	96	235
Newfoundlands	47	2,113		Skye Terriers	97	226
Welsh Corgis (Pembroke)	48	2,061		Brussels Griffons	98	219
Vizslas	49	1,867		Briards	99	216
English Setters	50	1,756		French Bulldogs	100	208

ceptional swimmer and diver, the web-footed Caõ de Agua, as the Portuguese call it, was used to carry messages between boats, to retrieve broken nets and to act as lifeguard for men washed overboard. Nearly extinct, the breed was revived in the 1920s and first imported to America in 1970. The Water Dog comes in black, white, brown and combinations of the three colors. Coats are curly or wavy. The tail is thick at the base, tapering to the tip.

MEXICAN HAIRLESS
Height: 11 inch average
Weight: 6-11 pounds

This Pinscher-like toy dog is hairless, except for a tuft on the head. It has erect ears and deep-set eyes that are either hazel, dark brown

or yellow. The head is slender, the muzzle long and pointed. The tail is long and carried horizontally. The Hairless is found in every color. The smooth skin must be protected from solar rays in the summer by applying suntan lotion. The dog's body temperature is 104 degrees, compared to a normal 101.2, to make up for the lack of insulation.

XOLOITZCUINTLI
Height: About 20 inches
Weight: About 24 pounds

This dog holds the record for the most eye-

Xoloitzcuintli puppy

stopping name (pronounced show-low-eats-QUEEN-tlee). There are only about a dozen in the United States and no more than 50 in its native Mexico. The sight of a "Xolo" is so unusual that one owner resorted to handing out printed pamphlets rather than answer the questions of bystanders when she walked the dog in New York City. Like the Mexican Hairless, the Xolo is smooth-skinned and superheated; the Aztecs are said to have used them as hot water bottles. Even more ancient inhabitants of Mexico buried clay effigies of the dog in human graves, apparently in the belief that they would guide the souls of the departed.

PICARDY SHEPHERD
Height: 21½-25½ inches
Weight: About 45 pounds

The Picardy is probably the rarest breed in the United States, where there are only a few specimens. Although traditionally used for guarding sheep in France, the dog is now employed there in police work instead of the Ger-

---

"When a dog bites a man, that is not news, because it happens so often. But if a man bites a dog, that is news."

—**JOHN B. BOGART,** *city editor of The New York Sun from 1873 to 1890.*

man Shepherd. (The reasons are practical as well as patriotic: the French believe that the Picardy is a better cop.) The Picardy's shaggy coat ranges in color from charcoal to light tan.

CANAAN DOG
Height: 19-24 inches
Weight: 40-60 pounds

The Canaan's lineage dates to Biblical days. After the dispersal of the Israelities, almost 2,000 years ago, the Canaan almost disappeared. Some were seen in the Negev Desert, as wild or partly domesticated animals. They were used by the Israelis fighting Arabs during the 1948 war for sentry and mine detection work and for locating wounded. When hostilities ended, they were trained as guide dogs for the blind. The first Canaans were brought to the United States in 1965. They are white with big markings in either black, brown or red. They also come in all shades of brown, black and

white hair. Tan points also appear on its smooth, glossy coat. The Bluetick has a highly developed treeing and trailing instinct for hunting coons. It also hunts fox, coyote and bobcat.

ENGLISH COONHOUND
Height: 21-25 inches
Weight: 45-65 pounds

The English is a fast hound who sounds a melodious voice when a coon is treed. It is particularly good on a cold trail, following the scent of an animal that has been there hours earlier. Any color is permitted, but the coat generally is tri-colored with red or blue ticking.

solids with white markings. The coat, harsh and flat, is of medium length. The Canaan is alert, aggressive and distrustful of strangers.

BLUETICK
Height: 23-35 inches
Weight: 70-90 pounds

This big hound gets its name from the blue effect produced by the interspersing of black and

Mutt versus Purebred

Call him what you will, mutt or mongrel, the dog of mixed ancestry has always been a subject of contention among dog owners. There are those who claim that natural selection produces a better animal than artificial selection; others insist that the mongrel, as one authority has put it, is nothing more than a dog that "has been designed without an architect" and exhibits all the defects of random construction.

Here is the case for and against the mongrel:

FOR

Since an estimated two out of every five mongrel puppies die within the first few weeks—for lack of the care lavished by humans on purebred dogs—the survivors are exceptionally strong and clever. Faults produced by inbreeding, such as nervousness, are not present in mongrels as often as in purebreds because the recessive genes do not come together as often. Many mongrels inherit useful hunting and protecting instincts from purebred parents. Often they have the best qualities of each parent. Although they may not be as good at any one task as a dog bred for it, the mongrel tends to be a better all-rounder, a dog for all purposes. The mongrel is alert, easily trained and friendly—unless taught to be otherwise.

AGAINST

Since the mongrel costs little or nothing, it is little valued by his owners, ill-treated, ill-fed and ill-supervised. It is the mongrel that spreads rabies and attacks domestic animals, giving all dogs a bad name. The mongrel may have been the toughest of its litter, in order to have survived, but it is not necessarily the best in terms of intelligence or disposition. A mongrel costs as much as a pedigree dog to feed and maintain. When the owner mates the dog, he is unsure what the offspring will be like—even in size—and usually unable to sell the puppies for very much. In general, acquiring a mongrel dog is like buying Brand X: Product reliability is not assured.

ILLUSTRATION BY BOB GALE

How to Say Bow-Wow in:

Chinese	Wung-Wung
Czech	Haf-Haf
Dutch	Waf-Waf
Finnish	Hau-Hau
French	Woa-Woa
German	Wau-Wau
Hebrew	Hav-Hav
Icelandic	Voff-Voff
Portuguese	Au-Au
Russian	Gav-Gav
Spanish	Jau-Jau

REDBONE
Height: 21-26 inches
Weight: 65-70 pounds

These solid reds track with alacrity and work well in the water. They are slightly taller at the shoulders than the hips. The medium-to-short coat is smooth and hard.

TREEING WALKER
Height: 25-35 inches
Weight: 60-70 pounds

Developed from the Walker Hound, the Treeing Walker, most experts agree, is the best of the

night hunters. Whereas the Walker is supreme as a fox hunter, the treeing variety is a coon specialist. The most desirable color is a white background with black and tan markings. The coat is smooth, fine textured, glossy and dense.

PLOTT
Height: 23-24 inches
Weight: 50-60 pounds

An all-purpose hound (although somewhat on the slow side), the aggressive Plott is particularly good on wild boar, bear, mountain lion and smaller game. It is the best fighter of the hounds. The short-haired, shiny coat is fairly thick and is dark-brown brindle. Some also have black saddles.

A GALLERY OF BREEDS

The chart on the following pages describes each of the 122 pure breeds recognized by the American Kennel Club. The breeds are arranged according to the groups in which they are normally listed in dog show catalogs. The chart also includes the eight breeds admitted to the Miscellaneous Class, the first step on the way to full recognition. Members of the class may compete at obedience trials but may not compete for championship points at conformation shows.

The popularity rank of each breed is based upon the number of dogs registered with the AKC during 1976. The Miscellaneous Class is not included in the rankings. For all dogs, the height measurements are from the withers, the highest point of the shoulders, to the ground. A guide to coat-color terms is on page 107.

SPORTING GROUP

POINTER
Origin: Europe. Developed in England around 1650. Most likely ancestors: Foxhound, Greyhound, Bloodhound and "Setting Spaniel." Formerly used to locate hares for Greyhound coursing, now to "stand" for shooters.

Height: Males 25-28 inches
Females 23-26 inches
Weight: Males 55-75 pounds
Females 45-65 pounds
Color: Liver; lemon; black; orange; any of these in combination with white
Popularity Rank: 84

GERMAN SHORTHAIRED POINTER
Origin: Germany. First recorded about 1860. Bred from German Bird Dog, various local scent dogs and English Pointers.

Height: Males 23-25 inches
Females 21-23 inches
Weight: Males 55-70 pounds
Females 45-60 pounds
Color: Liver; liver and white; liver roan
Popularity Rank: 25

GERMAN WIREHAIRED POINTER
Origin: Germany. Breed recognized around 1870. Resulted from crossing Pointer, Foxhound and Poodle stock. Retrieves as well as points. Coat is water- and brush-resistant. Imported to United States in 1920.

Height: Males 24-26 inches
Females smaller but not under 22 inches
Weight: Males 60-75 pounds
Females 50-60 pounds
Color: Liver and white spotted or ticked; solid liver; roan
Popularity Rank: 64

CHESAPEAKE BAY RETRIEVER
Origin: United States. Breed founded by Retriever pair from England shipwrecked in 1807 off Maryland coast and crossed with local Retrievers, probably Flat-coated and Curly-coated. Used for duck retrieving in icy waters.

Height: Males 23-26 inches
Females 21-24 inches
Weight: Males 65-75 pounds
Females 55-65 pounds
Color: Dark brown to faded tan or straw
Popularity Rank: 46

CURLY-COATED RETRIEVER
Origin: England. One of the oldest Retriever breeds, first exhibited in 1860. Probably descended from 16th century English Water Spaniel, retrieving Setters and others.

Height: 23½ inches average
Weight: About 65 pounds
Color: Black or liver
Popularity Rank: 120

FLAT-COATED RETRIEVER
Origin: England. "Wyndham," the first dog, exhibited in 1860, probably result of crossing Labrador Retriever, Newfoundland, Gordon Setter and Irish Setter.

Height: 23 inches average
Weight: 60-70 pounds
Color: Black; liver
Popularity Rank: 106

SPORTING GROUP

GOLDEN RETRIEVER
Origin: Scotland. Developed in 19th century from yellow Wavy-coated Retriever and Tweed Water Spaniel, crossed to Irish Setter, Bloodhound and Labrador. Recognized as separate breed in Britain in 1913.

Height: Males 23-24 inches
Females 21½- 22½ inches
Weight: Males 65-75 pounds
Females 60-70 pounds
Color: Golden (straw to red)
Popularity Rank: 10

LABRADOR RETRIEVER
Origin: Newfoundland. Imported to England in early 20th century and crossed with other Retrievers. Recognized as a separate breed in 1903.

Height: Males 22½-24½ inches
Females 21½-23½ inches
Weight: Males 60-75 pounds
Females 55-70 pounds
Color: Black; yellow; chocolate
Popularity Rank: 7

ENGLISH SETTER
Origin: England. Used for about 400 years. Probably produced by crossing Spanish Pointer, Water Spaniel and Springer Spaniel.

Height: Males about 25 inches
Females about 24 inches
Weight: Males 60-70 pounds
Females 50-60 pounds
Color: White; black, white and tan; black and white; blue belton; lemon and white; lemon belton; orange and white; orange belton; liver and white; liver belton
Popularity Rank: 50

GORDON SETTER
Origin: Scotland. Known since about 1620. Named for Duke of Gordon, who bred them as gun dogs in late 18th century.

Height: Males 24-27 inches
Females 23-26 inches
Weight: Males 55-80 pounds
Females 45-70 pounds
Color: Black with tan markings
Popularity Rank: 58

IRISH SETTER
Origin: Possilbly result of crossing English and Gordon Setter, Pointer and Spaniels. Known since 18th century in red-and-white coloration; solid red bred in 19th century. Imported to United States for hunting grouse, quail and other birds.

Height: Males about 27 inches
Females about 25 inches
Weight: Males about 70 pounds
Females about 60 pounds
Color: Mahogany or chestnut red
Popularity Rank: 4

AMERICAN WATER SPANIEL
Origin: United States. Bred in Midwest, probably from Irish and English Water Spaniels and Curly-Coated Retrievers. "Springs" game and retrieves from water. Recognized as a breed in 1940.

Height: 15-18 inches
Weight: Males 28-45 pounds
Females 25-40 pounds
Color: Liver or chocolate
Popularity Rank: 90

SPORTING GROUP

BRITTANY SPANIEL
Origin: France. A traditional breed, lacking tails since 19th century. Breed reconstituted in 20th, partly through crosses with Pointers. Imported to United States in 1931.

Height: 17½-20½ inches
Weight: 30-40 pounds
Color: Orange and white; liver and white
Popularity Rank: 17

CLUMBER SPANIEL
Origin: England. Probably resulted from crossing Spaniel stock with the Basset Hound. Named for Clumber Park, estate of Duke of Newcastle, where it was bred. Shown in England since 1859 and registered in United States since 1883.

Height: 16-19 inches
Weight: Males 55-65 pounds
Females 35-50 pounds
Color: White and lemon; white and orange
Popularity Rank: 114

COCKER SPANIEL
Origin: England. Considered the smallest of the sporting dogs. Once known as the "Cocking Spaniel" for its adeptness at hunting woodcock. Flushes game birds and retrieves. Exhibited since 1880s in United States.

Height: Males about 15 inches
Females about 14 inches
Weight: Males about 27 pounds
Females about 25 pounds
Color Black; parti-color; ascob
Popularity Rank: 5

ENGLISH COCKER SPANIEL
Origin: England. Recognized as distinct from American Cocker Spaniel in 1946. Larger than the American breed.

Height: Males 16-17 inches
Females 15-16 inches
Weight: Males 28-34 pounds
Females 26-32 pounds
Color: Parti-color; solid colors; roan
Popularity Rank: 66

ENGLISH SPRINGER SPANIEL
Origin: England. Named for its hunting technique: flushing game by springing on brush. Recognized as a breed in England in 1902. Began appearing at field trials in United States after 1924.

Height: Males about 20 inches
Females about 19 inches
Weight: Males 49-55 pounds
Females 44-50 pounds
Color: Liver and white; black and white; tri-color
Popularity Rank: 20

FIELD SPANIEL
Origin: England. Modern breed heavily influenced by Cocker and Sussex Spaniel crosses. Imported to United States in 1880s.

Height: About 18 inches
Weight: About 35-50 pounds
Color: Black; liver; mahogany; roan
Popularity Rank: 117

SPORTING GROUP

IRISH WATER SPANIEL
Origin: Ireland. Developed from traditional breeds and first exhibited in 1859. Used for retrieving ducks. Distinctive characteristics: curly topknot and rat tail. Tallest of the Spaniels.

Height: Males 22-24 inches Females 21-23 inches
Weight: Males 55-65 pounds Females 45-58 pounds
Color: Liver
Popularity Rank: 111

SUSSEX SPANIEL
Origin: England. Shown at least since 1862. Used for rough shooting on foot. Works slowly but has keen nose and "gives tongue" when it picks up the scent.

Height: About 15 inches
Weight: 35-45 pounds
Color: Golden liver
Popularity Rank: 121

WELSH SPRINGER SPANIEL
Origin: Wales. Known to hunters for several hundred years. Able to withstand extremes of temperature. Also called the "Starter."

Height: About 17 inches
Weight: About 40 pounds
Color: Red and white
Popularity Rank: 107

VIZSLA
Origin: Hungary. Bred since at least the tenth century. Almost extinct by end of World War I. Used for pointing and retrieving.

Height: Males 22-24 inches Females 21-23 inches
Weight: About 50 pounds
Color: Rusty gold
Popularity Rank: 49

WEIMARANER
Origin: Germany. Produced in early 19th century for big-game hunting. Ownership formerly restricted to members of an exclusive breed club. Imported to United States in 1929.

Height: Males 25-27 inches Females 23-25 inches
Weight: Males 60-70 pounds Females 55-60 pounds
Color: Gray
Popularity Rank: 39

WIREHAIRED POINTING GRIFFON
Origin: Holland. Developed in 1870s with coat adapted to swamp-hunting. First shown in England in 1888. Imported to United States around turn of the century.

Height: Males 21½-23½ inches
Females 19½-21½ inches
Weight: Males About 60 pounds
Females about 50 pounds
Color: Chestnut; gray and chestnut
Popularity Rank: 105

HOUND GROUP

AFGHAN HOUND

Origin: Sinai peninsula. Papyrus from 3,000-4,000 B.C. calls it "monkey-faced hound." Later appeared in Afghanistan, where it was a mountain hunter, enduring great extremes of temperature.

Height: Males 27 inches
Females 25 inches
Weight: Males about 60 pounds
Females about 50 pounds
Color: All colors
Popularity Rank: 30

BASENJI

Origin: Central Africa. Presented to the ancient Pharaohs as a gift. Rediscovered at end of 19th century. Barkless but "yodels."

Height: Males 17 inches
Females 16 inches
Weight: Males about 24 pounds
Females about 22 pounds
Color: Chestnut red; black; black and tan
Popularity Rank: 51

BASSET HOUND

Origin: France. Descendant of the old French Bloodhound and the St. Hubert hound. Used as a slow trailer of deer and small game and for flushing pheasant. Short legs allow it to work in dense brush and keep its nose, rated second only to Bloodhounds', close to the ground. Popularized in England in late 19th century.

Height: 15 inches maximum
Weight: 50 pounds average
Color: Any recognized hound color; commonly brown and white or red and white
Popularity Rank: 24

BEAGLE

Origin: England. Ancestors were scent hunters of pre-Roman era. From time of Elizabeth I, gentry used packs of Beagles to hunt hares and later foxes. Imported to United States—along with hares—to transplant the sport.

Height: Two varieties:
1) Maximum of 13 inches
2) More than 13 inches but not more than 15 inches
Weight: 13 inch variety: 15-18 pounds
15 inch variety: 18-24 pounds
Color: Tri-color most common
Popularity Rank: 6

BLACK AND TAN COONHOUND

Origin: United States. A scent hunter of raccoon probably descended from 11th century English Talbot Hound with Bloodhound and Foxhound crosses.

Height: Males 25-27 inches
Females 23-25 inches
Weight: 50-80 pounds
Color: Black and tan
Popularity Rank: 87

BLOODHOUND

Origin: Mediterranean countries. Praised by Claudius Aelianus in third century in **Historia Animalium** as a scent hunter. Modern development in England and United States, where often used to track fugitives and lost persons.

Height: Males 25-27 inches
Females 23-25 inches
Weight: Males 90-110 pounds
Females 80-100 pounds
Color: Black and tan; red and tan; tawny
Popularity Rank: 55

HOUND GROUP

BORZOI

Origin: Russia. Bred in 17th century from Arabian Greyhounds and Collie-type stock to produce coursing dog capable of withstanding Russian winters.

Height: Males 28 inches minimum
Females 26 inches minimum
Weight: Males 75-105 pounds
Females 55-90 pounds
Color: Typically white with black or tan
Popularity Rank: 52

DACHSHUND

Origin: Germany. Sausage-shaped dogs hunting badger appear in illustrations as early as 15th century. In World War I era, name temporarily Americanized to Badger Dog.
Height: Standard: About 9½ inches
Miniature: About 5 inches
Weight: Standard: 18-30 pounds
Miniature: Under 10 pounds
Color: Smooth and Long-haired varieties: Red; black and tan; chocolate and tan; dappled
Wirehaired variety: Wild boar most common
Popularity Rank: 8

AMERICAN FOXHOUND

Origin: United States. Developed from various hounds imported from Europe, some as early as De Soto's expedition to the Mississippi. Used for hunting in packs.

Height: Males 22-25 inches
Females 21-24 inches
Weight: Males about 60 pounds
Females about 50 pounds
Color: Typically tri-color or tan and white
Popularity Rank: 112

ENGLISH FOXHOUND

Origin: England. Mentioned in stud records kept by English Masters of Fox-hounds Association before 1800. Heavier than American Foxhound.

Height: Males about 25 inches
Females about 23 inches
Weight: 70-80 pounds
Color: Typically tri-color
Popularity Rank: 122

GREYHOUND

Origin: Egypt. Known since at least ninth century in England, where it was later bred for coursing and racing.

Height: About 28-32 inches
Weight: Males 65-70 pounds
Females 60-65 pounds
Color: Any color
Popularity Rank: 104

HARRIER

Origin: England. Used for hare hunting by the non-elite, who followed the packs on foot. May have been introduced after the Conquest by the Normans. Probably related to the Foxhound.

Height: About 19-21 inches
Weight: About 40-50 pounds
Color: Tri-color
Popularity Rank: 119

HOUND GROUP

IRISH WOLFHOUND
Origin: Ireland. Mentioned in ancient Irish manuscripts and used for centuries to hunt wolf and large elk. Breed reconstituted in 19th century to restore its combination of power and speed.

Height: Males 32 inches minimum
Females 30 inches minimum
Weight: Males about 160 pounds
Females about 120 pounds
Color: Gray; brindle; red; black; white; fawn
Popularity Rank: 56

NORWEGIAN ELKHOUND
Origin: Norway. Remains found in Viking graves. Used traditionally for hunting large game, including elk and bear. First shown in 1877, when a number of local Norwegian varieties began to be merged into a standard breed.

Height: Males 20½ inches
Females 19½ inches
Weight: Males about 55 pounds
Females about 48 pounds
Color: Gray and black
Popularity Rank: 32

OTTER HOUND
Origin: England. Known since about 1200 but most fully developed in 19th century, when hunting of otter with dog packs was popular. First imported to the United States about 1900.

Height: Males 24-27 inches
Females 22-26 inches
Weight: Males 75-115 pounds
Females 65-100 pounds
Color: Usually grizzle or sandy with black and tan spots
Popularity Rank: 115

RHODESIAN RIDGEBACK
Origin: South Africa. Developed by Boers, who crossed European breeds with native dogs that had a "ridge" on the back formed by hairs growing forward. Used as guard dog and for hunting lion and other game. First introduced into United States in 1950.

Height: Males 25-27 inches
Females 24-26 inches
Weight: Males about 85 pounds
Females about 65 pounds
Color: Wheaten
Popularity Rank: 70

SALUKI
Origin: Middle East. Known since ancient times for its speed and kept, along with hawk, for hunting gazelle and antelope. Brought to England in 19th century, where used for coursing and racing.

Height: Males 23-28 inches
Females smaller
Weight: 40-60 pounds
Color: White; cream; fawn; golden; red; grizzle and tan; tri-color; black and tan
Popularity Rank: 73

SCOTTISH DEERHOUND
Origin: Scotland. Legendary hunting companion of the Highland clan chieftains. Known since the 16th century, breed was reconstituted in the 19th. Used in the United States for hunting coyote and wolves.

Height: Males 30 inches minimum
Females 28 inches minimum
Weight: Males 85-110 pounds
Females 75-95 pounds
Color: Gray
Popularity Rank: 102

| **HOUND GROUP** | **WORKING GROUP** | |

WHIPPET
Origin: England. Developed in 19th century from Greyhounds and various Terriers. Used for coursing and racing, whence the nickname, "the poor man's race horse."

Height: Males 19-22 inches
Females 18-21 inches
Weight: 25-30 pounds
Color: Any color
Popularity Rank: 63

AKITA
Origin: Japan. Hunting breed developed in the 17th century. Once owned exclusively by nobles and the Imperial family. Care of Akita and manner of addressing ritually prescribed.

Height: Males 26-28 inches
Females 24-26 inches
Weight: Males about 85-100 pounds
Females about 75-85 pounds
Color: Any color
Popularity Rank: 60

ALASKAN MALAMUTE
Origin: Alaska. A sled dog used for centuries as basic transport in northwest Alaska. Admired by Russian and English explorers for its endurance and affectionate nature.

Height: Males about 25 inches
Females about 23 inches
Weight: Males about 85 pounds
Females about 75 pounds
Color: Light gray to black with white markings; white
Popularity Rank: 31

BEARDED COLLIE
Origin: Scotland. A traditional sheep and cattle dog from the Scottish-English border country. Saved from extinction by resurgence of interest in recent years. Possibly an ancestor of Old English Sheepdog. Joined Working Dog Group in 1977, becoming the 122nd breed.

Height: 20-22 inches
Weight: 40 pounds
Color: Black; gray; brown with white markings
Popularity Rank: 65

BELGIAN MALINOIS
Origin: Belgium. Outgrowth of traditional herding stock. Emerged in late 19th century. Distinguished from Belgian Sheepdog and Belgian Tervuren by its short coat.

Height: Males 24-26 inches
Females 22-24 inches
Weight: Males 65-75 pounds
Females 55-65 pounds
Color: Fawn to mahogany overlaid with black
Popularity Rank: 118

BELGIAN SHEEPDOG
Origin: Belgium. Bred in late 19th century in village of Groenendael from traditional sheep herding dogs. Distinguishing characteristic is long black coat. Imported to United States in early 20th century for police work.

Height: Males 24-26 inches
Females 22-24 inches
Weight: Males 65-75 pounds
Females 55-65 pounds
Color: Black
Popularity Rank: 79

WORKING GROUP

BELGIAN TERVUREN
Origin: Belgium. Similar to Belgian Sheepdog except that it was bred in town of Tervuren and has different coat color. Imported into United States in 1940s and registered as a breed separate from the Belgian Sheepdog in 1959.

Height: Males 24-26 inches Females 22-24 inches
Weight: Males 65-75 pounds Females 55-65 pounds
Color: Fawn to mahogany with black overlay
Popularity Rank: 85

BERNESE MOUNTAIN DOG
Origin: Switzerland. Brought to Switzerland by the Romans. Traditionally used to pull weaver's carts to market in the Berne Canton. Breed reconstituted around 1900 and became popular house pet among Swiss.

Height: Males 23-27½ inches
Females 21-26 inches
Weight: Males 80-105 pounds
Females 75-80 pounds
Color: Black with brown and white
Popularity Rank: 91

BOUVIER DES FLANDRES
Origin: Belgium. A traditional cattle-herding dog, first shown in 1910, from the region of Flanders. Breed almost wiped out by fighting there in World War I.

Height: Males 23½-27½ inches
Females 22¾ inches minimum
Weight: Males 90-110 pounds
Females 80-95 pounds
Color: Fawn to black; pepper and salt; gray and brindle
Popularity Rank: 62

BOXER
Origin: Germany. Developed from Bulldog and Terrier strains in the 19th century. Bred for fighting—name derives from use of front paws in combat—and bull-baiting, then for police work. First registered in United States in 1904.

Height: Males 22½-25 inches
Females 21-23½ inches
Weight: Males about 70 pounds
Females about 60 pounds
Color: Brindle; fawn (light tan to deep red)
Popularity Rank: 26

BRIARD
Origin: France. Traditional sheepdog—mentioned in 12th-century records–from region of Brie, used to guard flocks against wolves. Now found throughout France as herding and guard dog. Breed standardized around 1900.

Height: Males 23-27 inches
Females 22-25½ inches
Weight: Males 80-90 pounds
Females 70-80 pounds
Color: Black: gray; tawny; combinations of any two of these colors
Popularity Rank: 99

BULLMASTIFF
Origin: England. Bred in late 19th century from Bulldogs and Mastiffs to provide large, aggressive dogs for estate gamekeepers warding off poachers. Recognized in England as a purebred in 1924, in United States in 1933.

Height: Males 25-27 inches
Females 24-26 inches
Weight: Males 110-130 pounds
Females 100-120 pounds
Color: Red; fawn; brindle
Popularity Rank: 75

WORKING GROUP

COLLIE
Origin: Britain. Developed from a traditional sheep herding dog and bred in two varieties—Rough (long-haired) and Smooth (short-haired). Popularized by Queen Victoria in 19th century and known widely in United States by the 1880s.

Height: Males 24-26 inches
Females 22-24 inches
Weight: Males 60-75 pounds
Females 50-65 pounds
Color: Sable and white; tri-color; blue merle and white
Popularity Rank: 11

DOBERMAN PINSCHER
Origin: Germany. Produced before 1900 from sheep dog stock mixed with Rottweilers, Terriers and others. Used for guarding, policework and military duty. Named after the founding breeder, Louis Dobermann.

Height: Males 26-28 inches
Females 24-26 inches
Weight: Males 70-75 pounds
Females 60-65 pounds
Color: Black and tan; red; blue; Isabella
Popularity Rank: 3

GERMAN SHEPHERD
Origin: Germany. Developed from traditional farm dogs under the supervision of the parent club, the Verein für Deutsche Schäferhunde, formed in 1899. Used in many countries after World War I for guarding, law enforcement and guiding because of its intelligence and amenability to training.

Height: Males 24-26 inches
Females 22-24 inches
Weight: Males 80-85 pounds
Females 65-70 pounds
Color: Black and tan; gray-sable; golden-sable
Popularity Rank: 2

GIANT SCHNAUZER
Origin: Germany. Developed in Bavaria from the Standard Schnauzer, probably through crossings with traditional sheep and cattle dogs and with the Great Dane. Used for cattle driving. Almost unknown outside its native region until early 20th century, when it began being used for police work.

Height: Males 25½-27½ inches
Females 23½-25½ inches
Weight: 70-95 pounds
Color: Black; pepper and salt
Popularity Rank: 78

GREAT DANE
Origin: Germany. Known in German as the *Deutsche Dogge*, it was bred for 400 years as a boar hound. Possibly a descendant of the English Mastiff and the Irish Wolfhound.

Height: Males 30 inches minimum
Females 28 inches minimum
Weight: Males 135-160 pounds
Females 120-135 pounds
Color: Brindle; fawn; blue; black; harlequin
Popularity Rank: 18

GREAT PYRENEES
Origin: France. Its fossil remains in Europe date from 1,000 B.C. Guarded flocks in Pyrenean Mountains from wolves, bears and other predators. Also used by smugglers to carry contraband across the French-Spanish border. Bred in the United States since 1933.

Height: Males 27-32 inches
Females 25-29 inches
Weight: Males 100-125 pounds
Females 90-115 pounds
Color: White
Popularity Rank: 53

WORKING GROUP

KOMONDOR
Origin: Hungary. Served for about 1,000 years as a guard dog for herds and flocks, although recorded breeding began only about a century ago. Heavy, corded coat developed as a protection against predators.

Height: Males 25 inches minimum
Females 23½ inches minimum
Weight: Males about 95 pounds
Females about 80 pounds
Color: White
Popularity Rank: 109

KUVASZ
Origin: Hungary. Derived from Tibetan stock and bred as hunting dogs by Hungarian nobles from 15th century. Later used for herding and guarding.

Height: Males 28-30 inches
Females 26-28 inches
Weight: Males 100-115 pounds
Females 70-90 pounds
Color: White
Popularity Rank: 102

MASTIFF
Origin: England. Fought alongside ancient Britons against Roman invaders. Kept by Anglo-Saxon peasants for control of wolves. Also used for pit combats against bull and bears, for hunting large game and for guard duty.

Height: Males 30 inches minimum
Females 27½ inches minimum
Weight: Males about 200 pounds
Females about 170 pounds
Color: Apricot; fawn; brindle
Popularity Rank: 71

NEWFOUNDLAND
Origin: Newfoundland. Developed by fishermen from European breeds, possibly the Great Pyrenees. At home in frigid waters. Served as beast of burden. Most modern strains produced in England.

Height: Males about 28 inches
Females about 26 inches
Weight: Males about 160 pounds
Females about 120 pounds
Color: Black; bronze; white and black (Landseer type); gray
Popularity Rank: 47

OLD ENGLISH SHEEPDOG
Origin: England. Bred in Cornwall, Devon and Somerset as cattle and sheep dogs, probably at least as early as 18th century. Bearded Collie may have been an ancestor.

Height: Males 22½ inches minimum
Females smaller
Weight: Males about 125 pounds
Females about 75 pounds
Color: Gray; grizzle; blue; blue merle with or without white markings
Popularity Rank: 22

PULI
Origin: Hungary. Possibly derived from the Tibetan Terrier. Used for sheep driving and guarding along with the other Hungarian working dogs, the Komondor and the Kuvasz.

Height: Males about 17 inches
Females about 16 inches
Weight: About 25-30 pounds
Color: Black; gray; white
Popularity Rank: 77

WORKING GROUP

ROTTWEILER
Origin: Germany. Named after town of Rottweil in the region of Württemberg, where it was brought by Romans. Used as a cattle and cart dog. Breed reconstituted after 1910 and employed in police work.

Height: Males 23¾-27 inches
Females 21¾-25¾ inches
Weight: Males 110-130 pounds
Females 85-100 pounds
Color: Black with tan; mahogany brown
Popularity Rank: 57

SAINT BERNARD
Origin: Switzerland. Probably descended from Molossus breed introduced to Europe from Asia by the Romans. Name taken from the Great St. Bernard Pass in Alps, where snow rescue missions have been performed since 17th century.

Height: Males 27½ inches minimum
Females 25½ inches minimum
Weight: Males about 200 pounds
Females about 145 pounds
Color: Red and white; brown and yellow
Popularity Rank: 19

SAMOYED
Origin: Siberia. Used by nomads for reindeer herding and pulling sleds. Accompanied early Arctic explorers on expeditions to both poles.

Height: Males 21-23½ inches
Females 19-21 inches
Weight: Males 55-75 pounds
Females 45-55 pounds
Color: White; biscuit; cream
Popularity Rank: 29

SHETLAND SHEEPDOG
Origin: Shetland Islands. Derived from Collies brought to the islands from Scotland and crossed with Spaniels and dogs from Iceland.

Height: 13-16 inches
Weight: 20-30 pounds
Color: Black; blue merle; sable with white
Popularity Rank: 12

SIBERIAN HUSKY
Origin: Siberia. Kept as sled dogs by Chukchi nomads. Imported to Alaska after 1910 and used for sled racing and Arctic rescue work.

Height: Males 21-23½ inches
Females 20-22 inches
Weight: Males 45-60 pounds
Females 35-50 pounds
Color: Silver gray; red; black; white; tan and black
Popularity Rank: 14

STANDARD SCHNAUZER
Origin: Germany. Bred from Poodle, Spitz and Pinscher stock to serve as a rat catcher. First exhibited as Wirehaired Pinschers in 1879. Breed renamed for "Schnauzer," the first prize-winner.

Height: Males 18½-19½ inches
Females 17½-18½ inches
Weight: Males 40-50 pounds
Females 30-40 pounds
Color: Pepper and salt; black
Popularity Rank: 72

WORKING GROUP

**CARDIGAN
WELSH CORGI**
Origin: Wales. Traditional herding dogs whose function was to nip at heels of cattle to keep them spread over pasture land in Cardiganshire.

Height: 10-12 inches
Weight: Males about 33 pounds
Females about 28 pounds
Color: Red; sable; brindle; black; tri-color; blue merle
Popularity Rank: 88

**PEMBROKE
WELSH CORGI**
Origin: Wales. Cattle dogs from Pembrokeshire. Differ from Cardigan Welsh Corgi in having shorter body and finer coat texture. Tail is docked.

Height: 10-12 inches
Weight: Males 30 pounds
Females 28 pounds
Color: Red; sable; fawn; black and tan
Popularity Rank: 48

TERRIER GROUP

AIREDALE TERRIER
Origin: England. Developed in Yorkshire for hunting badger, weasel and other small game. Modern Airedale resulted from cross between now extinct black-and-tan breed and the Otter Hound.

Height: Males about 23 inches
Females slightly smaller
Weight: Males 50-60 pounds
Females 45-55 pounds
Color: Black with tan; grizzle with tan
Popularity Rank: 35

AMERICAN STAFFORDSHIRE TERRIER
Origin: England. Produced by crossing Bulldog and Terrier stock. Used for dog fighting in "the pit." Imported after 1870 to the United States, where also known as Pit Bull Terrier.

Height: Males 18-19 inches
Females 17-18 inches
Weight: Males 55-70 pounds
Females 40-55 pounds
Color: Any color. (These colors are not encouraged: more than 80 percent white; black and tan; liver)
Popularity Rank: 74

AUSTRALIAN TERRIER
Origin: Australia. First exhibited in 1885 under the name of Australian Rough. Possibly descended from mixing of Cairn, Dandie Dinmont, Irish, Yorkshire ad Skye Terriers. Used for hunting small game, tending sheep and guarding.

Height: About 10 inches
Weight: 12-14 pounds
Color: Blue-black and tan; red
Popularity Rank: 67

BEDLINGTON TERRIER
Origin: England. Developed at Bedlington in County of Northumberland in 19th century as a badger hunter.

Height: Males 16½ inches
Females 15½ inches
Weight: 17-23 pounds
Color: Blue; sandy; liver; either of the three colors with tan
Popularity Rank: 86

BORDER TERRIER
Origin: Great Britain. Bred from native Terriers in the region of the Cheviot Hills, on the border between England and Scotland, to protect domestic animals from foxes. Intended to have legs long enough to keep up with a horse yet short enough to follow a fox "gone to ground."

Height: Males 13-15½ inches
Females 11½-14 inches
Weight: Males 13-15½ pounds
Females 11½-14 pounds
Color: Red; grizzle and tan; blue and tan; wheaten
Popularity Rank: 108

BULL TERRIER
Origin: England. Product of a cross between Bulldog and white English Terrier (now extinct) with some Pointer stock. Colored variety developed around 1835, white variety around 1860. Used for dog fighting.

Height: About 18½ inches
Weight: 35-55 pounds
Color: White variety: White Colored variety: Brindle typical
Popularity Rank: 68

TERRIER GROUP

CAIRN TERRIER

Origin: Scotland. Developed from the traditional working terrier on the Isle of Skye. Used for all-weather hunting of otters and foxes in rocky countryside.

Height: Males about 10 inches
Females about 9½ inches
Weight: Males about 14 pounds
Females about 13 pounds
Color: Any color except white
Popularity Rank: 38

DANDIE DINMONT TERRIER

Origin: Great Britain. Breed first recorded around 1700 in English-Scottish border country. Named after Dandie Dinmont, character in a Sir Walter Scott novel, who owned several. Used for otter and badger hunting.

Height: 8-11 inches
Weight: 18-24 pounds
Color: Pepper; mustard
Popularity Rank: 96

FOX TERRIER

Origin: England. An old breed consisting of two varieties, Smooth and Wire, that probably developed from different stock. Until recently the two varieties were widely interbred. Used to flush foxes hiding from the hound pack.

Height: Males 15½ inches maximum
Females smaller
Weight: Males about 18 pounds
Females about 16 pounds
Color: Predominantly white with colored patches
Popularity Rank: 44

IRISH TERRIER

Origin: Ireland. First shown in 1879. Used to hunt large and small game and retrieve in water. Served as messenger and guard dog in World War I.

Height: About 18 inches
Weight: Males about 27 pounds
Females about 25 pounds
Color: Red; wheaten
Popularity Rank: 94

KERRY BLUE TERRIER

Origin: Ireland. Native to County Kerry. Used for hunting, retrieving and herding sheep and cattle. Became well-known in United States in 1920s.

Height: Males about 18½ inches
Females slightly smaller
Weight: Males 33-40 pounds
Female slightly less
Color: Blue-gray
Popularity Rank: 76

LAKELAND TERRIER

Origin: England. Developed in Cumberland County in the English Lake District for hunting, together with hounds, foxes that threatened livestock. Known for persistent pursuit of quarry in underground burrows.

Height: Males about 14½ inches
Females slightly smaller
Weight: About 17 pounds
Color: Blue; black; blue and tan; black and tan; red; red grizzle; grizzle and tan
Popularity Rank: 101

TERRIER GROUP

MANCHESTER TERRIER

Origin: England. Developed around the city of Manchester for rat hunting and coursing by crossing native Terrier stock with Whippet, Greyhound or Italian Greyhound. Since 1959 registered as same breed as Toy Manchester Terrier although latter shown in Toy Group.

Height: Standard: About 17 inches
Toy: 10-12 inches
Weight: Standard: 12-22 pounds
Toy: 12 pounds maximum
Color: Black and tan
Popularity Rank: 81

MINIATURE SCHNAUZER

Origin: Germany. Resulted from crossing Standard Schnauzer with Affenpinscher. A separate breed at least since 1899. Used for rat catching.

Height: About 13½ inches
Weight: Males about 17 pounds
Females about 14 pounds
Color: Salt and pepper; black and silver; black
Popularity Rank: 9

NORWICH TERRIER

Origin: England. Popular among Cambridge University undergraduates in 1880s. Imported to the United States after World War I. Used for fox and rabbit hunting.

Height: About 10 inches
Weight: 11-12 pounds
Color: Red; wheaten; black, tan and grizzle
Popularity Rank: 93

SCOTTISH TERRIER

Origin: Scotland. An ancient breed, known as the "Scottie," first standardized round 1880. Imported to United States shortly afterward.

Height: About 10 inches
Weight: Males 19-22 pounds
Females 18-21 pounds
Color: Black; gray; sandy; wheaten
Popularity Rank: 34

SEALYHAM TERRIER

Origin: Wales. Named for estate where breed developed in latter 19th century as a badger, otter and fox hunter. First shown in United States in 1911.

Height: About 10½ inches
Weight: Males 23-24 pounds
Females slightly less
Color: All white; white with head markings
Popularity Rank: 110

SKYE TERRIER

Origin: Scotland. Native to Isle of Skye, where long coat developed as protection against animal bites. A popular pet of nobility in 16th century.

Height: Males about 10 inches
Females about 9½ inches
Weight: 23-30 pounds
Color: Black; blue; platinum; fawn; cream
Popularity Rank: 97

TERRIER GROUP

SOFT-COATED WHEATEN TERRIER
Origin: Ireland. Known for two centuries and considered a possible ancestor of the Kerry Blue Terrier. First imported to the United States in 1946 and registered as a breed in 1973.

Height: Males 18-19 inches
Females slightly smaller
Weight: Males 35-45 pounds
Females slightly less
Color: Wheaten
Popularity Rank: 80

STAFFORDSHIRE BULL TERRIER
Origin: England. Developed from a cross between Bulldog and Terrier stock in the early 19th century for the sport of dogfighting. Has appeared at shows in United States since 1975.

Height: 14-16 inches
Weight: Males 28-38 pounds
Females 24-34 pounds
Color: Red; fawn; white; black; blue; any of these colors with white; any shade of brindle with white
Popularity Rank: 92

WELSH TERRIER
Origin: Wales. Known previously as the Old English Terrier or Black-and-Tan Wirehaired Terrier. Developed for hunting otter, fox and badger. First shown and brought to United States in 1880s.

Height: Males about 15 inches
Females slightly smaller
Weight: About 20 pounds
Color: Black and tan; grizzle and tan
Popularity Rank: 69

WEST HIGHLAND WHITE TERRIER
Origin: Scotland. Bred for at least several hundred years. Formerly called the Roseneath Terrier and the Poltalloch Terrier, after places in Scotland where intensive breeding carried on.

Height: Males about 11 inches
Females about 10 inches
Weight: 15-18 pounds
Color: White
Popularity Rank: 42

TOY GROUP

AFFENPINSCHER
Origin: Germany. Known since at least 17th century. Sometimes called the "monkey dog." Recognized as a breed in the United States in 1936.

Height: 10¼ inches maximum
Weight: 7-8 pounds maximum
Color: Black; black and tan; red; gray
Popularity Rank: 113

BRUSSELS GRIFFON
Origin: Belgium. Developed from a cross between Affenpinscher and a common Belgian farm dog, the Stable Griffon. Later crossings with the Pug produced Smooth- as well as Rough-coated varieties. Used as rat catchers.

Height: About 8 inches
Weight: 12 pounds maximum
Color: Rough-coated variety: Red and black; black Smooth-coated variety: Red and black
Popularity Rank: 98

CHIHUAHUA
Origin: Mexico. Probably the descendant of dogs kept by the Toltecs and Aztecs, before advent of Spaniards, as pets and for religious ceremonies. Portraits of them preserved in ancient rock carvings. Modern breed, derived from specimens discovered about 1850, divided into Long-coated and Smooth-coated varieties.

Height: About 5 inches
Weight: 6 pounds maximum
Color: Any color
Popularity Rank: 21

ENGLISH TOY SPANIEL
Origin: England. Possibly derived from a breed imported from Far East and crossed with native Spaniels. Known since 16th century and popular as a royal pet.

Height: About 9½ inches
Weight: 9-12 pounds
Color: King Charles type: Black and tan
Ruby type: Red
Blenheim type: Red and white
Prince Charles type: White, black and tan
Popularity Rank: 116

ITALIAN GREYHOUND
Origin: Italy. A dwarfed version of the Greyhound. Known for 2,000 years and popular as a pet in ancient Rome. Modern breed developed in Britain in 19th century.

Height: 13-15 inches
Weight: 6-10 pounds
Color: Any color
Popularity Rank: 82

JAPANESE CHIN
Origin: China. Bred in Japan, probably from dog imported from China, by the nobility. First brought to West by Commodore Perry in mid-19th century. Also known as Japanese Spaniel.

Height: About 9 inches
Weight: About 7 pounds
Color: Black and white; red and white
Popularity Rank: 88

TOY GROUP

MALTESE
Origin: Malta. A Spaniel-type breed known on the island since ancient times. A favorite pet of the upper classes, some of whom carried the dog in their sleeves.

Height: About 5 inches
Weight: Under 7 pounds
Color: White
Popularity Rank: 41

MINIATURE PINSCHER
Origin: Germany. Known for several centuries but intensively bred only since end of 19th century. A scaled-down version of the Doberman Pinscher, often used as watchdog.

Height: 8-11 inches
Weight: 6-8 pounds
Color: Red; black with tan and red; brown with yellow or rust
Popularity Rank: 61

PAPILLON
Origin: Italy. Developed in France in 17th century, where breed was popular at court of Louis XIV. Formerly called the Dwarf Spaniel. Modern name (French for "butterfly") taken from wing-like set of the ears.

Height: 8-11 inches
Weight: 6-8 pounds
Color: White with patches of color
Popularity Rank: 83

PEKINGESE
Origin: China. Known since at least eighth century in the Imperial household, where it was considered sacred and sometimes referred to as the "lion dog." Discovered by British troops looting Peking palace and brought to West.

Height: About 8 inches
Weight: 14 pounds maximum
Color: Any color
Popularity Rank: 15

POMERANIAN
Origin: Germany. Probably bred down in size from Scandinavian sled and herding dogs. Shown in the United States since 1892.

Height: About 5-6 inches
Weight: 3-7 pounds
Color: Any color
Popularity Rank: 23

PUG
Origin: Probably China. Developed in England, where it was introduced by Dutch East India Company traders.

Height: About 13 inches
Weight: 14-18 pounds
Color: Fawn; black
Popularity Rank: 36

TOY GROUP*

SHIH TZU
Origin: China. Records of the breed date from seventh century. Favorite of Chinese royalty. Imported to England about 1930 and to United States after World War II.

Height: 9-10½ inches
Weight: 9-16 pounds
Color: Any color
Popularity Rank: 27

SILKY TERRIER
Origin: Australia. Resulted from a cross between a Yorkshire Terrier and an Australian Terrier. First shown in its native county in 1907. Intended as pet but also used for rat catching.

Height: 9-10 inches
Weight: 8-10 pounds
Color: Blue and tan
Popularity Rank: 45

YORKSHIRE TERRIER
Origin: England. A relative of the Skye Terrier, first shown in 1861. In late 19th century, popular as an upper-class pet. Brought to the United States about 1880.

Height: 6½-7½ inches
Weight: 7 pounds maximum
Color: Steel blue and tan
Popularity Rank: 16

*For Toy Manchester Terrier see page 99.
 For Toy Poodle see page 105.

NON-SPORTING GROUP

BICHON FRISE
Origin: Canary Islands. Decended from Water Spaniels brought to the Canaries by Spanish sailors, who referred to them as Tenerife Bichons. Re-imported to continent in 1300s by Italian sailors. Favored by French and Spanish nobility and portrayed by Goya and other painters.

Height: 8-12 inches
Weight: 10-15 pounds
Color: White; white with cream; white with apricot
Popularity Rank: 54

BOSTON TERRIER
Origin: United States. Founding father was "Hooper's Judge" of Boston, Massachusetts, the progeny of a Bulldog and an English Terrier. Line developed in 1870s and won official recognition in 1893.

Height: 14-15 inches
Weight: 25 pounds maximum
Color: Brindle with white; black with white
Popularity Rank: 28

BULLDOG
Origin: England. Bred for ferocity, rather than beauty, from the 13th century until 1835, when bullbaiting was banned in England. In modern times, a symbol of toughness for the British nation, Yale football teams.

Height: Males about 16 inches
Females about 14 inches
Weight: Males about 50 pounds
Females about 40 pounds
Color: Brindle (red preferred); white; fawn; piebald (parti-color)
Popularity Rank: 37

CHOW CHOW
Origin: China. Name derives from Pidgin English. Known since at least 150 B.C. Unique characteristic is a blue-black tongue, whence its Chinese name, the "black-mouthed dog." Possibly derived from combination of Tibetan and Siberian breeds. First brought to England in 18th century.

Height: 19-20 inches
Weight: 55-70 pounds
Color: Any clear color (red most popular)
Popularity Rank: 40

DALMATIAN
Origin: Named for Dalmatia, on the Adriatic Coast, now a part of Yugoslavia. Formerly a carriage dog, it became favorite mascot of hook-and-ladder companies when firemen still depended on real horse power.

Height: 19-23 inches
Weight: Males 55-65 pounds
Females 45-55 pounds
Color: White with black spots; white with liver spots
Popularity Rank: 33

FRENCH BULLDOG
Origin: France. Smaller than the English Bulldog, which undoubtedly provided a large part of its heredity. Bat ears are a distinctive feature. An influential sire of French Bulldogs in America, Ch. Nellcote Gamin, was imported in 1904.

Height: About 11½ inches
Weight: 28 pounds maximum
Color: Brindle; fawn; white and brindle; white
Popularity Rank: 100

NON-SPORTING GROUP

KEESHOND
Origin: Holland. Derived from Arctic stock and related to the Samoyed and the Pomeranian. Used traditionally as barge dogs on the Rhine. Named for "Kees," mascot of 18th-century Dutch political movement led by Kees de Gyselaer.

Height: Males 18 inches
Females 17 inches
Weight: Males about 40 pounds
Females about 35 pounds
Color: Gray and black
Popularity Rank: 43

SCHIPPERKE
Origin: Belgium. Bred from a much larger black sheepdog several hundred years ago. Before 1888, breed was called Spitske or Spits. Name later changed to Schipperke, Flemish for "little captain," because dogs commonly used to guard canal boats. Docked tail traced to 1690, when, according to legend, a shoemaker punitively chopped off a dog's tail, setting a new fashion.
Height: 12-14 inches
Weight: 18 pounds maximum
Color: Black
Popularity Rank: 59

LHASA APSO
Origin: Tibet. Bred as a watchdog in Lhasa, the seat of the Dalai Lama. Substantial coat evidently developed because of harsh climate.

Height: Males 10-11 inches
Females 9-10 inches
Weight: About 16 pounds
Color: Golden; sandy; honey; dark grizzle; slate; smoke; parti-color; black; white; brown
Popularity Rank: 13

TIBETAN TERRIER
Origin: Tibet. Considered bringers of luck for 2,000 years and associated with a Shangri-La myth because its native valley was cut off from outside world by an earthquake in 14th century. Reached the West from the "Lost Valley" as a result of dogs being given to travelers as good luck charms. Bred in India in 1920s and in England since 1937.

Height: 14-16 inches
Weight: 18-30 pounds
Color: Any color
Popularity Rank: 95

POODLE
Origin: Germany. English name taken from German **Pudel,** meaning a puddle dog or one that likes splashing in water. Related to Water Spaniels. Standard variety used traditionally as water retriever. Coat sheered

to improve swimming, but stylish clipping eventually won dog great popularity in France, whence it came to the United States. (At shows only English Saddle Clip or Continental Clip are allowed for dogs more than a year old.) Miniature Poodle and Toy Poodle are considered same breed as Standard Poodle, differing only in size. Toy is shown in Toy Group.

Height: Standard: Over 15 inches
Miniature: 11-15 inches
Toy: 10 inches maximum
Weight: Standard: 45-64 pounds
Miniature: 14-18 pounds
Toy: About 6 pounds
Color: Any solid color
Popularity Rank: 1

MISCELLANEOUS CLASS

AUSTRALIAN CATTLE DOG
Origin: Australia. Used for herding cattle on large ranches. Possibly related to the Australian wild dog (dingo), the Collie and the Kelpie. Also called the Blue Cattle Dog.

Height: About 18 inches
Weight: About 33 pounds
Color: Mottled blue with black and tan markings

AUSTRALIAN KELPIE
Origin: Australia. Sheep herding dog derived from the dingo and the Border Collie. Noted for sharp sight, hearing and scent. Also called the Barb.

Height: 17-20 inches
Weight: 25-30 pounds
Color: Black; black and tan; red; red and tan; fawn; brown; blue

BORDER COLLIE
Origin: Britain. A sheep herder's dog for at least 400 years. Distinctive characteristic: forelegs shorter than hind legs.

Height: 19-21 inches
Weight: 30-50 pounds
Color: Typically black with white markings; gray; blue merle

CAVALIER KING CHARLES SPANIEL
Origin: England. Essentially a return to the longer-headed form of the English Toy Spaniel as it existed in the 17th century. Resulted from a breeding program begun in 1926.

Height: 12-13 inches
Weight: 13-18 pounds
Color: Red; white with red markings; white, black and red; black and tan

IBIZAN HOUND
Origin: Spain. Named for Ibiza, one of the Balearic Islands. Possibly a descendant of the ancient Egyptian Greyhound. Noted for keen hearing and jumping ability.

Height: 22½-27½ inches
Weight: 42-52 pounds
Color: White; red; lion; white with red; white with lion

MINIATURE BULL TERRIER
Origin: England. A scaled-down model of the Bull Terrier. Retains muscularity and tenacity of the larger breed.

Height: 14 inches maximum
Weight: 20 pounds maximum
Color: White; brindle with patches

MISCELLANEOUS CLASS

SPINONI ITALIANI
Origin: Italy. Used for pointing and retrieving. Popular with hunters in Italy but quite rare in the United States.

Height: 23-26 inches
Weight: 50-75 pounds
Color: White with orange or liver markings

TIBETAN SPANIEL
Origin: Tibet. Noted for longevity, some living to 24 years. Considered so valuable in 18th century that they were sent as tribute to Chinese emperors. Imported to United States in 1966.

Height: 9-10 inches
Weight: 9-15 pounds
Color: Any color

Color Coding the Breeds

Breeders use a peculiar argot to describe coat colors. These are some of the more mysterious terms:

ASCOB — An acronym for "Any Solid Color Other than Black" (Cocker Spaniels only).

BELTON — A white background flecked with darker hairs, such as orange belton and blue belton (English Setters only).

BLUE MERLE — A mixture of blue, gray and black, producing a marbled effect.

BRINDLE — Black hairs evenly mixed with hairs of a lighter color, such as brown, gray or tan.

FAWN — Varies from brown to golden tan.

GRIZZLE — Iron or bluish-gray.

HARLEQUIN — White background with small patches (Great Danes only).

ISABELLA — Light straw color (Doberman Pinschers only).

LION — Buff-colored, like the king of the jungle.

LIVER — Dark reddish-brown.

PARTI-COLOR — Two or more colors.

RED — Varies from red to brown, including chestnut and dark mahogany.

ROAN — Mixture of colored and white hair, such as blue roan.

SABLE — Lacing of dark brown and black hairs.

TRI-COLOR — White, black and tan.

WILD BOAR — Gray with silvery highlights.

5

To Be a Champion, It Takes a Winning Way
SHOWING

Showing

Where the Competition is Dog-Beat-Dog

Those who witness a dog show or an obedience trial for the first time are often surprised by the enthusiasm, the intense crowd passion that it can evoke. Football or hockey fans, even in their more uninhibited moments, display no greater frenzy than the partisans of a Sealyham Terrier that is about to take Best in Show. As a participant sport, dog competitions may be more esoteric than bowling, but there seems to be some natural inclination for dog owners everywhere to test their animals against each other to settle the old argument: "My dog is better than your dog."

No one can be certain when the sport of dogs began, but credit for the "first" is usually given to a show held in Newcastle-on-Tyne, a city in the northeast of England, in 1859. Only Pointers and Setters competed. Six years later the first field trials were held, according to a quaint scoring system: "Nose, 40; pace and range, 30; temperament, 10; staunchness before, 10; behind, 10."

The sport remained at a modest level until 1873, when the Kennel Club held a four-day show at London's Crystal Palace—the Madison Square Garden of that era—for nearly 1,000 animals. In the next year, the first formal "Code of Rules for the Guidance of Dog Shows" was issued. By 1877 dog showing had also become popular in the United States; the initial West-

Westminster's first show displayed 35 breeds and offered two Scottish Deerhounds for sale at $50,000.

D.P. FOSTER'S "LION"

MR. JONES'S SIBERIAN BLOODHOUND "BRUNO."

Miss B. WEBB'S "REX" $1000.00

WAGNER'S "NELLIE"

"MUNGO"

THE REV. MR. MACDONNA, WITH HIS DOG "MUNGO."

ESQUIMAUX DOG

MR. JOHN E. T. GRAINGER'S SETTER "NELLY" AND HER PUPS, VALUED AT $5,000.

TWO-LEGGED DOG — PUG "REX." — THE ONLY ESQUIMAUX IN THE SHOW.

The First Westminster Had It All

The original Westminster Dog Show in 1877 saw some rather original entries, including a two-legged dog and a "Siberian Bloodhound" named Bruno. Queen Victoria contributed to the occasion by entering her Scottish Deerhounds.

minster Kennel Club show in New York included more than 35 breeds. The first American obedience trials were organized in 1933—by a Poodle owner who wanted to prove that the breed was not too sissified to do an intelligent day's work. Today dog competition is so popular that the American Kennel Club estimates that there are more than 1,700 authorized all-breed and "specialty" shows annually and more than 1,000 obedience trials.

Kennel Club in Texas to the Windward Hawaiian Dog Fanciers' Association—have carried the passion for dogs to remote places. Myriad specialty clubs devoted to a single breed and obedience clubs have sprung up. The Finger Lakes German Shorthaired Pointer Club in New York, the Multnomah Irish Setter Association in Oregon, the Enchanted Poodle Club in New Mexico, the Shreveport Collie Fanciers in Louisiana and the Upper Snake River Valley Dog

The number of entries in dog shows has risen dramatically in the last three decades, signifying a fundamental shift from a hobby of the monied elite to a popular pastime. Clubs dedicated to the sport of purebred dogs have proliferated. While prestige names like the Westminster or the International Kennel Club of Chicago still maintain their hegemony, smaller groups of devotees—from Maine's Penobscot Valley Kennel Club to the Heart of the Plains

Training Club in Idaho testify to the widespread devotion to purebred canines.

Degrees of Excellence

The Ph.D.s of the purebred dog world are the animals entitled to wear the initials "Ch." for champion. To attain that exalted degree, a dog must win 15 "points" in competition with others at shows recognized by the American Kennel Club. The number of points awarded in any show depends upon the breed and the number of dogs entered; the more dogs competing, the more points—up to a maximum of five. Among a champion's credits must be two wins at "majors," shows offering three or more points. Dogs that reach the magic number of 15 are said to have "finished," a genteel term redolent of elite schools.

Dog shows are essentially beauty contests, but in the other forms of competition brains and temperament are more important than good looks. Obedience trials test the ability to heed commands exactly and to serve as a responsive companion. Beginners are awarded the title of Companion Dog (abbreviated C.D. and used after the name) if they achieve qualifying scores in three trials for such elementary tasks as heeling and sitting. To be awarded the Companion Dog Excellent (C.D.X.) the animal must get

A dog pursues an obedience degree by scaling a wall after retrieving a dumbbell.

Though exhibitors still have their aristocracy, their numbers no longer include only the idle rich.

high marks at more complicated tasks, such as retrieving over a high jump. Next comes Utility Dog (U.D.), an altogether too pedestrian title considering the array of required tasks, including locating articles by scent. The ultimate is the title of Obedience Trial Champion (O.T.Ch.) There is also a special title for the canine with the high-performance nose: Tracking Dog (T.D.).

The truly aristocratic dog—the body beautiful, the intelligent companion, the keen scenter—would thus have its name written as follows:

Ch., O.T.Ch. Rover T.D.

Such lushly adorned names are cherished on pedigree certificates and flaunted in advertisements for stud service.

Dogs may also prove their mettle at field trials, where hunting breeds chase, ferret, flush, point and retrieve a variety of furred and feathered game. Herding dogs, especially in Europe, compete at sheep trials, moving the flock and rounding up strays with startling precision. In New England, in the mountains of California, and in the Arctic, sled dogs compete in races such as the Iditarod Trail Race from Anchorage to Nome, Alaska, a test of stamina as much as speed. But for most dog owners, the universe of competition is the local show ring, before the eyes of the judge.

How a Judge Decides

Judging dogs at shows, as almost all who have

Common Faults

Under show rules, some conditions, such as lameness, deafness and blindness, lead to automatic disqualification. Males are ineligible if both testicles have not descended into the scrotum or they have been castrated, and females if they have been spayed. Dogs are also barred if their appearance has been changed artificially, unless the breed standard allows it.

Besides these universal rules, each breed has specific disqualifying faults. The fault may be in height; a Shetland Sheepdog may not be less than 13 nor more than 16 inches (measured from the shoulder to the ground). It may be in color; a white-coated German Shepherd is disqualified, as is a blue-eyed Samoyed. Or it may be in some other structural or behavioral trait; a Toy Manchester Terrier may not compete if its ears have been cropped or cut.

In addition, for each breed there are several less serious faults that would cause a dog to be penalized but not ruled out of competition. These are some of the most common faults, in the colorful vernacular of the judging fraternity:

APPLE HEAD. A doomed or rounded skull.
BOSSY. Having shoulder muscles that are overly developed.
CHINA EYE. An eye whose iris pigmentation is blue. (Not a fault in some breeds, notably the Dalmatian.)
COWHOCKS. Heels (hocks) that are turned toward each other instead of facing straight back.
DEWCLAW. A vestigial fifth toe on the inside of the leg. It is acceptable or preferred on some breeds, but in most the dewclaw is removed by surgery when the dog is young.
DISH FACE. A depression between the nose tip and the stop.
DOWN IN PASTERN. Having a foreleg whose "wrist" (pastern) is at an angle from the vertical.
DUDLEY NOSE. Brown or flesh colored nose rather than black.
EAST-WEST FEET. Feet that turn outward, giving the dog a Charlie Chaplin look.
EWE NECK. A thin or poorly curved neck, resembling that of a sheep.
FIDDLE FRONT. Legs that turn out at the elbows and in at the pasterns with the toes outward—roughly the outline of a violin.
GOOSE RUMP. A rump (croup) that slopes too steeply.
HACKNEY ACTION. A gait in which the dog lifts its front feet too high, suggesting the movement of a hackney horse.
HAW. A reddish membrane, sometimes called the third eyelid. It gives that morning-after look to Bloodhounds, in which the trait is permissible.
PADDLING. An outward, swimming type of action by the forefeet when the dog is moving. If the legs cross over each other, the motion, also abnormal, is called "weaving."
PAPER FOOT. A flat foot, lacking sufficiently thick pads.
SHELLY. A body that is too narrow and lacks sufficient bone. A heavy-set, thick-looking body is termed "cloddy."
THROATINESS. Having too much loose or wrinkled skin under the throat. Just the right amount of tautness is called a "dry neck."
UNDERSHOT JAW. A lower jaw that protrudes so that the front teeth are beyond the front teeth of the upper jaw. The opposite condition is called overshot (or pig-jawed) and is faulted in every breed.
WRY MOUTH. A mouth whose upper and lower jaws are out of alignment.

When judgment is at hand, everybody's nervous. Each breed's standard is so complex that the judge must possess an intuitive sense of the Total Look—a close approximation of the breed's ideal.

done it agree, is more of an art than a science. The American Kennel Club's "Guidelines for Dog Show Judges" candidly admits that "A judge's decisions, while based on the standard of the breed, are subjective . . . . It is impossible to tell someone how to judge a dog." Some attempts have been made to develop mathematically precise judging criteria, by requiring that each part of the dog be awarded a certain number of points: 15 for the head, ten for the ears, and so on. Apart from the time-consuming nature of such calculations—it might be difficult for a judge to get through the usual 20 to 25 dogs an hour even with the aid of a computer— mathematical precision is ill-suited to gauging the intangible qualities that make some dogs obvious winners and leave others "out of the ribbons." Judging by the numbers may also penalize unfairly the dog who is, taken as a whole, more than the sum of his parts.

Almost all judges agree that their essential attribute is an "eye" for a dog, a certain sensibility sharpened by practice and knowledge.

Judges, in other words, are both born *and* made.

But the process of judging is by no means totally subjective. The judge measures the dog against the "standard" for the breed, a kind of Platonic ideal that no dog may actually reach but which all strive to reach. Standards are quite detailed. The German Shepherd's, for example, covers three and a half printed pages. It prescribes general appearance, character, head (including ears, eyes and teeth), neck, forequarters, feet, proportion, body (including chest, ribs and abdomen), topline, tail, hindquarters, gait, transmission (the flow of muscle action as the dog moves) and color. Each standard is formulated by the so-called "parent club" of a breed and approved by the AKC, which recognizes changes from time to time that the parent club membership may desire. (Debates over modifications can be as heated as political controversies.) But many of the standards have remained unchanged since first published in 1929.

Some fashions in dog breeding work subtle alterations in breed characteristics that are not

WESTMINSTER
KENNEL CLUB
21st Annual
Dog Show
1897
FEB'Y 22, 23, 24, 25
MADISON SQUARE GARDEN

yet officially recognized. Cocker Spaniel fanciers, for example, have evidently developed a taste for luxuriant coats, especially on the legs and lower portion of the body, in apparent contravention of the standard, which says that the dog should not be "feathered . . . so excessively as to hide the Cocker Spaniel's true lines and movement or affect his appearance and function as a sporting dog." Many judges implicitly accept the trend of the times, at least to the extent of not seriously penalizing those with fuller coats.

What, then, does a judge look for? In general, the judge seeks a dog who is "typey," that is, who personifies the distinguishing characteristics of its breed. The dog's features must be balanced, harmonious and in proportion. The dog should have "soundness," a quality that most judges find difficult to define. It should be in good condition: healthy, not over- or underweight and covered by a well-maintained coat. The dog should also look capable of doing what its breed is intended to do. The Great Dane, for example, should exhibit the powerful build of a boar hunter rather than the delicacy of a lap dog.

To determine these qualities, the judge examines the dog from various angles, looks in its mouth, feels under the coat for unseen muscle and bone structure—a good judge, it is said, develops "animal hands"—and watches the dog move away from him and toward him. The toy dogs are put on a table for closer inspection. The judge is also examining the dog's style, carriage, bearing and, especially where breed standards mention it, personality. Shyness is a fault in a Doberman Pinscher, and in all dogs viciousness (to people, not other dogs) is frowned upon. One of the main occupational hazards of show judging is being bitten; judges are distressed by dog bites, not only because

---

A **black dog** *in 18th century English slang was a counterfeit shilling coin.*

they hurt but because they tend to undermine the dignity of the sport. The postman may forgive and forget, but taking a piece out of the judge is unlikely to lead to stardom in the show world.

Cheating

Like many other sports competitors, dog exhibitors are sometimes carried away by a desire to win, so much so that they may try extracurricular methods of influencing the judge. Some of these methods are considered acceptable, if devious, as when an owner carefully trims the dog's coat to disguise a deformity of the back or legs. Such stratagems rarely deceive experienced judges, who learn to search under the hair for the tell-tale signs of structural defect.

In other cases, the cover-up is attempted inside the ring. An exhibitor may try to hide a missing tooth by opening the dog's mouth for inspection in such a way that not all the teeth are visible; the knowledgeable judge may have to open the mouth himself to get a closer look.

Exhibitors may also wage psychological warfare. Some owners will slyly drop a hint that the dog is undefeated in past competitions or that it needs only one more success to be a champion. They may also stand just outside the ring, making nasty remarks, in conversation meant to be overheard by the judge, about the opposing dogs. Exhibitors sometimes bring along a claque of friends and relatives to applaud wildly whenever the judge passes by their dog. Even at large shows, like Westminster, there are dogs obviously favored by most of the audience. Judges maintain that they are not swayed by such extraneous considerations, and probably some kinds of attempted persuasion have the reverse effect on the annoyed official. But there must be times when a judge wonders whether, after giving the ribbon to a dog other than the

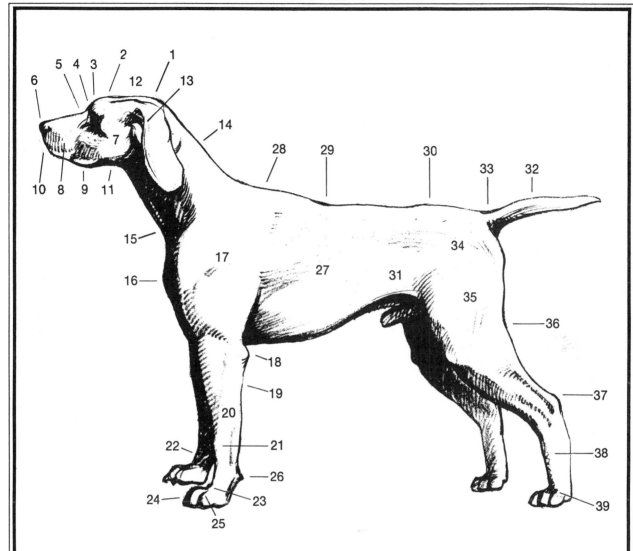

Points of the Dog

TECHNICAL TERMS

(1) Apex of Skull	(13) Set of Ear	(27) Ribs
(2) Skull	(14) Neck	(28) Wither
(3) Groove	(15) Dewlap	(29) Back
(4) Temples or Frontal Bones	(16) Brisket	(30) Loin
(5) Stop	(17) Shoulder	(31) Belly
(6) Nose	(18) Elbow	(32) Tail
(7) Cheek	(19) Calf	(33) Set of Tail or Stern
(8) Cushion	(20) Forearm	(34) Hip Joint
(9) Chop or Flews	(21) Knee	(35) Thigh
(10) Underjaw	(22) Pastern	(36) Stifle
(11) Corner of the Jaw	(23) Forefeet	(37) Hock
(12) Corner of the Eye	(24) Toes	(38) Pastern
	(25) Knuckles	(39) Hind-foot
	(26) Heelknob	

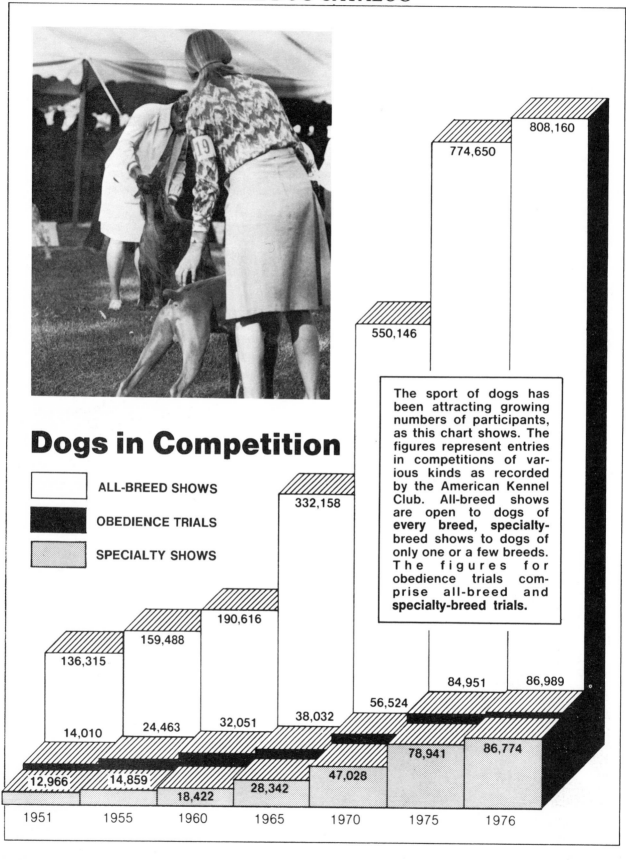

Dogs in Competition

ALL-BREED SHOWS

OBEDIENCE TRIALS

SPECIALTY SHOWS

The sport of dogs has been attracting growing numbers of participants, as this chart shows. The figures represent entries in competitions of various kinds as recorded by the American Kennel Club. All-breed shows are open to dogs of **every breed, specialty-breed shows to dogs of** only one or a few breeds. The figures for obedience trials comprise all-breed and **specialty-breed trials.**

	1951	1955	1960	1965	1970	1975	1976
All-breed shows	136,315	159,488	190,616	332,158	550,146	774,650	808,160
Obedience trials	14,010	24,463	32,051	38,032	56,524	84,951	86,989
Specialty shows	12,966	14,859	18,422	28,342	47,028	78,941	86,774

crowd favorite, he will be able to leave the ring unscathed.

Most of these tactics are considered relatively harmless, but the exhibitors may resort to outright deception, a practice known as "faking." To fake, in the eyes of the American Kennel Club, is to change the appearance of the dog "by artificial means except as specified by the standard for its breed." Since breeding itself is a contrived procedure, why should the exhibitor balk at going a few steps further? The assumption underlying the rule is that the desire to reach the ideal represented by the breed standard must have some limits. Otherwise, exhibitors might resort to all sorts of cutting and pasting to produce the perfect dog.

A common method of faking is to enhance the coat color by dyeing or to ensure that the white portions are whiter-than-white by applying bluing or chalk. There have been times when a judge, patting a dog, created a cloud of chalk dust. Illicit efforts to redecorate the animal have also been uncovered by judges who applied a damp cloth to the coat. Some exhibitors have gone so far as to give a dog clandestine surgery to improve its appearance. Golden Retrievers, for example, can have trichiasis—an

Dog exhibitors have their own tradition of cheating. "Faking" is the practice of artificially changing a dog's appearance. Chalking the coat of a white dog is one method often used.

ILLUSTRATION BY KIMBLE P. MEAD

The Circuit

STEP 1. The members of a breed are entered in separate "classes" for males (dogs) and females (bitches). The classes are arranged as follows:

Puppy (subdivided into 6-to-9 month-olds and 9-to-12 month-olds)

Novice (entrants who have won no show points previously)

Bred by Exhibitor (entrants bred and owned by those showing them)

American-breed (entrants bred in the United States)

Open (unrestricted)

The judges' choices in each of the male classes compete against each other for Winners Dog. The females compete for Winners Bitch. The Winners Dog and Winners Bitch each may earn up to five show points, depending on the number of entrants in the classes, toward the 15 required for a championship. The runnerup male is Reserve Winners Dog; the runnerup female is Reserve Winners Bitch.

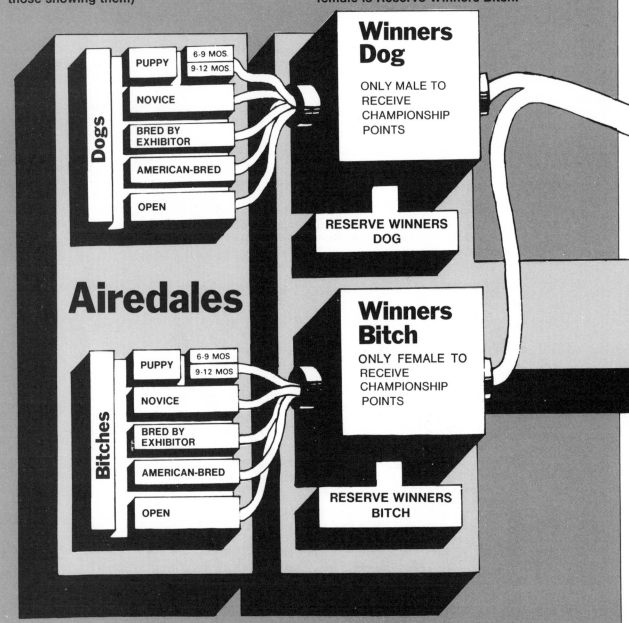

STEP 2. The Winners Dog and Winners Bitch are judged in the same ring with those that are already champions—the Specials. The judge selects one competitor as Best of Breed, awarding it a purple-and-gold ribbon. Another is picked as Best of Opposite Sex (opposite from the Best of Breed, that is), and either the Winners Dog or the Winners Bitch is named Best of Winners.

Usually the choice for Best of Breed is one of the Specials, but if either the Winners Dog or Winners Bitch is chosen, it automatically becomes Best of Winners also.

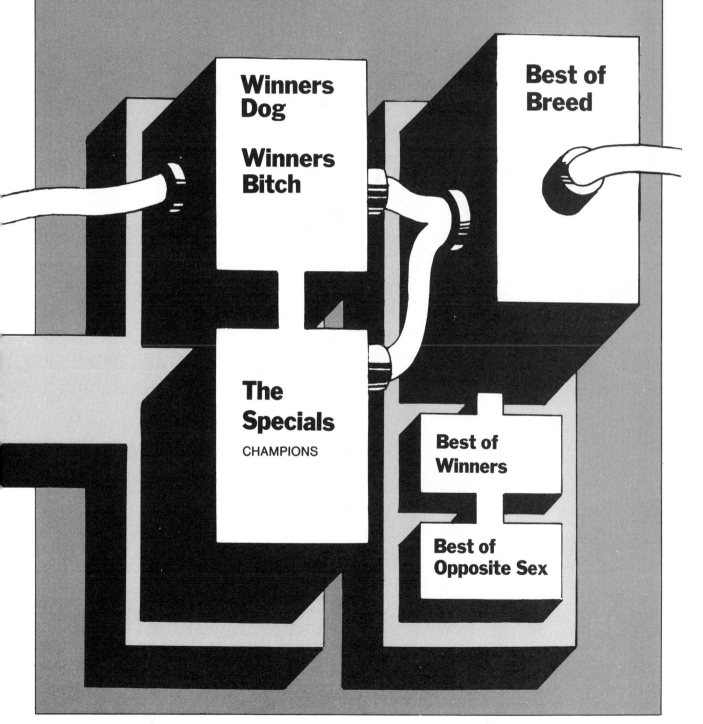

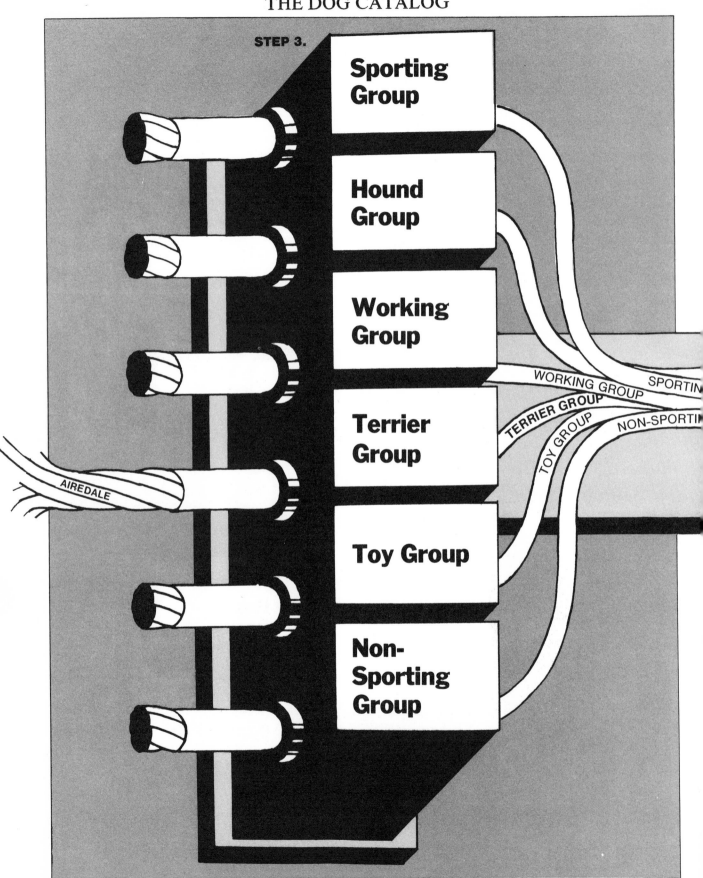

STEP 4.

Best in Show

HOUND GROUP
GROUP
GROUP

STEP 3. Each Best of Breed goes into the ring to compete for the group title (Group I) and its blue rosette. The second, third and fourth place dogs are designated Group II, Group III and Group IV.

STEP 4. The groups—Sporting, Hound, Working, Terrier, Toy, Non-Sporting—send their winners into the ring, where the judge selects one as the Best in Show and awards it a red-white-and-blue rosette.

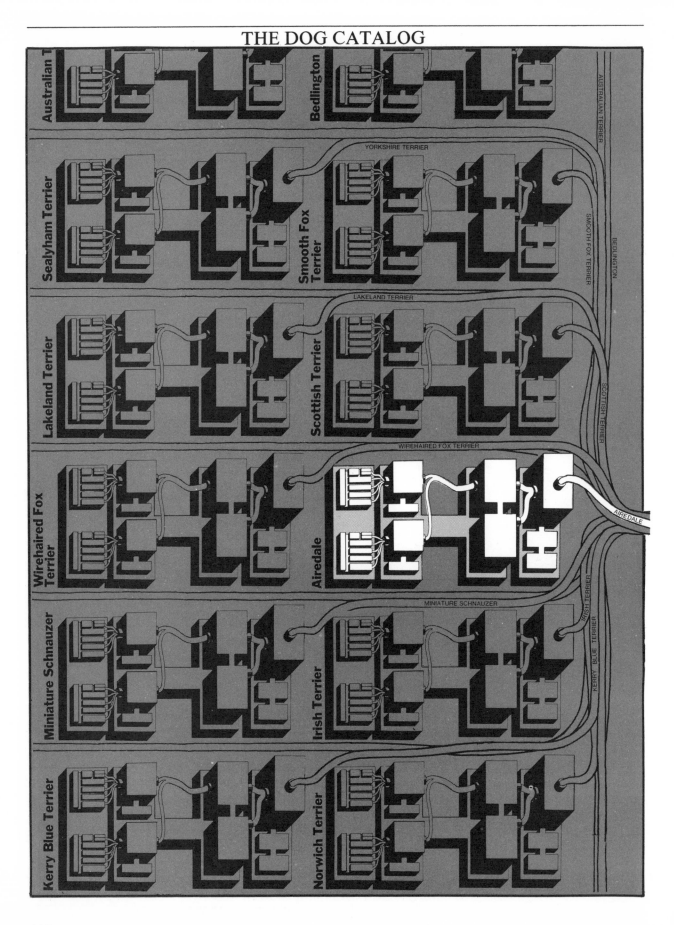

The show as a whole is an enormous winnowing process, sometimes involving thousands of dogs. The best dog in each of the breeds must be chosen, then the best dog in each of the six groups, then the best of the group winners. Before the group stage is reached, the sorting out proceeds simultaneously in a number of breeds at once, presenting the spectator with a 20- or 30-ring circus.

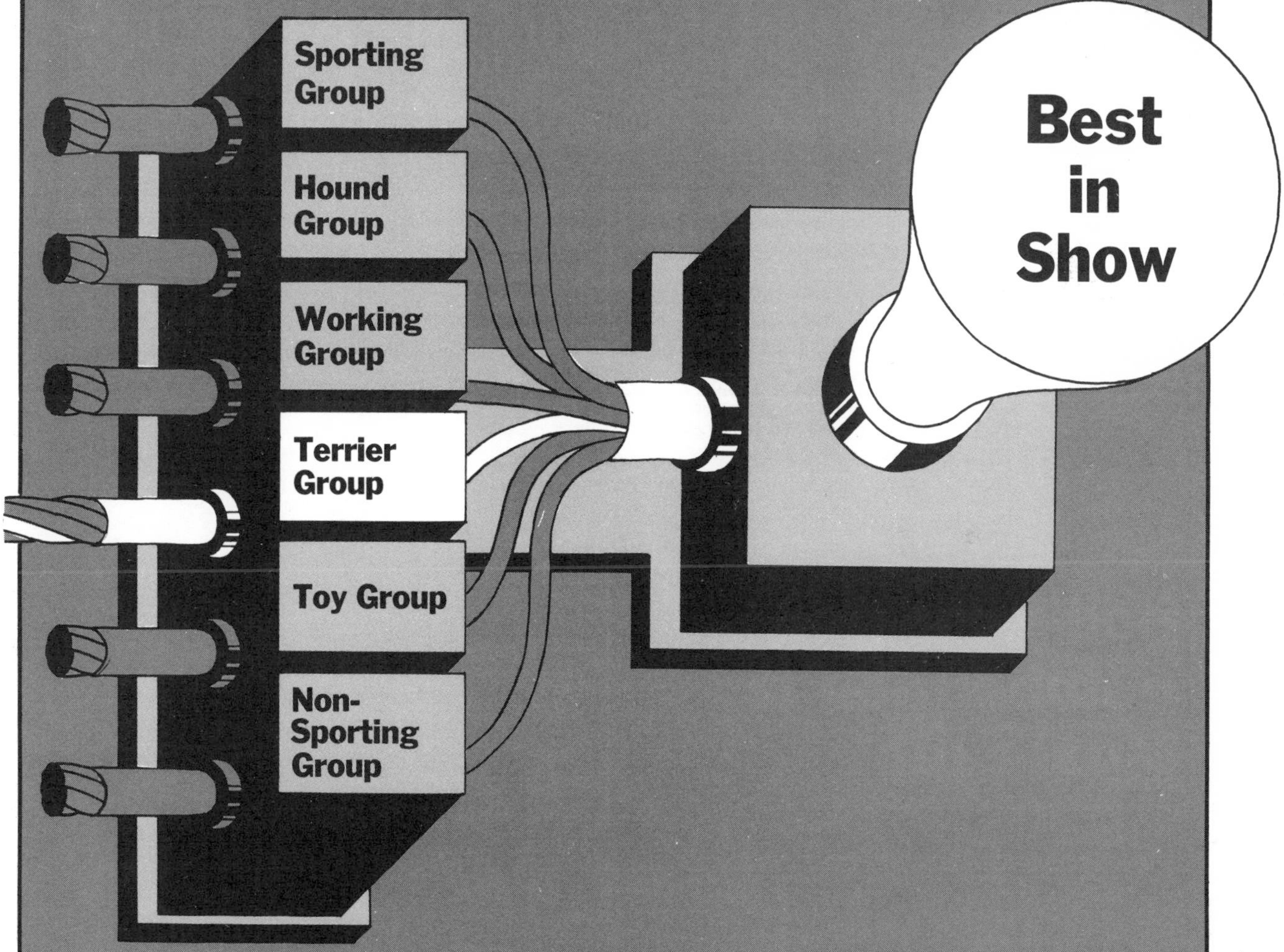

Sporting Group

Hound Group

Working Group

Terrier Group

Toy Group

Non-Sporting Group

Best in Show

The Show Circuit: Main Events

Name of Show		Location	Spring	Summer	Fall	Winter
Superstition	1	Mesa, Arizona			●	●
Kern County	2	Bakersfield, California	●			
Santa Ana Valley	3	Cypress, California	●		●	
Sun Maid	4	Fresno, California	●			
Channel City	5	Goleta, California		●		
Beverly Hills	6	Los Angeles, California		●		●
Orange Empire	7	San Bernadino, California		●		●
Silver Bay	8	San Diego, California		●		
		Del Mar, California				●
Golden Gate	9	San Francisco, California	●			●
Santa Clara Valley	10	San Jose, California			●	●
Santa Barbara	11	Santa Barbara, California		●		
Ventura	12	Ventura, California		●		●
Tampa Bay	13	Tampa, Florida		●		●
Atlanta	14	Hampton, Georgia	●	●		
International Kennel Club of Chicago	15	Chicago, Illinois	●	●		
Hoosier	16	Indianapolis, Indiana	●		●	
Louisville	17	Louisville, Kentucky		●		●
Maryland	18	Baltimore, Maryland			●	
Eastern Dog Club	19	Boston, Massachusetts				●
Detroit	20	Detroit, Michigan				●
Boardwalk	21	Atlantic City, New Jersey				●
Monmouth County	22	Oceanport, New Jersey	●			
Trenton	23	W. Windsor Twsp., NJ	●			
Westbury	24	Brookville, New York			●	
Westminster	25	New York, New York				●
Westchester	26	Tarrytown, New York		●		
Chagrin Valley	27	Chagrin Falls, Ohio		●		
Western Reserve	28	Cleveland, Ohio				●
Ravenna	29	Ravenna, Ohio		●		
Portland	30	North Portland, Oregon		●		●
Harrisburg	31	Carlisle, Pennsylvania		●		
		Harrisburg, Pennsylvania				●
Bucks County	32	Erwinna, Pennsylvania	●			●
Philadelphia	33	Philadelphia, Pennsylvania				●
Western Pennsylvania	34	Pittsburgh, Pennsylvania	●			
Devon	35	Whitehorse, Pennsylvania			●	
Texas	36	Dallas, Texas			●	●
Old Dominion	37	Reston, Virginia	●		●	●

*"Let Hercules himself do what he may
The cat will mew and dog will have his day."*

—WILLIAM SHAKESPEARE, Hamlet

abnormality in which the eyelashes touch and irritate the eyeballs—corrected by surgery. That may in fact be a humane action, but the operation technically disqualifies a dog from being shown. Similarly, in Terrier breeds the owner may attempt to make the ears fold over properly by removing a bit of cartilage surgically. Tails may be "fixed" to improve their carriage. (Docking—clipping—the tail is a permissible alteration in some breeds, however.)

The careful judge will look for scars and other signs of plastic surgery and, if necessary, call in a veterinarian for confirmation. Exhibitors are liable to be disciplined for deceptive practices, but the lure of a big win will always tempt some to try to improve upon nature.

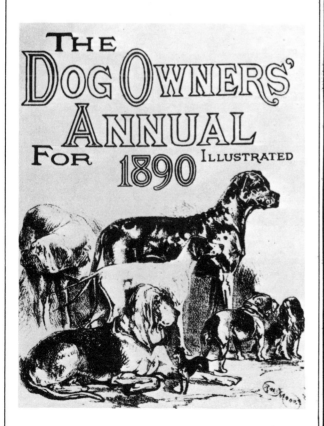

The Price of Success

Many people dream of turning their pet into a show champion, but they soon awake to the reality of cost. Producing a champion is more than a labor of love; it also requires a heavy investment in capital, from $500 to $3,000, depending upon how many shows it takes to amass the necessary 15 points. The money goes for entry fees, traveling and grooming expenses and paying for a professional dog handler.

Acquiring the services of a dog handler increases the chances of winning at shows. The handlers are expert at accentuating a dog's good points in the ring and obscuring its faults. The most sought-after handlers may charge $20,000 or more for a year's "campaigning" with a dog, traveling from show to show. They may handle dozens of dogs at a time, building a lucrative practice.

Some exhibitors recoup their investment by running breeding establishments or stud services and charging fees commensurate with a dog's show record. But for many persons of modest means showing dogs is simply an addiction that drains financial resources and brings nothing in return but an array of ribbons, suitable for framing. They find themselves keeping up not with the Joneses but the Rockefellers. Serious exhibitors often maintain kennels of show dogs, have substantial private incomes, and belong to upper-crust clubs that sponsor events in much the same spirit that medieval aristocrats hosted jousting tournaments. The Westchester (New York) Kennel Club, for example, holds a show each September on the grounds of a Hudson River estate, at which the club's 17 members — 10 of them from Wall Street — preside in white trousers and blue blazers. The atmosphere of many fashionable shows, in fact, demonstrates that the horsey set is also the doggie set.

Fletcher's Dozen

Walter R. Fletcher has covered thousands of dog shows for The New York Times. *He selects these as the dozen greatest show dogs of recent decades:*

Mrs. Cheever Porter's Irish Setter

Ch. Milson O'Boy

In five-year period, starting in 1934, named best-in-show 11 times, winner of group 46 times and best-of-breed 103 times . . . Considered by many the greatest show dog of his breed.

Mrs. Sherman Hoyt's Standard Poodle

Ch. Nunsoe Duc de la Terrace of Blakeen

In 18 times shown in the United States, won nine best-in-show awards, including Westminster in 1935, and 16 group titles . . . The first Poodle ever to win the New York classic.

James M. Austin's Smooth Fox Terrier

Ch. Nornay Saddler

Imported from England and first shown here in 1937, won 56 best-in-show awards by 1941 . . . Career total (59 times best-in-show) a record for a Terrier that stood for 32 years.

Louis Murr's Borzoi

Ch. Vigow of Romanoff

Never beaten for best-of-breed in 77 appearances in late 1930's . . . Best-in-show 21 times . . . Won-group 67 times.

H.E. Mellenthin's Cocker Spaniel

Ch. My Own Brucie

Won best-in-show at Westminster two years in a row (1940 and 1941) . . . Influenced many Cocker bloodlines.

Dr. and Mrs. R.C. Harris' Boxer

Ch. Bang Away of Sirrah Crest

Won 121 best-in-show awards, including Westminster in 1951.

Mr. and Mrs. Len Carey's Doberman Pinscher

Ch. Rancho Dobe's Storm

Never defeated for best-of-breed . . . Won best-in-show 17 times out of 25 times shown . . . Took Westminster in 1952 and 1953 . . . Retired at 38 months old.

Sunny Shay's and Dorothy Chenade's Afghan Hound

Ch. Shirkhan of Grandeur

The first of his breed to win Westminster (1957) . . . Offspring won many titles.

Mr. and Mrs. C.C. Venable's Pekingese

Ch. Chik T'sun of Caversham

Took 127 best-in-show awards in the United States, 11 in Canada . . . Once won best-in-show 14 times in 46 days . . . Retired after winning Westminster in 1960.

Dr. Milton E. Prickett's English Springer Spaniel

Ch. Chinoe's Adamant James

Won best-in-show 60 times, 47 of them in one year (1971) . . . Captured Westminster in 1971 and 1972, the first to take a double since Ch. Rancho Dobe's Storm.

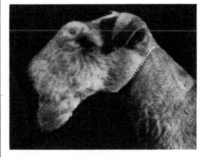

Mrs. V.K. Dickson's Lakeland Terrier

Ch. Red Baron of Crofton

Won Westminster in 1976 for his 75th best-in-show . . . The greatest winning Terrier since Ch. Nornay Saddler, three decades earlier.

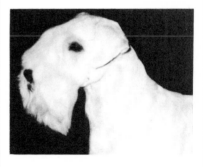

Mrs. Dorothy Wimer's Sealyham Terrier

Ch. Dersade Bobby's Girl

The top winning female in the history of dog shows in the United States (51 best-in-show awards) . . . Retired after winning Westminster in 1977, the first Sealyham to do so in 41 years.

6

Your Command Isn't Always Its Wish
TRAINING

Training

When Nature Meets Nurture

The notion that fish have to swim and birds have to fly contains a biological truth that applies to dogs as well—namely that animals behave, at least at times, according to instinct. But what is it that dogs "have" to do? Apart from their obvious penchant for prancing about on four legs, dogs display some skills that seem to come naturally and others that must be learned. Distinguishing between the two is important for dog training, because there is no need to waste time elaborately teaching a puppy to do what it will do instinctively as soon as it is old enough. There are notable examples of Bloodhounds, for example, who followed a cold trail successfully on their first try, having never benefitted from formal education during puppyhood in the theory of tracking. Many water dogs, like the Newfoundlands, will, when they are ready, act upon their natural bent for exhuberant splashing about in ponds without having had swimming lessons, and there is almost no way of keeping Retrievers dry when they are within reach of a mudhole. On the other hand, if a breed of dog is known to have an instinctive knack for doing something, it is possible to perfect his abilities, to teach him to do well what he will do anyway.

An instinct is essentially an inherited behavior trait, an innate predisposition to behave in a given way under a given set of circumstances. When a dog acts on instinct, it is following an inner command rather than one that comes from outside, from its master. Although they may get somewhat better after practice, dogs do not, for example, need to be taught how to mate. And when the litter arrives, the mother does not need to be instructed in maternal care.

Most canine instincts originally served some evolutionary purpose, giving the dog a survival advantage. Sexual behavior has obvious advantages for a species that wants to continue to exist, but the utility of some other instincts is not so clear. Many dogs circle about a number of times before lying down, which has been speculatively interpreted as an instinct derived from a time when the animal had to make a bed for itself by flattening tall grass. Burying bones is probably an instinctive form of prudence, putting some food aside for hard times ahead.

Male dogs evidently found it useful to identify their territories by urinating on trees, an instinctive pattern that somehow got transferred to fire hydrants (from a dog's point of view a tree trunk and a hydrant are not much different) when canines became city-dwellers. Not all instincts, obviously, are as useful as they once were.

Some dog behavior that at first glance seems instinctive may not be so. Pointers seem to have an inner need to stand transfixed when they spot game, but just staring at the bird would

Aim for the possible: fetching, not reading.

Dogma *has nothing to do with dogs. It comes from the Greek* **dokein,** *"to seem good."*

not have done the dog much good before he teamed up with a human hunter. Chasing the quarry is much more practical. It has been suggested that, rather than behaving instinctively, the Pointer is being hypnotized by the bird's movements. A more likely explanation is that the Pointer's rigid response is the result of artificial selection by man of some less exaggerated behavioral trait.

Many such instincts have been preserved or intensified because people considered them useful. Terriers, in their natural state, apparently had some instinct for killing the rodents whose burrows they excavated, but selective breeding magnified that drive. Although the urge to kill is innate, dogs often need to learn how to kill skillfully—for example to guard all the holes of the burrow to prevent a badger's escape. He may learn from experience or a person may teach him.

There is a standing argument about whether dogs have a homing instinct. Stories abound of dogs who jumped out of the car miles from home in unfamiliar territory and miraculously returned. There is no scientific proof of a homing instinct akin to that of pigeons; one plausible theory is that lost dogs simply move about randomly, a pattern which leads *some* of them in the right direction. (We tend not to hear stories about the dogs lost miles from home who never made it back.) The dogs probably recognize landmarks and follow promising sounds and smells once they find themselves in the general vicinity of home.

Apart from his instincts, a dog's intelligence also has great bearing on what he can be trained to do. Numerous experiments have attempted to determine exactly how intelligent a dog is, as defined by his ability to solve simple problems. In general, dogs have not performed impressively, especially compared to primates (apes and chimps). They have difficulty finding their way out of all but the simplest mazes, and their memory is not keen. In one experiment, a dog was tied up in view of three boxes and allowed to observe meat being placed in one of them. The dog could not remember which box to go to if he was unleashed more than 30 minutes later. Dogs may, however, remember smells better than sights.

Dogs do not seem to be able to count. Mothers may not even notice one or two puppies removed from the litter. Some coonhunters insist that their dogs have been able to keep track

ILLUSTRATION BY DEBBIE HALL

Truffle Hunting

The truffle, a mushroom-like, subterranean growth that is the jewel of French cuisine, once was hunted exclusively with a pig, who rooted them out of the forest floor. But that method is being rapidly replaced by the use of dogs, whose nose for truffles has proven to be superior. Professional truffle hunters, using only one dog, have been said to find as much as 150 to 200 kilos, whose retail value would be thousands of dollars, in a single week. Although pigs dig by instinct and by appetite, the dog must be trained for the task. But dogs do have one distinct advantage: they do not have to be restrained, as the pig does, from immediately consuming its precious discovery.

A Reader's Guide to Training Manuals

The how-to-do-it literature on dog training is enormous. Here are some titles representative of the genre:

Daglish, Eric Fitch
Training Your Dog,
Arco, 1976.

David, L. Wilson,
Go Find,
Howell, 1974.

Davis, Henry P.,
Training Your Own Bird Dog,
Putnam 1969.

English, Margaret,
*A Basic Guide to Dog Training
and Obedience,*
Grosset & Dunlap, 1975.

Johnson, Glen R.,
Tracking Dog, Theory and Methods,
Arner, 1975.

Knap, Jerome J. and Alyson,
Training the Versatile Gun Dog
Scribner's, 1974

Koehler, William,
*The Koehler Method of Open Obedience
for Ring, Home and Field,*
Howell, 1970.

Landesman, Bill and Kathleen Berman,
How to Train Your Dog in Six Weeks,
Frederick Fell Publishers, 1976.

Loeb, Paul,
*Paul Loeb's Complete Book of
Dog Training,*
Prentice-Hall, 1974.

Maller, Dick,
21 Days to a Trained Dog,
Simon and Schuster, 1977.

Pearsall, Margaret E.,
*The Pearsall Guide to Succesful
Dog Training,*
Howell, 1973.

Saunders, Blanche,
The Story of Dog Obedience,
Howell, 1974.

Siegal, Mordecai and Matthew Margolis,
Good Dog, Bad Dog,
Holt, Rinehart and Winston, 1970.

Wolters, Richard A.,
*City Dog: Revolutionary Rapid
Training Method*
Dutton, 1975

of the number of coons they chased up a tree. But many of the hunters, who are otherwise more partial to their hounds than the quarry, concede that in general the coons seem smarter than the dogs.

Dogs are certainly smart enough to communicate to humans, although the famous "talking dog" exists mainly in jokes like this one:

A trainer takes his dog to see a theatrical agent about booking a talking dog act. To impress the dubious agent, the trainer asks the dog: What keeps rain out of the house? The dog answers, "Rrroof!" The agent is still skeptical, so the trainer poses another question: "Who is the greatest baseball player of all time?" The dog replies: "Rrruth!" Unimpressed by this monosyllabic display, the agent sends the man and dog away. Outside the office, the dog turns to the trainer and asks: "Should I have said DiMaggio?"

What sideshow feats of eloquence dogs have accomplished are probably mere "acoustic imitation," not much more thoughtful than a parrot's and much less skillful. Dogs that do make imitative noises display no sign that they understand the sounds or even the concept of words. They may respond to words like "sit" and "stay" but only because they have learned to associate a response with the appropriate sound of a command. There was a dog owner in the 1920s who claimed that his German Shepherd understood 400 words—a vocabulary extensive enough for the animal to hold a reasonably articulate conversation on Aristotelian philosophy —but such claims have encountered well-deserved skepticism.

"Sir, a woman preaching is like a dog walking on his hind legs. It is not done well; but you are surprised to find it done at all."

—SAMUEL JOHNSON (1709-1784)

Dogs do, of course, send messages to each other and to humans by means of sounds and "body language." They can communicate that they wish to be followed to a lost child or calf. Such incidents cause the general intelligence of dogs to be overestimated by proud and perhaps astonished owners.

Teaching the Teacher

If there is a universal principle of dog training, it is that the owner needs to be trained first. Whatever the differences in instinct, intelligence and temperament, dogs are generally amenable to training, but not all persons are so suited. Many dogs, for example, are less likely to lose their patience during training sessions than their owners. So the length of training sessions often must be tailored to suit the needs of the human participants.

Once a person has himself well disciplined, he can proceed to deal with the animal. The basic choice is whether to use negative or positive methods. The negative theory, which emphasizes the importance of swift and sure punishment, once had many adherents, just as corporal punishment of school children did. But trainers seem to be changing to non-violent

Housebreaking the Puppy: Six Steps

Step 1. Barricade the puppy into a corner of the room where it will live and cover the entire floor area of the enclosure with newspaper. Make sure that the enclosure is large enough so that it can get a considerable distance away from its food bowl.

Step 2. When the puppy selects a target area on the paper, praise lavishly.

Step 3. Gradually reduce the paper around the target area and continue praising lavishly if the puppy stays accurate.

Step. 4 Shrink the target to a single sheet. Watch the puppy closely and grab it as it makes a move for the paper. Transfer the paper outside and put puppy on it. (Remember to yardbreak the puppy as well by choosing the same outdoor location each time.)

Step 5. When the puppy has become accustomed to asking to go outside, dispense with the paper.

Step 6. Train yourself to walk the dog regularly.

ILLUSTRATION BY KIMBLE P. MEAD

The Education of a Seeing-Eye

A masterpiece of the art of training is the guide dog for the blind. The concept first emerged in Germany, after World War I, when blind veterans were given dogs taught to negotiate the obstacles of everyday life. Today, in the United States, the dogs are trained and provided to blind persons free by several charitable organizations. German Shepherds are most common, but other intelligent, even-tempered dogs are used, including Golden Retrievers, Labrador Retrievers, Collies, Bouviers des Flandres, and Boxers.

The training process is long and elaborate and costs about $4,000 for each dog. Suitable puppies are "adopted" by families until they are more than a year old. (Many 4-H Clubs sponsor puppy-raising programs.) Then comes the formal training, which takes from three to six months. The difficulty is in teaching the dog not only to avoid obstacles himself but to remember the person he is leading. The trainer, for example, must reprimand a dog by saying "No!" if it walks around a pole without leaving room for him to pass. He must teach it to stop for hazards, such as low-hanging branches and clotheslines, that threaten only the dog's human companion. A crucial task is avoiding cars. The dog's tendency to go around obstacles might leave the blind person squarely in the path of an oncoming vehicle; the dog learns that the car is an impediment that must move itself out of the way. (Most difficult to avoid are other human beings, whose movements are even less predictable than those of cars.) The dog must learn to stop at curbs and intersections, to find doors, to retrieve articles dropped by its master and to remain undistracted by traffic, noises and other animals.

The training is also unique in that the dog must learn to exercise discretion, to interpret a command in light of what it can see but its master cannot. The dog obviously must not obey a command to go forward if that would take man and dog into the flow of traffic or off the edge of a train platform.

In the final stages the trainer may work blindfolded to test the dog's trustworthiness.

As a sightless person does, he relies on the dog's movements, sensed through the rigid harness, to guide him. The last step is to train the blind person and his dog together, a process that takes about a month of live-in learning. By graduation, the two have come to operate as a team, a perfect man-dog unit.

Leading the Deaf Through a Maze of Sounds

Although blind persons have long had the tasks of daily living eased by the assistance of a guide dog, the deaf or hearing-impaired have struggled on without canine help. Now, however, the American Humane Association has begun training "hearing dogs" who compensate for their owners' sensory deprivation in much the same way that a seeing-eye dog does.

The hearing dogs — selected from mixed as well as pure breeds, often from the local shelter — are given a standard two-week obedience course followed by special "auditory awareness" training. The dogs are taught to be sensitive to the sounds of alarm clocks, crying babies, knocks on the door, smoke alarms—even the sound of a wallet falling out of a pocket onto the floor.

The trainer races the dog to the source of the sound until, after a while, the animal realizes there is something special about it. When living with its deaf owner, the dog will rush back and forth between him and the sound source to alert him. In the case of the alarm clock, the dog nudges the owner to awaken him or, if a small dog, jumps on the bed.

Training takes three to four months at the association's Denver headquarters and combines the skills of a dog trainer and an educator for the deaf. Training dogs costs about $1,800 each, but they are provided free to deaf persons. The association relies on contributions.

The program, which began experimentally in 1976, grew rapidly because of the demand for hearing dogs. The program has encountered only minor difficulties; one of them was a dog that developed motion sickness from jumping on his owner's water bed when the alarm rang each morning.

When punishing or rewarding always be consistent.

ILLUSTRATION BY DEBBIE HALL

methods that stress the importance of what psychologists call "positive reinforcement," the rewarding of desirable behavior so that the dog will *want* to act as he should. The advantage of positive reinforcement is that 1) the owner does not feel quite so much like a sadist and 2) the dog avoids doing naughty things even when the owner is not around. The spare-the-rod-and-spoil-the-dog school frequently produced an animal that was devious and tended to fear the owner, who was associated with punishment.

To teach a dog control, the owner must learn to control himself in a variety of ways. For one thing, he must force himself to an unusual degree of consistency. Using the command *Come* on one occasion and *Here* on another may seem reasonable, but the dog is likely to become confused and do neither. The owner must also learn to control his natural laziness. If the dog is breaking the rules by unwarranted barking at 2 AM, the owner must rouse himself and silence the offender, even though he would just prefer to turn over in bed and overlook the incident. Otherwise, the dog will get the message that wee-hours barking is permitted.

What should be the dog's reward? Fortunately, dogs, unlike people, are not very mercenary and would rather perform for love than material things, like food. Well-fed dogs do not really need the extra calories from tidbits tossed as a door prize for coming when called. On the other hand, they do need and enjoy affection, so the positive reinforcement school prescribes effusive verbal praise and physical comforting: ear rubbing, chest patting and head scratching. After a while, though, verbal praise should be sufficient.

Old Dogs and New Tricks

The saying that "You can't teach an old dog new tricks" is one of those adages that long seemed self-evident. But most trainers today disagree. They might, in fact, put it the other way around: You can't teach a very young dog anything. Dogs that are less than four to six months old have short concentration spans, making it difficult to do any sustained training, and some specialized trainers, those who teach performing dogs for example, prefer dogs over two years old. Although it is easier to instill good habits relatively early, dogs of any age can always learn. Sometimes, however, in extreme old age, they tend to lose inhibitions that have been trained into them and revert to youthful behavior, having, in effect, a second puppyhood.

ILLUSTRATION BY KIMBLE P. MEAD

Golden Tonka, Obedience Champion

To the average owner, frustrated in his attempt to even housebreak a dog, the spectacle of a canine trained well enough to capture obedience trial prizes is nothing short of miraculous. And the most miraculous of these is a female Golden Retriever named Golden Tonka. For three straight years, 1974, 1975 and 1976, Tonka was top dog for obedience in the United States, accumulating along the road to stardom perfect scores (200 points) in six trials. In one year alone, 1976, she was the high scorer in 48 trials. The climax of her career was in July, 1977, when she became the first dog to earn the title of Obedience Trial Champion, a new designation created by the American Kennel Club only that month.

Tonka displayed her skills at a memorable performance at the 1977 Westminster Dog Show in Madison Square Garden. "For some reason she is a ham," her owner and trainer, Russell H. Klipple of Parker Ford, Pa., has observed. "Applause is like a shot in the arm to her." Responding to that appreciative crowd, Tonka retrieved objects by jumping over hurdles — never by taking the easy path around them. She located objects that had been scent-marked by her owner, sorting them from among similar objects with uncanny precision. But her best "trick" was her absolute responsiveness from a distance to Klipple's hand signals; he could make her get up, sit down, walk and jump by merely lifting a finger—as if the dog were attached to his hand by marionette strings.

For all her robot-like perfection, it was apparent that Tonka was as playful as other dogs and that training had not taken the spirit out of her. In between disciplined obedience feats, Tonka would frolic about by her owner's side, jumping up to have her head scratched. It was as if Tonka was trying to prove that, despite everything, she was, so to speak, human.

One difficulty with positive reinforcement is that the trainer must wait for the dog to do something laudable of its own accord so that it can be rewarded. Moreover, refraining from becoming angry at the dog when it is chewing a chair leg may take above-average will power; positive reinforcement requires that the animal be distracted from its misdeeds, summoned and rewarded for coming. Some positive theories do, however, accept that, when caught in the act, a dog can be scolded, by saying *No!* or *Shame!* in a disapproving voice. (All commands should be given in a firm, decisive tone so that the dog does not think the trainer is unsure of himself; many people seem to adopt a wheedling tone, as if they do not really expect the dog to respond.)

There are training courses, manuals and methods beyond counting, but in all of them, there are four basic commands:

1. *Heel.* When a dog heels, it walks *with* a person rather than pulling ahead. The basic training technique is to yank a leash attached

to a choke collar to get the dog's attention whenever its mind begins to wander from the task of keeping pace with the walker.

2. *Come.* Dogs come to their owners more

or less naturally, assuming they do not hate them, so it is often unnecessary to do much more than reinforce and routinize that behavior. Sometimes an extra-long leash is used outdoors; if the dog does not respond promptly to the *come* command, a pull on the leash emphasizes the seriousness of the message.

3. *Sit*. Since dogs sit quite a bit without being commanded to do so, one method is to simply wait for it to happen, give the command belatedly and offer praise. The dog may be a bit puzzled at first about what it did to merit the plaudits, but eventually it catches on. At times

The Schutzhund

Training dogs to attack is frowned upon by many experts on the ground that insufficiently disciplined animals may endanger innocent persons. But a technique called *Schutzhund* (German for "protection dog") training, imported from Europe relatively recently, claims to produce a dog that will defend its owner diligently while remaining totally under control and non-vicious. The interest in Schutzhund training is a reflection of popular apprehension about crime and concern for personal safety.

The training, offered by various clubs, is a kind of post-graduate course for dogs, usually German Shepherds or Dobermans, that already possess the C.D.X. from obedience trials or a tracking title. The dog is taught to bark at an "attacker" in hiding and to fend off an assault on its owner. In the "courage test" the dog must pursue the attacker, biting his (protected) arm even though he tries to drive the dog away. When the attacker stops fighting, the dog must stop of its own accord. The successful dog earns a new title, SchH A, and various higher ones for more advanced training.

a little downward manual pressure on the rump may be necessary.

4. *Stay*. Essential to controlling a dog is being able to make it stand still while the owner moves away. The first step is to give the command and reward the dog with praise if it does not leap forward instantly. Gradually, the owner gets further and further away. A long leash may be used to flick the dog to remind it to stand if it begins to move.

Preserving the Furniture

To many, especially fastidious, persons the most annoying thing a dog can do is to jump on the furniture, putting muddy paw prints and hair all over a valuable sofa or chair. Unfortunately, furniture lounging is all too common, because dogs like the soft life, too, when they can get it. Sometimes they will even take to the furniture surreptitiously, when alone in the house, leaving only telltale indentations in the pillows.

ILLUSTRATION BY KIMBLE P. MEAD

To enforce the "four on the floor" rule, trainers have developed three basic methods:

1. *The Clothesline Method.* Tie a long clothesline to the dog's collar and let it wander around the room. As soon as it even looks longingly at the sofa, give what is known as a "corrective jerk," a short, sharp pull on the line. Repeat as needed until the dog considers lying on the floor not so bad, all things considered.

2. *The Mousetrap Method.* Place a half dozen mousetraps on the sofa and cover with sheets of newspaper. When the dog leaps onto it, the traps will spring, creating a clatter that will put the animal to flight—hopefully not onto the club chair.

3. *The Balloon Method.* This is a variation of the mousetrap method, especially useful for large surfaces, like beds. Tie a string across the bed and attach clusters of inflated balloons to the string. When the dog jumps on the bed, the claws will burst the balloons, frightening it away. Before using this method, one should ascertain that the dog does not have a craving for rubber. Balloons are hard to digest.

Methods 2 and 3 have the advantage of not requiring the owner to be in at the time the offense is committed, but they do have the disadvantage of requiring the home to be oddly decorated with mousetraps and balloons for some time.

Dutch: The Canine Narc

Perhaps the greatest narcotics dog was Dutch III, a German Shepherd who worked for the Washington, D. C. police. Dutch possessed not only a superior nose but an unusual determination. For example, on one case he barked at a cigarette box, indicating that he thought it contained narcotics. His partner looked inside, found nothing and returned it to the table. Annoyed, the dog took the case in its mouth and bit down. Out fell two packets of heroin that had been hidden by a false bottom.

Using his nose like an X-ray machine, Dutch sniffed through the doors of forty closed lockers to find the one containing a heroin cache. Even a packet dangling out a window by a string failed to fool him; he simply sat down by the windowsill to mark the spot.

As a fully-trained police dog, Dutch knew that guns and other weapons can be important pieces of evidence. So if he encountered one in his search for narcotics, he would bark to alert his partner and resume his main task of finding the drugs.

Under the Gun, Performance Counts

Dogs have been trained to disarm a person without injuring him. Here a highly-disciplined canine demonstrates how to remove a pistol from the hands of an "assailant."

7

The Vet Takes Pains to Cure
HEALTH

Health

Trotting Along With the March Of Medicine

The profession which now spends a large part of its time ministering to the medical needs of dogs was hardly concerned with them at all less than a century ago. The name "veterinarian" derives from a Latin word for draft animals, and, indeed, the early practitioners devoted themselves to maintaining the health of economically important agricultural beasts, particularly cattle and horses. As the first president of Cornell University sailed for Europe in 1868 on a faculty-recruiting mission, Ezra Cornell, the university's founder, supposedly shouted at him from the dock, "Don't forget the horse doctor."

Today, in the minds of most people, a veterinarian is a "dog doctor," and the impression is statistically accurate. Less than 10 percent of the nation's 30,000 veterinarians devote themselves exclusively to "large animals" (livestock), while about two thirds are in private practices that deal entirely or partly with "small animals" (dogs and cats), according to a survey by the American Veterinary Medical Association. The rest are in research and government programs. Three quarters of the 4,000 animal hospitals in the country specialize in pet care. The rise of

Canine Care: Questions and Answers

Dr. Harold M. Zweighaft, director of the Tri-Boro Animal Hospital in New York City and a member of the House of Delegates of the American Veterinary Medical Association, reports on some of the questions of current concern in the field of canine health:

1. What vaccinations should a puppy be given?

It has been said that ten experienced, competent veterinarians in one room will yield 11 vaccination programs. There is more truth than humor in that statement. The core of the controversy is the puppy itself. Today's ethical vaccines—vaccines produced by a reputable pharmaceutical or biological firm where quality controls are rigidly enforced—are all standardized and effective. But puppies presented for vaccination vary widely as to breed, size, age, health, parasite population and remnants of maternal immunity. These variations make it impossible to devise an effective vaccination program to cover all puppies. Most doctors today agree that, given a healthy, non-parasitized (no worms) pup in a satisfactory nutritional state, vaccination with a trivalent vaccine at ten to 12 weeks of age, repeated four to six weeks later, will confer an effective, long-lasting immunity—up to 15 months. (A trivalent vaccine protects against three diseases: distemper, hepatitis and leptospirosis.)

Unfortunately, not all puppies are healthy, free from worms, mites or fleas and in excellent nutritional condition when their vaccinations are started. Urban pups are subject to different stresses and virus concentrations than are their suburban counterparts. Farm puppies are in a class by themselves.

Continued on page 153

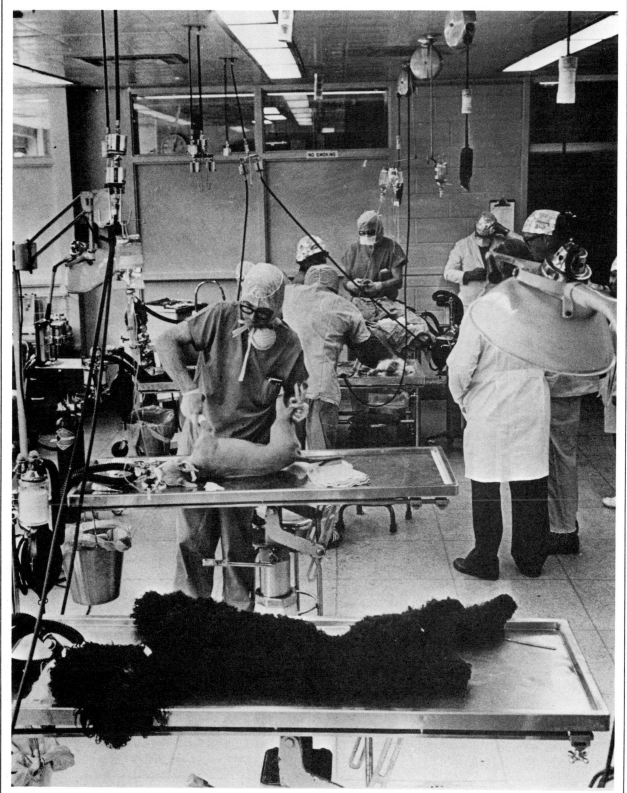

Veterinarians at work at the Animal Medical Center, the world's largest small animal hospital, which offers around-the-clock service on Manhattan's East Side.

the small animal practice bespeaks the importance of pets in modern American society. It has also helped to overcome the argument that women were unsuited for the profession because they lacked the requisite strength; grappling with a Yorkshire Terrier obviously takes less muscle than wrestling with a horse. (About 500 veterinarians are women.)

The profession is also much better educated than in the days of Ezra Cornell, who had to go as far as Edinburgh to find a competent teacher of veterinary medicine, James Law. Professor Law was horrified by what he found in New York. In a speech in 1893, he complained that totally untrained persons "were licensed to poison, maim, and slay the flocks and herds of the Empire State, and heartily did they avail

The Healing Art: At the Forefront...

A man phones from Geneva, Switzerland, to make an appointment for his dog to be treated. A woman from California brings her dogs in a chauffeured limousine for an examination. The medical mecca that has drawn these travelers is the Angell Memorial Hospital in Boston, one of the world's foremost treatment centers for canines and other small animals.

Founded in 1915, Angell has been a pioneer in developing surgical techniques, identifying diseases and devising treatments. Today it handles 800 surgical cases every month, from simple spayings to the implantation of heart pacemakers. The operating rooms, recovery rooms, isolation wards and intensive care facilities are stocked with equipment as complex and expensive as in a hospital for humans — an electrocardiograph, an x-ray generator that costs $67,000 and surgical lights at $4,000 each. (Dogs and cats are not the only patients: on a typical day, a premature puppy was sharing a special care room with two owls and a snake.)

There is a specialist for almost every ailment among the staff of 17 full-time veterinarians and eight consultants, who treat not only the pets of rich persons from afar but the neighborhood animals from Boston's inner city and referrals from other veterinarians as well. Like any hospital, Angell also has interns—an annual crop of eight competitively chosen veterinary school graduates who, in the words of the Chief of Staff, Dr. Gus Thornton, "gain a tremendous amount of experience in a short time under proper guidance and with good equipment." Angell is also a prime testing ground for new drugs. It runs clinical trials to determine, for example, the effectiveness of new antibiotics. The hospital, which moved to a new building in 1975, is supported by the Massachusetts Society for the Prevention of Cruelty to Animals. The hospital is named for a founder of the society.

Visiting hours in the patient wards are from 10 AM to 2 PM each day, but if the owners cannot come the attendants talk to the animals and pet them so that they do not feel abandoned. The bars of the cages are sometimes decorated with get-well cards.

"People are impressed that all this technology is available for dogs," said a hospital official. "But there's a lot of human touch, too."

...And at the Front Door

Although Dr. Charles F. Kaufman opened his veterinary practice in 1974, almost no one has brought a dog or cat to his office. That is because he brings his office to them.

Dr. Kaufman and his associates, known collectively as "the Mobile Vet," cruise the neighborhoods of Brooklyn and lower Manhattan in three customized vans, making house calls from 9 AM to 9 PM. Each van is equipped with a veterinarian, an assistant, an examination table and enough medical equipment to do minor surgery. For major operations the vans pick up animals and deliver them to a surgical theater at the headquarters, where a telephone dispatcher records vehicular movements with pins on a street map.

Dr. Kaufman began his service because, "I had worked in the city and seen what a hassle it was for people to get a vet. I also wanted to start a practice for myself with very little money. For the price of a truck, I was in business." The main attraction was convenience: older persons, the handicapped, and people with large dogs or with many animals found it easier to pick up the telephone than to transport themselves to an office. The price, moreover, was competitive. The $15 house call fee was about the same as charged by Dr. Kaufman's stationary colleagues.

In three years, two more vans were added, and the main obstacle to expansion now is recruiting enough veterinarians willing to work peripatetically. "It's harder work, and it takes more self-confidence," says Dr. Kaufman. "In a hospital you're protected by the staff. In the home, you're dealing with people on their own turf. You have to be able to handle yourself, both personally and professionally."

Using animal power to help animals, the ASPCA ambulance rolled along New York's cobblestone streets in the 1890s in search of sick dogs.

Tick

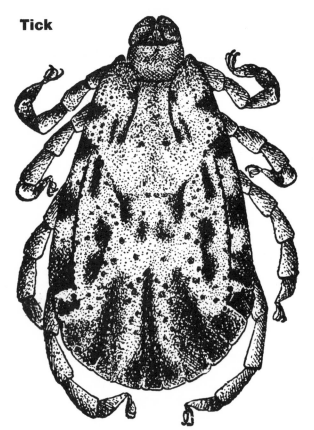

The tick spends much of its life attached to a dog's skin, gorging itself on blood.

The flea's highly adapted lifestyle has helped make it the most common external parasite of dogs.

Both are shown enlarged hundreds of times.

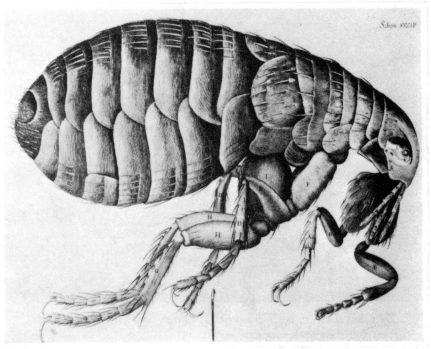

Flea

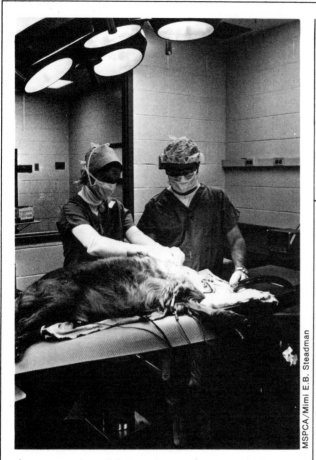

A surgeon (on right) and a technician work on a dog in one of the operating rooms at Angell Memorial Hospital in Boston.

"In his grief over the loss of a dog, a little boy stands for the first time on tiptoe, peering into the rueful morrow of manhood. After this most inconsolable of sorrows there is nothing life can do to him that he will not be able somehow to bear."

JAMES THURBER

Canine Care: Questions and Answers

2. How serious is heartworm disease?

Heartworm infection or dirofilariasis varies in importance according to geography. California and the Midwest are relatively free of this canine parasite. The East Coast from Florida to Canada, however, is heartworm country.

An infected dog has the mature worms living in the upper right chamber of its heart. The worms may be several inches long, and several dozen may live in the right auricle and the large blood vessels attached to it. Infant worms (microfilaria) circulate throughout the blood vessels of the body. These infant worms are picked up by a mosquito when biting the dog. The microscopic infants are transmitted to another dog when the mosquito bites again several days later. (Fortunately, these worms will not develop in humans.) After several months, the infected dog will lose weight, develop a cough, and may have fainting spells.

Early cases can be treated. Most importantly, heartworms can be prevented by maintaining the dog on diethylcarbamazine tablets or liquid during and after the mosquito season. It is necessary to make sure that the dog is free from heartworms prior to starting the preventive medications, because they will kill any adult worms already in the heart, causing them to fall into the lungs where they may create a fatal embolism (blockage). A simple blood test will determine whether the disease is present. In some areas a series of two negative blood tests is advisable before starting the medication. *Continued on page 157*

themselves of the opportunity." Today's veterinary students undergo a thorough four-year postgraduate course and often intern in an animal hospital. Many branch out into specialities such as dermatology, cardiology, ophthalmology, neurology and radiology. The demand for specialists is such that some have begun hanging out their own shingles instead of practicing in the big hospitals. (Some veterinarians are unhappy about this trend because they feel that it will suggest to the clients that the general practitioner is somehow not competent to deal with all patients.) In fact, the demand for animal doctors of all kinds is growing so rapidly that professional groups estimate another 10,000 veterinarians will be needed in the 1980s.

Being hospitalized often gives a patient that caged-in feeling.

Medi-Pet's Policy of Prevention

A national health plan for people is probably a thing of the distant future in the United States, but for dogs the prospects may be somewhat better. Medi-Pet, a medical plan covering dogs and cats, was founded in California in 1976 by Paul E. Murray, Jr., a retired official of the Bank of America, whose goal is to extend the program nationwide. It is modeled after a "health maintenance organization," in which subscribers pay a fixed annual fee for treatment at the organization's facilities.

Medi-Pet, which reports having about 1,200 subscribers in the San Francisco area, charges an annual fee of about $70. In return, the pet owner is assured medical and surgical treatment except for breeding and cosmetic procedures. There are also some additional charges, such as $4 a day for in-patient care at one of the organization's three hospitals. To be eligible, a pet must be between 16 weeks and seven years old, vaccinated and free of pre-existing ailments.

Mr. Murray says that he devised the plan because veterinary hospitals are operating at less than capacity while many pet owners are refusing their animals medical treatment: "The average owner will elect to put the pet to sleep when the bill gets above $300, our research shows. I want to take the economics out of the decision about whether an animal lives or dies. Under Medi-Pet, the healthy animals support the unhealthy animals." Mr. Murray believes that the health plan will encourage preventive medicine since owners will be more likely to take their pet to the veterinarian at the first sign of illness.

In adapting the concept of pre-paid medical care to the needs of animals, Mr. Murray made at least one concession in the direction of health insurance: the application blank for Medi-Pet bears a striking resemblance to a Blue Cross form.

Miracle Cures Are Now in the Bag

Most of the wonder drugs that have been discovered in the quest for cures for human diseases have also found their way into the veterinarian's little black bag. The following is a guide to the medicines that are used for treating dogs.

● ANTIBIOTICS

Examples: Penicillin
Streptomycin
Tetracycline
Chloramphenicol
Erythromycin

Action: Destroy bacteria or prevent them from reproducing. These drugs do not affect viruses.

Application: Pneumonia, kidney and liver infections, abscesses.

● CORTICAL STEROIDS

Examples: Hydrocortisone
Prednisolone
Prednisone
Triamcinallone

Action: Reduce inflammation. Available in pills, liquids, sprays or ointments.

Application: Dermatitis, asthma, arthritis, allergies.

● ANTICONVULSANTS

Examples: Dilantin
Phenobarbital
Mylepsin

Action: Increase the threshold of activity within brain cells, preventing over-excitation in the form of convulsions or tremors.

Application: Epilepsy, slow-growing brain tumors, distemper convulsions.

● DIURETICS

Examples: Lasix
Naturetin
Diuric
Esadrix

Action: Cause an increase in water excretion by the kidneys, eliminating excess fluids from the lungs, abdomen or limbs.

Application: Heart failure (to rid lungs of fluid), dropsy or ascites (to drain abdominal cavity), kidney diseases.

● ANESTHETICS

Examples: Surital
Pentothal
Fluothane
Halothane
Metofane
Nitrous Oxide

Action: Depress conscious areas of the brain, preventing awareness of pain, and cause relaxation of voluntary muscles.

Application: Surgery.

● ANTICANCER DRUGS

Examples: Nitrogen mustards
Cytoxin
Vincristine
6 Mercaptopurine
L-Asparaginase

Action: Prevent the reproduction of malignant cells for varying periods. These drugs also adversely affect normal cells to some extent.

Application: Tumors, including carcinoma and mastocytoma, and lymphosarcoma (leukemia).

● ANABOLIC HORMONES

Examples: Winstrol
Durabolin

Action: Increase metabolic efficiency in older animals.

Application: Osteoperosis (softening of bones because of improper metabolism of calcium), liver and kidney malfunctions.

● ANALGESICS AND NARCOTICS

Examples: Aspirin
Morphine
Demerol
Butazolidine

Action: Alleviate pain

Application: Arthritis, tumors, broken legs, sprains.

A conscientious owner tries to save a puppy from a trip to the dog dentist. Most dogs' built-in need to gnaw keeps their teeth clean.

The educational system is having difficulty keeping the supply equal to the demand. There are only a handful of veterinary schools in the United States—19 to be exact—and some of them have ten times as many applicants as student places. Dean Robert M. Marshak of the University of Pennsylvania Veterinary College has described the selection process as "wrenching." Since all the schools are state-supported, out-of-state applicants are generally given a lower priority and often find that they have nowhere to go. The six New England states re-

Canine Care: Questions and Answers

3. What is immune-mediated disease?

Variation in immunity is a much investigated and discussed branch of medicine. The research has focused on the "immune-mediated diseases," which include allergy, hypersensitivity, lack of resistance to infection and certain degenerative diseases.

There are three forms of immunity dysfunction. Some animals are immune deficient. They will not respond to a vaccine and may develop distemper or hepatitis despite being given the proper vaccinations. Puppies with this condition may be constantly ill with various viral or bacterial infections and may even develop a fatal one before reaching adulthood.

A second form of dysfunction is too much immunity within the dog's system. Pups or even adults of this type will overreact to germs, pollens or dust. They are the highly allergic or hypersensitive dogs that are always scratching or coughing or having frequent and persistent bouts of vomiting and diarrhea.

The third type of dysfunction occurs when an animal becomes immune to parts of its own body, such as the blood cells or inner skin structures or joint linings. These conditions are termed auto-immune disease.

Sophisticated laboratory tests are necessary to confirm the presence of immune-mediated diseases. If diagnosed in early stages, these diseases can be alleviated but rarely cured. *Continued on page 159*

A surgeon at Angell Memorial Hospital treats a patient in the minor surgery room.

cently banded together to establish a regional veterinary school at Tufts University near Boston because of the difficulty their residents had in finding places. Some universities have also begun offering training as a veterinary assistant, a kind of paramedic, to help fill the shortage of clinical personnel.

As a result of the educational and research resources that have been devoted to veterinary medicine, the level of practice has become quite sophisticated. Pharmaceutical advances have armed the veterinarian with a broad spectrum of

Anatomy of an Appendage

Despite its advanced state, the science of dog anatomy has provided no clear explanation for why the dog has a tail. Some facts are not in dispute. The tail is essentially an extension of the cervical column, the dog's backbone, and consists of three to 23 vertebrae, depending upon the type of dog. Any curls or bends in the tail are caused by imbalances in tension in the muscles controlling it. But students of the subject disagree about what the tail was put there to do. One theory is that the tail acts as stabilizer and rudder when the dog is in motion, helping it to shift its center of gravity, to jump more easily and to turn at high speed. According to this argument, the docked-tail breeds developed a more spread-out stance in the rear to compensate for the lack of the natural stabilizer.

Evolution probably played a large part in tail development. Tufts of hair may have developed in some breeds to enhance the rudder effect. Northern dogs could have acquired their curled tails through natural selection, since extended tails tended to drag in the snow and eventually freeze. Tucking the tail between the legs in moments of fear may have originally been an instinctual response to protect the tail from being bitten by natural enemies.

Even the reason for tail wagging is hotly frequently debated by the experts. One explanation that has been offered is physiological: the tail acts as a pump, a backup heart so to speak, that keeps the dog's blood circulating properly in moments of stress. Proponents of this theory contend that long-tailed dogs survive heart ailments better than short-tailed varieties. Another proferred explanation is that wagging is a means of communication. It certainly communicates happiness, but why should the dog, before coming in contact with people, have needed to express its feelings of contentment? The reason, say some theorists, is that dogs hunted in packs, often in tall grass. The leader of the pack, by moving its tail from side to side, could signal to the followers its excitement at having picked up the scent of game. (Oral communication at that point would have frightened off the prey.) In later eons, the dog came to associate the tail wagging with the excitement of seeing its owner again and other happy occasions.

Definitive explanations are also lacking for the dog's habit of chasing and chewing its own tail. Some believe that this is a late behavioral adaptation to domestication. That is, the dog chews its tail to get attention from people who wonder why it chews its tail.

chemical weapons, from anticancer drugs to birth control pills. Dogs now enjoy therapeutic equipment like back braces (for Dachshunds with sagging spines) and leg casts with built-in wheels so that the animal can move about. Dentistry, from simple removal of tooth tartar to complicated root canal operations, is available. Orthopedic surgery can remedy otherwise crippling bone ailments. Some dogs have been fitted with hearing aids, and weak or broken ear cartilage has been stiffened with plastic implants. There are even veterinarians who practice acupuncture on dogs.

The advances in veterinary science have sometimes proven two-edged, because much of the elaborate medical care now available is also expensive. Many owners are reluctant to invest possibly hundreds of dollars in laboratory tests, surgery and hospital charges, especially when, viewed in cold economic terms, the cost of a new dog would be less than that of repairing the old one. But affection often defeats economic logic, especially when an ill dog becomes a *cause célèbre*.

Journalistic chestnuts about the sick-child-too-poor-to-pay-for-an-operation are now matched by stories about dogs in similar straits. A classic instance was the discovery of an ownerless Collie with its thigh bone broken, apparently by an automobile, in the town of Babylon, New York, in the fall of 1977. The area's newspaper, *Newsday,* reported that the dog would probably be put to death unless an owner came forward; the town could not justify spending an estimated $200 for orthopedic surgery. The dam of sympathy burst. Contributions began flowing into the town hall, where the regular animal welfare fund was down to its last $25, and within a few days enough had been collected to send the dog to a surgeon, who used a metal plate and screws to join the fractured pieces of bone. The dog was then adopted by a local family. The operation cost $412, but almost twice that much had been contributed within a few weeks. The Collie may have reason to be thankful that it did *not* have an owner when its accident occurred.

Fourteenth-century veterinary science was in the same primitive state as medicine itself.

Canine Care: Questions and Answers

4. How safe are flea collars?

The advent of flea collars and tags has helped to reduce the tick and flea population of dogs and cats. But they have not completely eliminated the problem, and they have introduced new problems in some instances.

Most dogs tolerate flea collars quite well. In some cases, however, the collar can cause a severe dermatitis around the neck. Prompt removal of the collar and appropriate treatment will clear up the dermatitis. Other dogs may absorb the toxic ingredient in the collar (organic phosphates) and can become quite ill. They may even develop convulsions.

It is dangerous to administer worming medications to a dog wearing a flea collar or tag because some worming preparations contain substances similar to that in the collar and may cause an overdose in the dog. The substances in the collars can also adversely affect the action of an anesthetic. If a dog is scheduled for surgery, the veterinarian should be informed that it was wearing one.

Tales like these of miraculous cures have helped to create a somewhat romanticized image of the modern veterinarian as the kindly person who saves the lives of lovable animals. When he was dean of the University of Georgia College of Veterinary Medicine in 1974, Dr. Richard B. Talbot remarked sarcastically that the institution "is a nice place. That's because it's full of veterinarians. And . . . veterinarians are a bunch of really nice guys." But some members of the profession are concerned that, because he is associated with pet care, the veterinarian's true contribution to human welfare is masked. "We find ourselves confronted," Dr. Talbot contended, "with the wide-spread, simplistic notion that veterinary medicine as science, art and applied research is dedicated to the objective of innoculating and spaying pet canines." He and other veterinarians argue that the treatment of dogs has had benefits for human medicine as well. The discovery that B vitamins cure pellagra in humans was helped by a veterinarian's discerning, in 1916, a connection between that disease and "black tongue" in dogs. Cardiac catheterization (inserting tubes through blood vessels to the heart as part of a surgical procedure) was invented by a veterinarian, as was the technique of pinning bones to heal fractures.

Medical treatment of dogs has also helped to eradicate or control some of the approximately 200 "zoonotic diseases," afflictions that may be transmitted from animals to man. The most notorious of these diseases, and for centuries the most dreaded, is rabies, which is usually transmitted to human victims through bites.

The very name (from the Latin *rabere,* "to rave") conjures up the horrible death, usually within a week, that it inflicts upon canine and human victims. Rabies is a virus that attacks the central nervous system, causing wild and aggressive behavior, paroxysms and fatal paralysis. A dysfunction of the swallowing muscles produces the inability to drink that gave rabies its other common name: hydrophobia, or fear of water. (Some rabies victims have grown frenzied at the mere sound of running water.)

There was no treatment for rabies until the

late 19th century, when the French scientist Louis Pasteur began experiments in which dogs were made immune to rabies by being innoculated over a period of time with weakened forms of the virus. (Pasteur used dried brain segments of an infected rabbit to make his vaccine.) By giving the animals progressively more virulent strains, he built up their resistance so that when they were bitten by a carrier no symptoms appeared. He was even able to demonstrate that the immunity could be produced *after* the victim was bitten but before the virus had a chance to attack the nervous system, a finding that is the basis of the treatment used today. In 1885, the first human bite victim was cured of rabies by a series of 12 innoculations of the Pasteur vaccine.

Relatively little progress was made in rabies treatment after Pasteur, apart from the introduction of a safer vaccine made from duck embryos in the 1950s. That was because rabies virtually died out among the dog population in North America and many European countries in the 20th century. Quarantines, muzzling orders and vaccination of dogs helped make rabies a rare occurrence.

But in the 1970s, there has been at least one breakthrough: the discovery that rabies virus could be positively identified in suspect dogs by microscopic examination of a small sample of skin taken from the dog's facial area. The conventional method of diagnosis was to keep the animal under observation until it developed the symptoms of rabies or to kill it on mere suspicion and autopsy the brain. When perfected, the new technique will allow doctors to decide quickly whether to begin treatment without having to sacrifice the animal. Early diagnosis in the dog also prepares the way for developing an effective cure for rabid animals.

The medical advances may be coming just in time, because rabies is having a worldwide resurgence, not primarily as a canine disease but as an epidemic among wildlife. Before 1951, all cases of human rabies in the United States were caused by either dog or cat bites. But since then dog-borne rabies has been virtually unknown, while a growing number of bats, skunks, foxes, raccoons and other wild animals have been reported as carriers.

Wildlife rabies poses a particular threat to man and his pets in Europe, where the epidemic, mainly among foxes, has been moving steadily westward from its suspected source: the fox population in the Arctic regions of the Soviet Union. The disease has spread from Poland into Germany, where about 6,000 persons a year are being treated for rabies, and across the Alps into Italy.

Some countries, hoping to contain the outbreak, are offering bounties to fox hunters, although the only effective barrier so far has been water. Britain, which imposes a six-month quarantine on all imported animals, has been spared by its traditional bulwark against all European invasions, the English Channel. But there are growing fears that a rabid animal will be smuggled into the country or enter accidentally with a ship's crew. Once its natural defense line has been breached, Britain is particularly vulnerable to the disease because of its large native fox population. The epidemic could spread quickly from these animals to the hounds and horses of the fox hunters. (One characteristic of a rabid fox is that it loses its fear of man and may wander aimlessly near habitations.)

The British government has stringent emergency plans to eradicate all wild animals within a five-mile radius of a rabies outbreak. But the ultimate answer to the rabies threat, many experts believe, is a vaccine for wildlife. Scientists in the United States are now perfecting such a vaccine, which, because wild animals will not report for vaccination, will take the form of a timed-release capsule that can be hidden in bait.

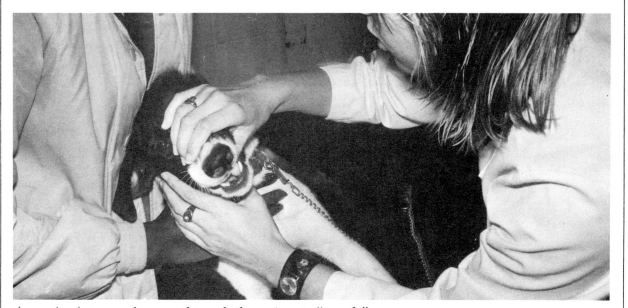

A veterinarian must do more than ask the patient to "say ah."

Just as animal medicine helps protect humans against rabies, many of the medical discoveries that are made for humans also benefit dogs. For example the famous "Heimlich maneuver" for expelling food stuck in the throat has been tried successfully on dogs by its originator, Dr. H. J. Heimlich of Cincinnati. By pressing a fist on the abdomen just below the rib cage of the dog, he was able to force air from the lungs up through the trachea, dislodging the obstacle that prevented the dog from breathing. Similar experiments have indicated a way in which artificial respiration, as given to humans, might be adapted to dogs. In the experiments, the rib cage of a dog lying on its side was pressed down to expel air from the lungs. Then the fold of skin over the ribs was grasped in both hands and pulled up until the dog was almost lifted from the table, causing air to be sucked into the lungs. Dogs have also benefitted from antibiotic treatments developed for Rocky Mountain Spotted Fever, a potentially fatal disease that is endemic to the southeastern United States (despite its name) and is transmitted to both man and dogs by tick bites.

The governmental regulatory apparatus that has been established to control the marketing of drugs also operates to protect dogs from unreliable medicines. Any company desiring to sell a new canine medicine must first receive approval from the Federal Food and Drug Administration's Bureau of Veterinary Medicine. The company must prove, by submitting laboratory and clinical test results, that the drug is effective as well as safe.

Apart from the contagious diseases that dogs are usually vaccinated against, perhaps the most common canine disorder is parasites. The intestines, blood vessels and skin of the dog have become the favorite home of an entire bestiary of tiny creatures who could not exist without canines as part of their life cycle. These include worms — tapeworms, roundworms, whipworms, hookworms, heartworms — and an assortment of clinging insects: ticks, mites, lice and fleas. While treatments for all of these conditions exist, somehow a particularly notable outpouring of human ingenuity has been directed at the destruction of fleas, which are the most common external parasites. Collars, tags, sprays, shampoos, sticks and dips have been devised to eradicate them, but fleas have been even more ingenious. Although reduced in numbers, they have managed to survive — partly because of their ability to develop resistance to toxic agents and partly because they are so well adapted to their chosen habitat. The flea (there are several varieties) is an insect that lacks wings but can jump acrobatically. The adult nourishes itself by sucking blood from the dog, sometimes causing serious anemia in young or weak dogs and often transmitting diseases, such as tapeworm. Eliminating the flea would be easier if it lived its entire life on the dog, but the female usually lays its eggs elsewhere, perhaps in a carpet. The eggs hatch within two weeks, and the larvae spin cocoons in which they turn into full-fledged fleas, jumping onto the first dog that comes along. The flea thus must be pursued in all its haunts.

Even though the war against fleas is far from won, veterinary medicine has found cures for many of the most virulent diseases and parasites afflicting dogs. Yet it is often the ordinary household hazards that do the most damage. Even the venerable dog bone can be a menace. The powerful jaws of some dogs can shatter bones, causing intestines to be perforated by the swallowed splinters. (An uncooked shank or knuckle bone is relatively harder to shatter.) Chewing on painted toys can produce lead poisoning. In the garden are insecticides and pesticides that can be licked from grass and shrubs, and poisonous plants (like daffodil bulbs) that can be ingested. In the driveway may be pools of automobile antifreeze containing potentially deadly ethylene glycol, a substance whose aroma and taste dogs apparently find irresistible. Dogs have been known to get into the family's pill supplies, overdosing themselves with such potent drugs as amphetamine stimulants. First aid procedures may help, but it is often impossible to tell which substance was ingested. Taking the dog in for an examination is far better than wondering what to do until the veterinarian comes.

Intestinal Worms: A Rogues' Gallery

Pictured here are four common parasites that live in the intestines of dogs, causing symptoms such as gastrointestinal disturbances, weight loss and anemia. They are usually detected by examining fecal matter with a microscope for the presence of eggs, which are distinctive to each species of worm. In many instances, puppies are born already infected with worms from the mother.

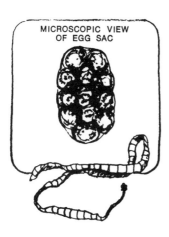

TAPEWORM

Scientific name: Dypylidium caninum
Length: Up to about two feet
Method of infection: Ingestion of an infected intermediate host, either animal, fish or flea
Treatment: Yomesan pills; arecoline (a purgative)

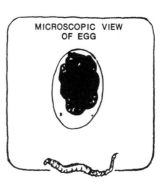

HOOKWORM

Scientific name: Ancylostoma caninum
Length: Up to about ¾ inch (thread-like)
Method of infection: Larvae in the soil are ingested by the dog or penetrate the skin
Treatment: Disophenol by injection or dichlorvos orally

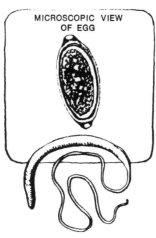

WHIPWORM

Scientific name: Trichuris vulpis
Length: Up to about ½ inch (thread-like)
Method of infection: Ingestion of larvae in the soil
Treatment: Pthalofene, either orally or by injection; Milibis tablets

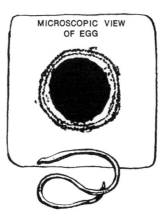

ROUNDWORM

Scientific name: Toxocara canis
Length: Four to seven inches
Method of infection: Dog ingests eggs or the larvae
Treatment: Administration of piperazine orally

8

At Times, Sex Can Be Artificial

REPRODUCTION

Reproduction

Giving the Creative Urge an Outlet

Among the many liberties that the dog surrendered when it accepted domestication was reproductive freedom. Except for "street matings" by strays and accidents resulting from supervisory failure, the appointed time, place and partner are now determined by man. There are even externally imposed age limits: the American Kennel Club does not ordinarily register litters if either parent was over 12 years old at the time of mating, if the female was under eight months, or if the male was under seven months. So carefully regulated is the dog's sex life, in fact, that some authorities have denied that it has one at all. Dr. A. Barton, a veterinarian, has argued for example, that "The very least that sex life seems to imply are freedom of choice of a sexual partner, a certain regularity of sexual routine, and conscious anticipation and planning for future sexual activity."

The issue may be merely semantic, however, because few doubt that, whatever the conditions imposed, the dog does engage robustly in sex whenever allowed. The man-made rules are clearly suppressing a well-developed instinct for propagating the species. The remarkably efficient procreation process calls forth none of the vain display that mark some animal courtships. Rather, it involves a complex series of hormonal changes that ensures that the female becomes fertile and amenable twice a year (in most cases) and that the male is particularly attracted at precisely those times. The onset of the fertile period is announced over a wide area by an olfactory broadcasting system that ensures the presence of a large variety of possible mates. That may have given the dog the evolutionary advantage of allowing natural selection to occur right at the time of mating; only the fittest get to father.

The strength of the reproductive instinct is appreciated by anyone who has ever tried to thwart it. A female in heat left unattended even momentarily may be found locked irretrievably in the "copulatory tie" with an enterprising male, an embarrassing moment for the dogs and a frustrating one for the owner unprepared for a litter. Fences are almost no obstacle. Males have surmounted them, dug under them or gone right through them in hot pursuit. There is little alternative to maintaining a 24-hour-a-day armed guard.

The majority of owners eventually shrink from the burdens of guardianship and have their females spayed, eliminating the ovaries, the uterus and the "heat cycle." Others, trying to preserve the possibility of breeding at a later date, resort to palliatives such as tablets that reduce the female's scent. (Some authorities argue that this is one odor that chlorophyll is powerless to mask.) Owners of males rarely take much interest in their reproductive behavior, usually resorting to neutering only in an attempt — successful on young dogs only — to cure personality defects such as over-aggressiveness.

There are two main reasons for humans' exerting control over canine reproduction: eugenics and profit. The litter produced by a carefully contrived mating between a male and female who both have "credentials" is valuable because the puppies are expected to inherit the desirable traits. It is a speculative business, but the market for reproductive services seems to be booming. Puppies of prize-winning parents fetch high prices, and it may be difficult to even get an appointment with a champion stud dog. Many stud owners reserve the right to examine the female for suitability or require health certificates to prevent possibly inferior puppies

Sod Poodle *is a colloquial name for the prairie dog, which is not a dog at all but a member of the squirrel family.*

Perpetual Calendar for Whelping

The perpetual whelping calendar is a device for quickly computing the date on which puppies are *likely* to arrive when the conception date is known. (The gestation period takes 63 days on average, although individual cases may deviate by a few days from the average.) To use the calendar, find the appropriate date in the row marked "conception," then read the date below in the row labeled "due." For example, a dog that conceives on January 5 is due to give birth on March 9.

Conception—Jan: 1 2 3 4 5 6 7 8 9 10 11 12 13 14 15 16 17 18 19 20 21 22 23 24 25 26 27 — 28 29 30 31
Due—March: 5 6 7 8 9 10 11 12 13 14 15 16 17 18 19 20 21 22 23 24 25 26 27 28 29 30 31 **April** 1 2 3 4

Conception—Feb: 1 2 3 4 5 6 7 8 9 10 11 12 13 14 15 16 17 18 19 20 21 22 23 24 25 26 — 27 28
Due—April: 5 6 7 8 9 10 11 12 13 14 15 16 17 18 19 20 21 22 23 24 25 26 27 28 29 30 **May** 1 2

Conception—Mar: 1 2 3 4 5 6 7 8 9 10 11 12 13 14 15 16 17 18 19 20 21 22 23 24 25 26 27 28 29 — 30 31
Due—May: 3 4 5 6 7 8 9 10 11 12 13 14 15 16 17 18 19 20 21 22 23 24 25 26 27 28 29 30 31 **June** 1 2

Conception—April: 1 2 3 4 5 6 7 8 9 10 11 12 13 14 15 16 17 18 19 20 21 22 23 24 25 26 27 28 — 29 30
Due—June: 3 4 5 6 7 8 9 10 11 12 13 14 15 16 17 18 19 20 21 22 23 24 25 26 27 28 29 30 **July** 1 2

Conception—May: 1 2 3 4 5 6 7 8 9 10 11 12 13 14 15 16 17 18 19 20 21 22 23 24 25 26 27 28 29 — 30 31
Due—July: 3 4 5 6 7 8 9 10 11 12 13 14 15 16 17 18 19 20 21 22 23 24 25 26 27 28 29 30 31 **August** 1 2

Conception—June: 1 2 3 4 5 6 7 8 9 10 11 12 13 14 15 16 17 18 19 20 21 22 23 24 25 26 27 28 29 — 30
Due—August: 3 4 5 6 7 8 9 10 11 12 13 14 15 16 17 18 19 20 21 22 23 24 25 26 27 28 29 30 31 **Sept** 1

Conception—July: 1 2 3 4 5 6 7 8 9 10 11 12 13 14 15 16 17 18 19 20 21 22 23 24 25 26 27 28 29 — 30 31
Due—September: 2 3 4 5 6 7 8 9 10 11 12 13 14 15 16 17 18 19 20 21 22 23 24 25 26 27 28 29 30 **Oct** 1 2

Conception—August: 1 2 3 4 5 6 7 8 9 10 11 12 13 14 15 16 17 18 19 20 21 22 23 24 25 26 27 28 29 — 30 31
Due—September: 3 4 5 6 7 8 9 10 11 12 13 14 15 16 17 18 19 20 21 22 23 24 25 26 27 28 29 30 31 **Nov** 1 2

Conception—Sept: 1 2 3 4 5 6 7 8 9 10 11 12 13 14 15 16 17 18 19 20 21 22 23 24 25 26 27 28 29 — 29 30
Due—November: 3 4 5 6 7 8 9 10 11 12 13 14 15 16 17 18 19 20 21 22 23 24 25 26 27 28 29 30 **Dec** 1 2

Conception—Oct: 1 2 3 4 5 6 7 8 9 10 11 12 13 14 15 16 17 18 19 20 21 22 23 24 25 26 27 28 29 — 30 31
Due—December: 3 4 5 6 7 8 9 10 11 12 13 14 15 16 17 18 19 20 21 22 23 24 25 26 27 28 29 30 31 **Jan** 1 2

Conception—Nov: 1 2 3 4 5 6 7 8 9 10 11 12 13 14 15 16 17 18 19 20 21 22 23 24 25 26 27 28 29 — 30
Due—January: 3 4 5 6 7 8 9 10 11 12 13 14 15 16 17 18 19 20 21 22 23 24 25 26 27 28 29 30 31 **Feb** 1

Conception—Dec: 1 2 3 4 5 6 7 8 9 10 11 12 13 14 15 16 17 18 19 20 21 22 23 24 25 26 27 — 28 29 30 31
Due—February: 2 3 4 5 6 7 8 9 10 11 12 13 14 15 16 17 18 19 20 21 22 23 24 25 26 27 28 **March** 1 2 3 4

from being sold under the "brand name" of the stud.

There are organizations that, in effect, license dogs to reproduce by certifying that they are free of hereditary disease. The Orthopedic Foundation for Animals examines hip X-rays for signs of the potentially crippling malformation known as dysplasia. Hips are ranked on a scale of one (no evidence of the defect) to four (severe dysplasia). When an advertisement for a stud service stipulates "X-rayed bitches only," it means that an OFA certificate will be required. Another organization, the Canine Eye Registry Foundation, warrants that no hereditary eye disease has been uncovered in an ophthalmological examination. Another mission of the foundation is to detect diseases that have become endemic to certain breeds or strains. The eye records, for example, have disclosed an unusually high incidence of progressive retinal atrophy in English Springer Spaniels. Many other breeds suffer from hereditary eye defects —they were found in 25 percent of the foundation's first 28,000 examination reports—and similar genetically transmitted diseases.

Both males and females are often taken from show to show until they become champions for

the sole purpose of setting them up in business as "producers." Some breeders believe that the true worth of a dog is not what it is but what its progeny turn out to be. In a 1976 memorial article for Ch. King's Creek Triple Threat, described as "the greatest Beagle of all time," *Showdogs* magazine said that

Tribute must be paid to Triple Threat the sire as well as to Triple Threat the show dog. At the time of writing, 47 champions claim [him] as their sire. There are at least a dozen within a point to several points of their titles. Numerous others have a few points each. There's a whole flock of youngsters who will soon be reaching show age, plus four new litters by him— one not yet born.

The same magazine celebrates the procreative powers of dogs by acclaiming as "top producers" those males whose offspring have won five championships in a calendar year and females whose offspring have won three.

With so much fame and fortune at stake, it is not surprising that the act of mating becomes more charged with significance for the owners than for the dogs who are being bred. When

Birth Control: Questions and Answers

Preventing dogs from reproducing has become an important function of veterinarians. Dr. Harold M. Zweighaft answers the questions most commonly asked about canine contraception.

1. Is there a pressing need to impose birth control on dogs?

The hue and cry frequently raised about the need for birth control is in a sense much ado about neutering. The dog population of all areas of the United States has remained remarkably constant for the last 20 years. The concept of a soaring canine population is emotional rather than factual. But many dogs are not properly supervised, which often makes it seem as if the dog population is getting out of hand.

Continued on page 174

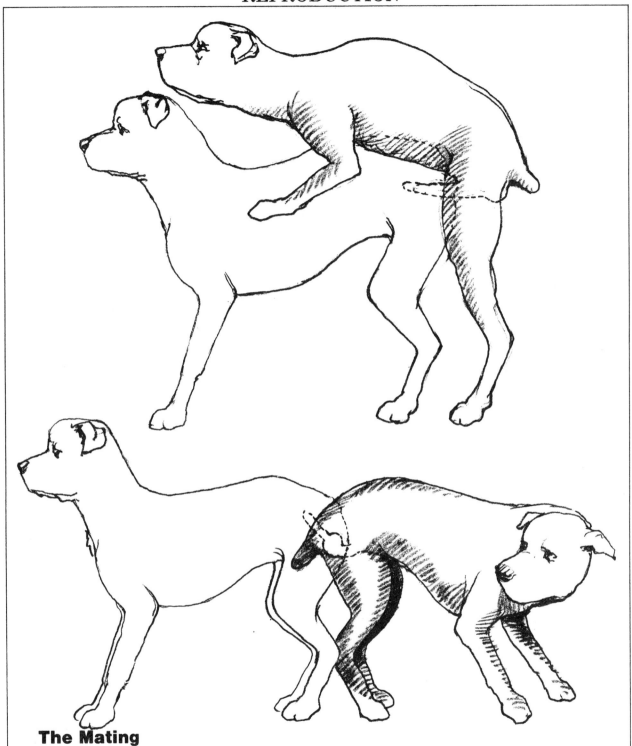

The Mating

The male mounts the female and begins thrusting motions. A slender bone in the penis facilitates entry before a full erection is achieved. When fully erect, the penis has a bulbous enlargement toward its base that would prevent entry. The purpose of the bulb is to effect the "copulatory tie," maintaining penetration about 15 minutes, until the sperm-rich portion of the seminal fluid is ejaculated. The male, still "tied" to the female, may dismount and face in the opposite direction.

The Spaying Operation

When a female dog is spayed, the ovaries and uterus are removed surgically to prevent her from having puppies. The basic steps in the operation are pictured here.

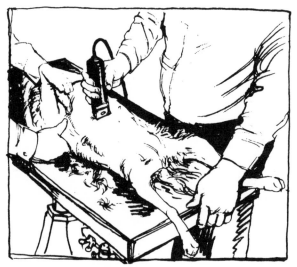

1. ANESTHESIA. The dog is anesthetized by an injection of a barbiturate, sodium pentothal. An endotracheal tube in the windpipe carries a mixture of anesthetic gas and oxygen that will keep the animal unconscious during the operation.

2. PREPARATION. The hair on the abdomen is removed with electric clippers. The skin is washed with antibacterial soap, then rubbed with liquid ether to remove fats and oils which may be trapping bacteria. It is also scrubbed with alcohol and painted with antiseptic solution.

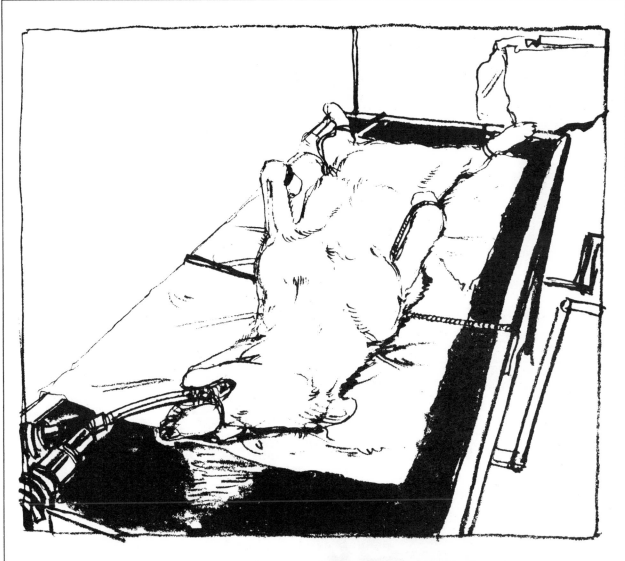

3. POSITIONING. The dog is secured to the operating table with nylon cords. The front feet are left in a forward position, rather than being tied back toward the head, to avoid restricting the expansion of the chest during breathing.

4. THE INCISION. An incision of about two to four inches, depending upon the size of the dog, is made in the abdomen. The edges of the incision are pulled back over a sterile drape and fastened with scissors-like clamps.

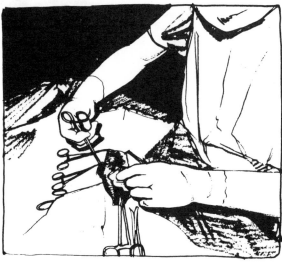

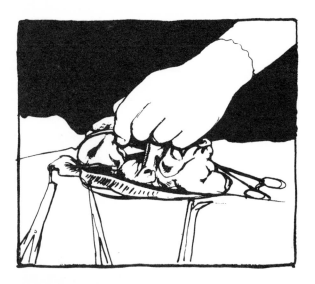

5. THE LIGATION. The ovaries and "horns" of the Y-shaped uterus are lifted from the abdomen. The blood vessels to the ovaries are "ligated" or tied off with catgut, enabling the ovaries to be detached from the body.

6. SEVERING. With the ovaries (A) and the uterine horns (B) laid back across the drape, the blood vessels leading to the lower portion of the uterus (C) are tied off and the organ is severed from the cervix, leaving only a "uterine stump."

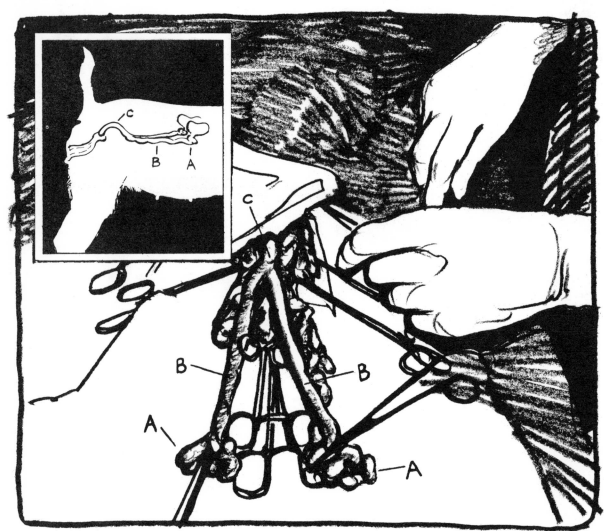

7. SUTURING. The incision is closed. First the lining of the abdomen (peritoneum) and then the muscle layers are sewn with an absorbable suture. Finally, the skin is sewn with a stainless steel wire suture, which is nonirritating. It will be removed 10 days later.

8. RECOVERY. The dog is placed in a recovery room with the endotracheal tube still in place to ensure that an air passage is left open. The dog awakens a few minutes after surgery is completed.

Birth Control: Questions and Answers

2. What is neutering?

Both male and female dogs can be neutered by means of surgical procedures performed under general anesthesia. The male is castrated: the testicles are removed through an incision just in front of the scrotum. Afterwards, the dog cannot father puppies, and his supply of male homones is severely diminished. (A small amount of the male hormone, testosterone, continues to be produced by the adrenal glands.) When performed on a dog under six months old, the surgery usually prevents aggressive behavior, restricts development of the penis and bladder, and may cause the dog to go through life with a urinary tract that is susceptible to infections.

If the surgery is done when the dog is over two years of age, no behavioral changes occur. Aggressive dogs remain aggressive, and dogs that constantly masturbate continue to do so. Obedience training may be helpful in overcoming these undesirable traits. Occasionally, castrated dogs will develop skin and coat problems or tend toward obesity unless the diet is restricted.

The female, when neutered, is said to have been "spayed." The term is derived from the Anglo-French *espeier,* meaning to cut or penetrate. The surgery is technically an ovario-hysterectomy. Under the anesthetic, the belly is shaved and scrubbed with soap and antiseptics. An incision is made in the abdomen, and the two ovaries and the uterus are removed. Recuperation in the hospital may take two to five days, depending on the dog's age and condition.

A spayed female will not only be unable to bear puppies but will no longer come into heat (estrus). If she has been spayed before her first heat period, her breasts will not develop appreciably. Females that are spayed before or just after the first heat period almost never develop tumors or cancers of the breasts. These tumors develop in some older, intact females due to the influence of the ovarian estrogenic hormones. Spaying also avoids uterine infections. Some adverse effects are seen in a small percentage of spayed dogs. A few will develop skin disorders or incontinence (dribbling of urine while resting or sleeping).

Continued on page 178

---

brought together, the two canines often find that they dislike each other. The female may refuse to accept the male, in which case the attendants use friendly persuasion, holding her in place while the stud earns his fee. There are dangers in forcing the issue, however. Males have been severely injured by bites from resentful females, and a famous stud was killed by a vengeful mate. Sometimes it is the male who refuses to cooperate with the breeding program, possibly from nervousness or inexperience. In that case it may be necessary to try again later or find another stud.

The financial arrangements associated with stud service are often quite complex. Typically, the stud owner will offer some guarantee of conception, such as an offer of a free second chance at the next heat if the first "service" does not produce a litter. Sometimes the stud owner will forego the fee in return for the opportunity to choose one or more puppies from the litter (often the "pick of the litter" is offered). But these arrangements so often break down into mutual recriminations that the American Kennel Club, in its general brochure, advises would-be breeders that their agreements "should be put in writing, clearly stating all circumstances and obligations surrounding the transaction" and that remedies must be sought in civil court if an unresolvable dispute occurs. The AKC does not regulate stud fees, and it refrains from umpiring disagreements.

Modern Methods

Although the mating of dogs generally adheres to tradition, efforts are often made to apply modern technology, such as artificial insemination. Artificial insemination was first performed successfully on a dog in the 18th century, but breeders have only recently begun to exploit intensively the advantages over natural methods. The chief advantage is that the male and female need not get along with each other. Besides overcoming the temperamental obstacles to mating, artificial insemination avoids the physical difficulties that are sometimes encountered when males and females are of quite different size (which can occur even in the same breed) or are so overweight as to make copulation seem like an exertion that is hardly worthwhile.

The artificial method also allows the semen to be examined for evidence of infertility, thereby resolving potentially acrimonious disputes about which partner is responsible for nonconceptions. Microscopic study may provide clues to the nature of contraception-inhibiting "sperm antibodies" in some females and may eventually enable breeders to influence the sex of puppies.

Even more revolutionary than artificial insemination is the freezing of semen for future use. Reporting in 1976, Dr. S. W. J. Seager, a veterinarian who has experimented with the technique, said that "since 1969 we have had over 700 puppies born from frozen semen and have developed five generations of dogs using this method of breeding. Semen frozen in 1968 shows little or no loss of motility (ability of the spermatozoa to move) at this time. Completely normal pups have been born from semen stored for 4½ years." Similar experiments were carried on from 1968 to 1976 by the Walter

Picking Out a Mate Without Picking Up a Defect

In selecting a mate for a dog, it is important to determine whether the potential partner has any of the dozens of diseases and defects that may be passed on from one canine generation to another. Several, like hip dysplasia, are found in all breeds, but many others seem to be associated with only one or a few breeds. These are some of the more common inheritable conditions and the breeds in which they are found:

Boxer	Gingival hyperplasia (overgrowth of gums)
Bulldog	Cleft palate
Collie	Collie eye anomaly (improper retinal development)
Cocker Spaniel	Glaucoma (swelling of eye caused by increase in interior fluids)
West Highland White Terrier, Cairn Terrier, Scottish Terrier, Labrador Retriever	Craniomandibular osteopathy (progressive calcification of jaw muscles)
Cocker Spaniel, Dachshund, Pekingese, Beagle	Intervertebral disc degeneration (slipped spinal disc)
Toy Breeds	Tracheal collapse (constricted windpipe) -and- Luxating patella (tendency of knee cap to slip out of joint)

Whelping the Litter

1. As the moment of birth approaches, the mother crouches in the delivery position with the vulva distended. Special hormones soften the cartilage in the pelvic region to make it easier for the puppies to pass through.

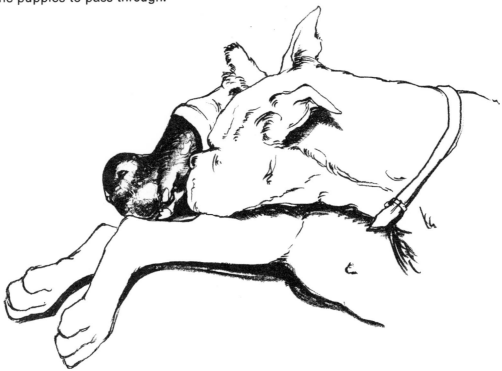

2. A puppy emerges, encased in a membranous sac that has protected it and lubricated its passage. The mother tears the sac away with her teeth. Intervals between the arrival of puppies in the litter may vary from a few minutes to hours.

3. The mother chews through the umbilical cord, which has nurtured the fetus, and licks the puppy to encourage it to begin breathing. She will generally also eat the afterbirth that emerges after each puppy.

4. The puppies begin sucking hungrily at the mother's teats. During the first 24 hours the milk contains colostrum, a substance rich in antibodies, from which the puppies will get most of their immunity during their initial six to 12 weeks of life.

Birth Control: Questions and Answers

3. Which dogs should be neutered?

Most authorities agree that males should not be routinely castrated but that such surgery should generally be reserved for testicular tumors or hormonal imbalances. (In contrast, cats kept as pets are commonly castrated to avoid the strong, objectionable odor from the urine that develops in a complete male.) Male dogs, in any case, do not present the inconvenience of going through cyclical heat periods as females do. They are always willing and almost always able.

Bitches are generally neutered as a convenience for the owners. The female usually goes through the heat period twice a year. The first heat can occur at from six to 10 months of age. The dog will exude a bloody vaginal discharge for about 10 days. In the next 10 days there may be a mucoid or clear discharge or none at all. Conception normally is possible between the ninth and the 13th day from the onset of the bloody discharge. It is the discharge and the courting males attracted to the females during the entire three-week period that most owners seek to avoid by having the dog spayed. In terms of contraceptive results, a well-held leash is as effective as the ovariohysterectomy.

The decision to spay may be deferred if the owner believes that the female has genetic qualities that ought to be passed on to offspring. Owners of purebred dogs have the option of continuing the line by selective breeding, and many owners of mixed breed dogs are rightly convinced that their female has traits worth perpetuating. In such cases, a hysterectomy is usually done only for medical reasons or later in life, when the female would no longer be used for breeding.

Continued on the next page

Reed Army Hospital Institute of Research as part of a program of breeding German Shepherds for military use. The experimenters found that, although the artificial method generally produced fewer puppies in each litter, females experienced similar conception rates whether mated naturally or inseminated with thawed semen. If banks of frozen semen ever come into general use, it would make it possible for outstanding sires to contribute their genes long after they are dead and prepare the way for mail order stud service, perhaps through catalogs in which prospective buyers could shop for paternal inheritance.

But whatever method is used, once conception has been achieved the breeder waits for the gestation period, approximately 63 days, to run its course. For dogs, the blessed event, referred to as whelping, usually turns out to be a series of events, resulting in litters as large as a dozen or more. To contain all these offspring, the owner often prepares a wooden whelping box with sides low enough for the mother to get in and high enough to keep the puppies from rolling out.

Despite the box's admirably functional proportions, it may seem less inviting than a broom closet or the area under a staircase. Lining the box with newspapers helps make it acceptable, because the mother-to-be seems to get a reassuring sense of nest-building from tearing them to shreds.

There are serious differences of opinion about how much midwifing is necessary during puppy delivery. Can nature be trusted or must humans intervene? Many owners take the middle ground and stand by for emergency duty if nature errs or maternal instinct fails to tell the mother what to do and when to do it.

The first critical point is shortly after the puppy emerges, individually wrapped, supermarket style, in what looks like a plastic bag. The bag, which protects the fetus and lubricates its exit, should be torn away promptly by the mother. If it is not, many owners will do it themselves. The second critical point is the umbilical cord separation. If the mother fails to chew it through, some owners will snip it with scissors. Lastly, the mother should lick the puppy roughly, cleaning it and stimulating it to begin breathing. If the mother is negligent, the owner may do the job (with a towel, not a tongue).

Another controversial whelping issue is whether the mother should eat the afterbirth, the placental lining that emerges after each puppy. Those who say she should argue that it contains hormones which promote the flow of mother's milk and strengthen maternal feeling, insuring that the puppies get good care. Others maintain that eating the afterbirth is unnecessary and that it is better for the mother's stomach to be empty and receptive to nourishing food at the start of nursing.

Owners often fill hot water bottles during the whelping vigil to guard against chilling of newborns, a leading cause of death, and also to prevent the mother from accidentally sitting on one puppy while moving her body around to bear another. Such accidents are frequently fatal. Puppies may arrive at intervals of minutes or of hours; some females take half a day to produce the full litter, much to the chagrin of the fatigued maternity ward attendants. Since it may be difficult to know when the whelping is complete, owners usually take the dog to the veterinarian when it seems to be over to make sure that no unborn puppies, a possible source of infection, remain.

Once the puppies are born, the mother's main function is to serve as an all-hours snack bar for the brood. They usually remain attached to mother's milk for about six weeks, although after the third many owners begin weaning them on semi-solid foods like baby cereal. (Throughout the period of upbringing, the father, if he is around, displays little interest in family life.) If the mother becomes ill or fails to produce adequate milk, the owner must resort to baby bottles and the commercial formulas for "orphan" puppies. Even when they are healthy and dedicated, mothers finally become tired of meeting the puppies' food demands and refuse further dining privileges. From that point onward, the new generation is left to suckle from the milk of human kindness.

Birth Control: Questions and Answers

4. Is there a "pill" for dogs?

There is a contraceptive pill for female dogs. It is a potent synthetic hormone (megestrol acetate) that will prevent the bitch from having her heat period. When the medication is stopped, the dog will come into heat and be capable of conceiving. A similar drug previously was withdrawn from use because it was found to cause an exceptionally high incidence of uterine infections in young and middle-aged dogs. The pill that is available (the identical substance is used to treat advanced uterine and breast cancers in women) should be used only under a veterinarian's supervision.

There is also a "morning after" treatment to prevent a dog from giving birth as a result of an unauthorized mating. It consists of injecting estrogenic hormones in dosages varying with the dog's weight and age. The treatment is 95 percent effective, but it can have side effects, such as breast tumors, cystic ovaries and uterine infections, and will bring the dog back into heat or prolong the heat.

9

The Joys of the Table Are Shared Below

NUTRITION

Nutrition

Vitamins, Minerals and That Certain Something

"All you add is love," reads the label of a popular dog food. It is merely a commercial slogan, yet is expresses a truth about the relationship between people and ther pets. Feeding the dog may by the single most important way that an owner shows his love. Everytime the bowl is put on the floor, the owner says, in effect, "Eat, eat, my puppy."

The love-food connection reveals itself in several ways. There may be an undue concern that the food be adequately nutritious, a concern that often translates into extreme brand consciousness and faddist devotion to various kinds of vitamin and protein supplements, coat conditioners, "high-energy" foods or "health foods." The owner may cook for his pet but take his own meals from the can. Most of all, the connection is apparent in the obsession with giving

the dog "something it likes."

The notion that a dog has taste preferences to which the owner should cater is relatively new and the singular product of an affluent, indulgent civilization. Watching a dog prove its wolf ancestry by devouring food in a few gulping mouthfuls hardly suggests that canines are discriminating in matters of taste. But much research has been devoted to the commercially vital subject of how well a dog can differentiate among tastes and whether it cares about what food tastes like. The results of that research indicate that the dog, if not exactly a gourmet, has surprisingly strong feelings about what it consumes.

Dogs are, of course, less finicky than cats. The reason, researchers believe, is that cats need much more protein and vitamins in their food. So that what seems like mere fussiness is actually a quest for better nutrition. In the dog's case, however, a naturally omnivorous beast has become selective about what it eats simply through satiation. The pet dog, in other words, suffers from a jaded palate, a condition unknown in the wild, when feeding took some effort on the dog's part other than approaching a dish.

Not all dogs are equally discriminating. Mini-ature Poodles have been found to be much more choosy than Labrador Retrievers, who are more particular than Beagles. Beagles' relative insensitivity seems remarkable, considering that they have been bred for olfactory discrimination, but Dr. Alan D. Walker of London, England, has argued that "having also been bred as pack dogs they may have an overriding

ILLUSTRATION BY KIMBLE P. MEAD

How Much Is Enough?

This chart, based on National Academy of Sciences data, indicates how much dry or canned food is required daily for maintenance by dogs of various sizes under normal conditions. Active dogs may require more food, sedentary dogs less. The daily ration should be doubled for dogs that are still growing. As a reducing diet, feed about 60 percent of the normal amount until the dog reaches the desired weight.

WEIGHT OF DOG IN POUNDS	AMOUNT OF DRY FOOD	AMOUNT OF CANNED FOOD
5	3 ozs.	11 ozs.
10	5 ozs.	1 lb. 2 ozs.
15	6½ ozs.	1 lb. 7 ozs.
20	9 ozs.	1 lb. 13 ozs.
30	12 ozs.	2 lbs. 9 ozs.
50	1 lb. 4 ozs.	4 lbs. 3 ozs.
70	1 lb. 12 ozs.	5 lbs. 14 ozs.
110	2 lbs. 10 ozs.	9 lbs. 1 oz.

(Note: Dry food generally contains about 10 percent water, canned food about 75 percent. Semi-moist is not included because brands vary considerably in water content.)

The Food Bowl Bonanza

Product	Company	Retail Sales in Millions of Dollars 1976
CANNED DOG FOOD		
Alpo	Liggett Group	$145.0
Ken-L Ration	Quaker Oats	90.0
Kal Kan	Mars Inc	82.0
Mighty Dog	Carnation	48.0
Friskies	Carnation	46.0
Recipe	Campbell	31.0
Cycle	General Foods	24.0
Vets	Liggett Group	22.5
Blue Mountain	Associated Products	21.0
Skippy, Premium	National Can	20.7
Skippy, Dr. Ross	National Can	19.0
Cadillac	U. S. Tobacco	19.0
Rival	Associated Products	17.0
Strongheart	Strongheart	15.6
Twin Pet	Allied Food	6.0
Calo	Borden	3.2
Laddie Boy	National Can	3.0
Hills	Riviana Foods	2.8
Ideal	Allied Food	2.5
Red Heart	Allied Food	2.5
Dash	Armour	...
Henny Pen	Allied Food	1.1
Jobo	Allied Food	1.1
All others		57.0
Total		$680.0
DRY DOG FOOD		
Dog Chow	Ralston Purina	302.0
Chuck Wagon	Ralston Purina	96.0
Puppy Chow	Ralston Purina	92.0
Gravy Train	General Foods	91.0
Friskies Dinner & Cubes	Carnation	60.0
High-Protein Dog Meal	Ralston Purina	55.0
Gaines Meal	General Foods	....
Jim Dandy Chunks & Ration	Jim Dandy	21.0 / 16.0
Hunt Club Walter Kendall	Standard Brands	15.0
Ken-L Ration Biskit & Meal	Quaker Oats	13.0
Alamo Brand	Liggett Group	10.4
Vets Nuggets	Liggett Group	10.0
Field & Farm	Ralston Purina	6.0
Strongheart	Strongheart	4.0
Purina Dinner Mix	Ralston Purina	3.5
All others		135.1
Total		$930.0

Product	Company	Retail Sales in Millions of Dollars 1976
MOIST DOG FOOD		
Ken-L Ration Burgers	Quaker Oats	103.0
Gaines Burgers	General Foods	85.0
Top Choice	General Foods	56.0
Ken-L Ration Special Cuts	Quaker Oats	30.0
Gaines Prime Variety	General Foods	16.0
Gaines Prime	General Foods	12.0
All others		3.0
Total		$305.0
WHOLE BISCUIT SNACK DOG FOOD		
Milk-Bone, Flavor Snacks	Nabisco	49.0
Liv-A-Snaps, Beef-Snaps, Char-O-Snaps, Chick-N-Snaps	Liggett Group	6.0
Say Cheese, People Crackers and Doggie Donuts	R. T. French's	5.0
Ken-L Ration Treats	Quaker Oats	4.7
Gaines Biscuits & Bits	General Foods	2.5
All others		17.8
Total		$85.0

The well-stocked dog food store caters to the bulk buyer.

tendency to compete for food, almost regardless of its more sophisticated qualities." There is some evidence that the older dog acquires a bit more *savoir faire* in culinary matters as the years go by, and there are indications that eating is more important in some dog families than in others. In an experiment, a group of Poodles were divided into two groups according to whether they were selective or non-selective about what they ate; the members of the choosier group turned out to be mainly each others' blood relatives. One important indication of taste preference is the finding that dogs become bored if they eat the same thing every day and, given a choice, prefer food that is new to them.

Dr. Walker maintains that "sensory perception is the principal factor determining choice of food in two-dish situations, appetence being a relatively constant factor." What does a dog sense as it munches its rations? The research

shows that it likes food served moist and rather warm — apparently because the archetypical canine hunter was not in a position to refrigerate his prey before eating it. Dogs seem averse to acids (few of them can tolerate citrus fruits) but indifferent to whether the food has been salted. They dislike bitter tastes yet do not respond immediately to sweetness, which may indicate that the canine candy addict has been trained by his "connection."

The animals most favored by dogs as a food source have been ranked by tests in this order: sheep, ox, horse, pig. The liver is the favorite edible organ. In general dogs prefer their meat well matured and gamey (another reason for burying their bones.) Dogs also accept vegetarian foods. They eat cereals readily, and some even find carrots an interesting change of pace. No scientific evidence has been found for the belief that garlic improves food flavor for dogs,

although, as in the case of candy, the dog that lives with garlic lovers may become conditioned to aromatic table scraps.

The Taste Makers

To the dog food manufacturer, creating a product with more taste appeal is like building a better mousetrap. In the hopes that pet owners will beat a path to their door, the manufacturers have created research establishments dedicated to both nourishing the dog and tantalizing its palate. The Gaines Nutrition Center in Kankakee, Illinois, for example, houses 400 dogs whose *raison d'etre* is to eat. There are 33 breeds (purebreds only are used because they have predictable normal weights against which test results can be measured) represented by dogs from puppyhood to old age. This cross-section of the pet dog population is fed and cared for according to a strict regimen, and visitors are

ILLUSTRATION BY KIMBLE

excluded to prevent possible disruption of the dogs' eating routine.

In this hermetically-sealed environment, the dogs are expected to concentrate on their assigned tasks, such as tasting recipes for new products. A Gaines research bulletin has described taste testing as follows:

There are usually forty dogs on a "preference panel." Most test series are conducted with each dog given a choice of two foods for two consecutive days; either

*The term **mongrel** for a dog of mixed breed probably derives from "mong," which in England is a dialect word for a mixture of animal feeds.*

Manufacturers gear their products to the pet owner's fantasies. These treats are shaped to look like people—policemen, firemen, dog catchers, mailmen and burglars—who have supposedly incurred the permanent wrath of dogs.

two Gaines products or a Gaines food and that of a competitor. The dogs are fed at the same time every day in identical pans. These are placed in reverse order each day of the test to avoid a left or right preference on the part of the dog. The food is weighed out by ounces and after 45 minutes the dishes are picked up and the leftover food weighed.

The preference results then go back to the technical researchers working on the product. This can be a lengthy procedure, especially when a new food is under development. By the time a product is ready for preference testing, the formula appears nutritionally sound and palatable. But suppose the dogs are indifferent to it. Is it flavor? And if so, which of the dozen or so major ingredients in the food? Or is it texture? Should the chunks be larger or smaller? Or should the kibble be harder or crunchier? The possibilities may seem almost endless but the humans take their best educated guess and try again.

Another complex procedure is used for "flavor validation," proving that a product la-

beled with a particular flavor, such as beef, can be distinguished by dogs from foods with other flavors:

It is done by feeding the dog in a big test booth, completely enclosed except for a two-way glass panel; a mirror on the inside and window on the outside. The dog can be observed but cannot see out and thus cannot be distracted. A sliding tray with six compartments for dishes is built into the booth underneath the window. The procedure starts by giving the dog portions of several different foods. Let's say the selection is chicken, beef, liver and three other types of meat; with beef as the food under test for flavor validation. If the dog attempts to eat anything but beef, an attendant watching through the window pulls the tray out of the booth. The dog is allowed to eat the beef and after a while realizes this is what he's supposed to do when in the booth. The foods are placed in different dishes each time so the dog is not conditioned to "place" but actually has to scent out the food he's to eat.

Next the actual foods are replaced by six different dog food products, each with a different ingredient as flavoring. One of the products contains beef. The dog should head straight for this one, eat it, and ignore the others. If he does this ten consecutive times with five other choices always available, the product can be labeled "beef flavored," or as containing beef as the primary ingredient. Since this test must be run in sequence, if the tenth time the dog decides to try another food or gets bored and won't eat anything, the test must start again from the beginning.

The companies that dominate the pet food industry are willing to invest so much effort in finding the perfect flavor because success may mean a larger share of the booming market. Americans spent about $2 billion on dog food in 1976, about three times what they had spent a decade earlier and more than they were

The Vital Ingredients

Shown below are the amounts of each nutrient that a dog needs every day for each kilogram (2.2 pounds) of its body weight. To find out if your dog is getting the proper amount of a given nutrient, multiply its weight by the amount shown on the chart and compare it with the label on the dog food.

For example, if your dog weighs 44 pounds and you want to know whether it is getting adequate protein, convert its weight into kilograms: $44 \div 2.2 = 20$.

Then multiply the number of kilograms by the number of grams of protein required: $20 \times 4.4 = 88$.

Now check the label of the dog food container to see how much protein there is in each serving. If the number of servings you provide contains less than 88 grams of protein, the dog is getting too little.

Key:	g=gram (.001 kilogram)
	mg=milligram (.001 gram)
	μg=microgram (.001 milligram)
	IU=International Units

Nutrient		Adult Maintenance	Growing Puppies
Protein	g	4.4	8.8
Fat	g	1.3	2.6
Minerals			
Calcium	mg	120.	260.
Phosphorus	mg	100.	210.
Potassium	mg	220.	220.
Sodium chloride	mg	330.	530.
Magnesium	mg	11.	22.
Iron	mg	1.30	1.30
Copper	mg	0.17	0.17
Cobalt	mg	0.055	0.055
Manganese	mg	0.110	0.22
Zinc	mg	0.110	0.22
Iodine	mg	0.033	0.066
Vitamins			
Vitamin A	IU	99.	198.
Vitamin D	IU	6.6	20.
Vitamin E (alpha tocopherol)	mg	2.0	2.2
Vitamin B_{12}	μg	0.7	0.7
Folic acid	μg	4.4	8.8
Thiamine	μg	20.	20.
Riboflavin	μg	44.	88.
Pyridoxine	μg	22.	55.
Pantothenic acid	μg	51.	99.
Niacin	μg	242.	397.
Choline	mg	25.	55.
Vitamin K	μg	33.	66.

Growing Together . . .

Are fat people more likely to have fat dogs? A study done at the Blue Cross Animal Hospital in Grimsby, England, concludes that they are. The study examined the relationship between the physiques of about 1,000 dogs of various breeds and their owners. It found that 25 percent of owners of normal weight had obese dogs but that a much larger proportion of overweight owners, 44 percent, had overweight dogs. (In the case of the dog, the veterinarians made a judgment of whether it was obese by feeling the fat layers around the ribs; in the case of the owner, they used less direct methods.)

When pets and owners are both obese it is apparently because they share a common lifestyle and eating habits. Overweight persons tend to be sedentary, and among the exertions they avoid is taking the dog out for exercise. Dogs who were kept in most of the day also may be eating out of boredom, a well-known syndrome in humans.

Moreover, fat dogs were getting too many high-calorie scraps from the family's richly laden table. Some owners, the study found, took pride in feeding their dogs the same food they ate. "Owners who feed entirely home-cooked food, some of it especially bought," the study concluded, "are probably motivated by feelings of emotional closeness to their pets and like to feel that they enjoy wholesome home-cooked food of a palatability almost acceptable to human beings." In some cases, "dogs played the part of spoilt and pampered children, receiving as many tasty morsels as could be crammed into them. A few owners were so dominated by their dogs' personalities that they were perpetually meeting demands for food."

The veterinarians at the hospital found that it required tact to convince overweight owners that their dogs needed slimming since they tended to regard them as "just right." Convincing the dominant personality in the pair may be even more diffcult.

laying out for breakfast cereal and baby food combined. No one is quite sure what caused the increase in sales. The dog population might have risen or owners might be buying larger and hungrier breeds. It may also be that owners have, in advertising terms, moved up-market. Once content to feed their dogs relatively inexpensive dry meal or even just table scraps, they seem to be switching to the more costly canned foods or the semi-moist variety, which comes packaged by the serving — a sort of canine convenience food.

The food companies recognize that it is the owner, not the dog, who must first be persuaded to try their brand. The industry's advertising budget for 1977 was about $125 million, much of which paid for dancing, prancing and paw-clapping dogs to show enthusiasm for the product on television. New brands are elaborately test marketed for human consumer appeal. The wide variety of flavors and types of food that each company sells — a typical supermarket devotes about 200 feet of shelf to pet foods — reflects the marketing principle that the more shelf space it occupies, the more the company will sell. Thus, a manufacturer may branch out into snack foods, diet foods (for those dogs that

An 1890s advertisement for puppy biscuits. Dog food is now a $2 billion a year business.

ate too much of the snack foods), food for older dogs and food for dogs that are pregnant. There are also special diets to keep show dogs at their competitive best. ("Remember," counsels the manufacturer of one brand, "nutrition

. . . And Taking It Off Together

For obese persons with obese dogs the only sensible alternative may be to change the common lifestyle that makes both overweight. Here are some suggestions by Dr. Judith S. Stern of the Nutrition Department at the University of California at Davis on how to lose weight with your dog:

1. Increase your normal activity rate. If you walk the dog only twice a day, go for another walk. Walk further than you usually do. That extra block will help you and the the dog burn up exces calories.

2. Try changing your eating habits and the dog's through behavior modification. Set a time and a place for meals and stick to the plan, eliminating impulsive, unplanned eating.

3. If you are both accustomed to snacking during the day, substitute something less caloric for yourself and offer the dog a smaller biscuit than usual.

4. Put less on your table when you eat. The less there is, the fewer scraps there will be for the dog.

Cooking for the Canine Gourmet

Although in the long run a dog is probably better off nutritionally if it eats out of the can every night, there are special occasions on which some people want to treat their pet as a gourmet and not just a gourmand. The following is a suggested menu of home-cooked dishes for such occasions. (The amount served should vary with the size of the dog.) "Hors d'ogs" are an appetizer that can conveniently double as a hiding place for unpalatable pills. "Canine Cantonese" combines liver, a favorite of dogs, with vegetables in the manner of the Orient. The dessert, "Pennsylvania Dutch Puppy Pretzels," is a new interpretation of the classic dog biscuit.

CANINE CANTONESE

Ingredients:

1/2 pound beef liver
1/4 cup all-purpose flour
1 egg, beaten with 1 tablespoon water (save the shell)
1/4 cup wheat germ
1 1/2 cups cooking oil
1 cup cooked string beans (save cooking liquid)
1 carrot, shredded
1/2 cup cooked chick peas
1/2 cup chicken stock
1/2 cup cooking liquid from string beans
1 tablespoon soy sauce
1 teaspoon cornstarch
2 cups brown rice cooked in beef bouillon

Directions:

1. Cut liver into half-inch cubes (if liver is partially frozen, it is easier to cut.)
2. Place flour in paper bag, add cubed liver and shake until liver is evenly coated.
3. Dip liver in beaten egg.
4. Roll liver in wheat germ until coated.
5. Heat oil in a wok. When oil is almost smoking, add the liver and stir-fry for about 2 minutes until brown. Remove liver and drain on paper towel.
6. Remove all but 2 tablespoons of oil from the wok. Add carrots, string beans and chick peas.
7. Mix vegetable cooking liquid and chicken stock with soy sauce, corn starch and pulverized shell (for calcium) and add to wok. Heat until sauce thickens. Add liver.
8. Cool and serve on top of brown rice.

CHÂTEAUNEUF-DU-PUP

Directions:
Fill the dog's bowl with fresh water.

HORS D'OGS

Ingredients:

1/4 cup cheddar cheese, grated
1/4 cup swiss cheese, grated
1/2 teaspoon brewer's yeast
2 tablespoons hydrogenated vegetable shortening
1/2 cup oatmeal, toasted

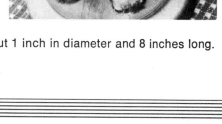

Directions:

1. Combine cheeses, brewer's yeast and shortening.
2. Using plastic wrap, shape mixture into a log about 1 inch in diameter and 8 inches long.
3. Roll log in toasted oatmeal.
4. Refrigerate. Slice into half-inch rounds and serve.

PENNSYLVANIA DUTCH PUPPY PRETZELS

Ingredients:

1 teaspoon brown sugar
2 teaspoons active dry yeast
2/3 cup water
3/4 cup whole wheat flour
3 tablespoons low-fat soy flour
1/4 cup non-fat dry milk powder
1   tablespoon desiccated liver powder
1 tablespoon bone meal flour with red bone marrow
1/4 cup non-fat dry milk powder
1 egg, beaten (use 1/2 in recipe, the other half to glaze the pretzels)
3/4 teaspoon salt
2 tablespoons cooking oil
3 tablespoons wheat germ

Directions:

1. Dissolve yeast in warm water. Add sugar.
2. Combine whole wheat flour, soy flour, all-purpose flour, liver powder, bone meal, dry milk powder and salt.
4. Add 1/2 beaten egg, oil, and yeast-water mixture. Mix.
5. Turn out on a well-floured bread board and knead until dough is firm.
6. Place in an oiled bowl, cover and let rise until almost doubled in bulk.
7. Punch down the dough, divide into 12 equal parts and roll into 1/2" thick ropes.
8. Shape into pretzels and place on greased cookie sheet.
9. Bake in preheated 375° oven for 15 minutes.
10. Remove from oven, brush with beaten egg and sprinkle with wheat germ.
11. Return to oven and bake at 300° for about 15 minutes, until pretzels are nicely browned and quite firm.
12. Let cool and store in a cookie jar.

is often the difference between the purple ribbon winners and the 'also rans'.")

Flavors proliferate in endless permutations and combinations intended to appeal to the owner's perception of what tastes good to his dog: beef with chicken, liver with bacon, ham and eggs, cheeseburgers (only junkfood for people). Dogs are presented with a variety of culinary styles: Western-style, Country-style (and perhaps one day Italian-style and Kosher-style). Coloring is added to insure, for example, that the burgers are suitably red, something that could only matter to the owner because dogs are believed to be color blind.

Consumers are so vulnerable to marketing

Cave canem *(beware of the dog) is a motto that was worked into the mosaic floors of many Roman houses. Some authorities now believe that it was not meant to warn against vicious canines but to prevent visitors from accidentally stepping on the family's diminutive Italian Greyhound.*

strategies that the food companies have legal battles over the names they can put on the labels. When the Quaker Oats Company began selling a dog food called Tender Chunks, it was sued in Federal court by the Ralston Purina Corporation, which contended that Quaker's product was infringing on the name of a Purina cat food, Tender Vittles. Quaker countersued and claimed that Purina, which leads the pet food industry with about one third of all sales, was trying to drive it from the market.

Reading Between the Lines

Although companies may make a Federal case out of a well-advertised product name, they are less likely to call attention to the fine print on the label. The list includes such less than appetizing ingredients as "animal liver and glandular meal," "soybean hulls," and "ethylenediamine dihydriodide." The labeling of dog foods is regulated to some extent by animal feed laws, which require accurate description of the package contents. But Jeris G. Eikenberry, the President of the Association of American Feed Control Officials, has candidly pointed out that "nothing in existing state or Federal regulation has anything to do with the regulation of quality. You can distribute, manufacture and offer for sale a pet food which is 'low quality', as long as it is properly labeled . . . . Quality is a matter of opinion."

Most dog owners have little opinion about the quality of the food they supply their pets, because they are not quite sure what went into it. They are certain that *escalopes de veau* have not been ground up to make dog meal, but they have only deeply repressed suspicions about the parts that probably were used. The National Academy of Sciences list of common dog food ingredients makes it clear that aside from grain, fish meal, vegetables and milk products, much of what gets into the can or bag is more or less the sweepings from the packing house floor. Such items as "carcass residue with blood, dry or wet, rendered, dehydrated, ground," and "chicken offal with feet, raw" or "poultry feathers, hydrolyzed, dehydrated, ground" are

BACKWARD PUPPIES NEED LACTOL

" *The nearest thing to bitch's milk* "

IF you have a backward, undersized or ailing puppy give him LACTOL — *the nearest thing to bitch's milk.* LACTOL is similar to bitch's milk in fat, proteins and carbohydrates. It has a similar taste and puppies simply lap it up. LACTOL builds good bone, strong teeth, firm flesh, promoting all round growth. Obtainable at Pet Stores, Chemists, Grocers and Corn Merchants. In two sizes: 3/6 & 10/6.

FINGER-SIZED PUPS REARED ON LACTOL

Mrs. Jean Aldcroft of East Didsbury, Manchester, writes: "I have reared a big litter of Pekingese puppies from birth on LACTOL. They were no bigger than my finger when born but thanks to LACTOL they came on wonderfully."

Manufacturers make what seem like spectacular claims about their products, but it's best to read labels carefully. This 1951 advertisement from a British magazine never substantiates its miraculous claims for the product.

obviously not the stuff of dog food commercials.

These ingredients are normally dignified on the labels and on television by the name of "byproducts." Indeed, apart from their rather gruesome provenance, the components of commercial food do supply the proteins, carbohydrates, fats, vitamins and minerals that the dog needs. Dog food sold as "complete and balanced" should have all the necessary nutrients in the proper proportions to support healthy life. Many veterinary nutrition experts recommend using the commercial food because diets of table scraps or even food specially prepared by the owner tend to become unbalanced.

One popular misconception that may bedevil home cooking is the belief that dogs can flourish on a diet of pure meat. Dogs are carnivores, to be sure, but in the wild they would normally eat the stomachs and intestines of their herbivorous prey, thereby ingesting the vegetable nutrients and fibers that they needed. For a dog, an all-meat diet would tend to be too low in calcium and too high in phosphorus. Dry commercial food is generally composed of about 40-50 percent grain (such as wheat and corn) and legumes (soybeans).

If the owner buys a commercial product, all that is left to his judgment is supplying the proper amounts daily. In general, the proper amount is related to body weight although the age, type and environment of the dog may vary the calculations somewhat. Growing puppies need about twice as much as adults on "maintenance" diets, and the lower metabolic rate of the aging dog makes it prudent to feed him less. Dogs who spend most of the day confined in an apartment require less food than dogs out chasing sheep or rabbits or those in "stress" conditions, such as gestating and lactating females. Nervous dogs use more food energy than placid ones, and dogs who spend most of their time outdoors in cold climates can burn up as much as 90 percent more calories than dogs in temperate regions.

Following these guidelines may seem simple, yet overfeeding seems to be the rule. Obesity is the commonest canine nutritional disorder. The dog evidently suffers from an overabundance of love.

A Home Remedy for "Fat Dog Disease"

A weight reduction program for a specific dog should be developed in consultation with its veterinarian, but these are some general hints on feeding for trimness by Dr. Harold M. Zweighaft:

People can become fat because of psychological or glandular disturbances. Dogs, being unable to open refrigerators, depend on their owners to make them a victim of what I call "fat dog disease." The overweight dog is faced with severe health handicaps. It is prone to diabetes, heart failure, hormonal malfunctions and many other pathological conditions.

Before considering what to do about the extra pounds, a discussion of the ounce of prevention would be in order. The mature dog should be fed twice daily. A small morning feeding and a larger evening feeding are desirable. Feeding times should be constant.

Experimental evidence indicates that when food is left out, the dog will eat intermittently until its caloric requirements are satisfied. If the dog is trained to eat within a short period of time, it will develop the habit of bolting the food and overeating. Ideally, then, the early feeding should be offered in the morning. If not eaten, the food should remain throughout the day until the evening meal. The night feeding should remain available all night or until eaten. There is nothing wrong with a dog preferring to save some food for a 2 am snack!

An adequate diet for a normal, mature dog should be a balance: low in carbohydrates, low in fats and rich in high-quality protein. The early feeding could provide protein in the form of hard boiled or scrambled eggs (cooking the eggs eliminates "avadin," an anti-vitamin in the whites that will destroy some of the B-complex vitamins within the dog's body); cottage cheese; sour cream or yogurt; or cooked cereal, such as oatmeal, Wheatina, Farina or Pablum. (The instant hot cereals are fine for hurried, harried mornings.)

The late feeding should offer a protein-carbohydrate mixture consisting of meat and kibble or meal, which provides bulk and calories. Liquid salad or cooking oil such as safflower, peanut or corn oil should be added. As a rule of thumb, an active, 30 pound dog should get one half pound of meat (ground beef, table scraps such as steak, roast beef, turkey and chicken, or a quality canned meat listing beef or horsemeat as the first ingredient) plus two tea cups of kibbled biscuit or moist dog food. Add one or two tablespoons of liquid oil.

This is a good diet for a mature dog from six months to nine years of age. Consult a veterinarian for advice on feeding your dog if it is younger or older. Dogs with liver, kidney or heart disease as well as a variety of other illnesses will require specially prescribed diets. Younger, active dogs need proportionately more food than older, sedentary animals. An owner can "eyeball" his dog for weight stability. If the dog is thin, increase the total amount of food. Conversely, the pudgy dog should have its total amount of food decreased by 25 to 30 percent.

Pity the dog with fat dog disease. His owner complains "I only feed him a little bit once a day." That "little bit" is always an enormous daily total of calories. It takes will power for people to lose weight, and it takes determination to ignore soulful eyes and nudging noses to help dogs lose weight. To lose weight, the dog must be slightly hungry all the time. If the dog gets just what it needs, it will stay fat. On a calorie-deficient diet, stored fats and carbohydrates are used up, and over a period of time the dog will shed pounds. It is that simple.

The twice-a-day feeding schedule is imperative for weight loss. The early morning feeding of cheese, eggs or cereal should be a small quantity. The later meal should consist of meat in some form but not the kibble or moist food. (These preparations are enormously high in calories.) All-bran or shredded wheat should be mixed with meat to provide bulk and roughage without supplying excess calories. If the dog remains heavy, reduce the total amount of food further, perhaps another 25 percent. Additional snacks are prohibited. Those little tidbits slipped from the dinner table add calories and retain pounds.

10

It's Hard to Put Teeth into It

THE LAW

The Law

Private Pets and Public Enemies

The legal institutions that regulate the relationship of man and dog fall into two general categories: those that protect the man against the dog and those that protect the dog against the man. The dog has usually needed more protection than the man, but he has not always gotten it. Under Roman law, dogs were classified as *ferae naturae,* wild animals, belonging to whomever took them. As the centuries passed, the dog was grudgingly promoted to the category of *domitae naturae,* domestic animals regarded as property. Even then the law did not place the canine among the highly esteemed beasts that provided food and horsepower, but in a lowlier subdivision. In the 18th century the great English legal commentator Sir William Blackstone could refer contemptuously to "dogs of all sorts, and other creatures kept for whim and pleasure" as having "no intrinsic value."

That meant that while horse and cattle thieves would suffer dire consequences, capital punishment was unlikely to be meted out for dog rustling; it was even debatable whether stealing a dog amounted to larceny. One could do what one liked to another man's dog without being liable to a civil suit, because no court would award damages for harming something of no value.

Early laws governing dogs protected man, not dog. Roman law classified dogs as wild animals.

June 23, 1959

G. W. JONES

DOG MUZZLE

Filed April 3, 1957

2,891,504

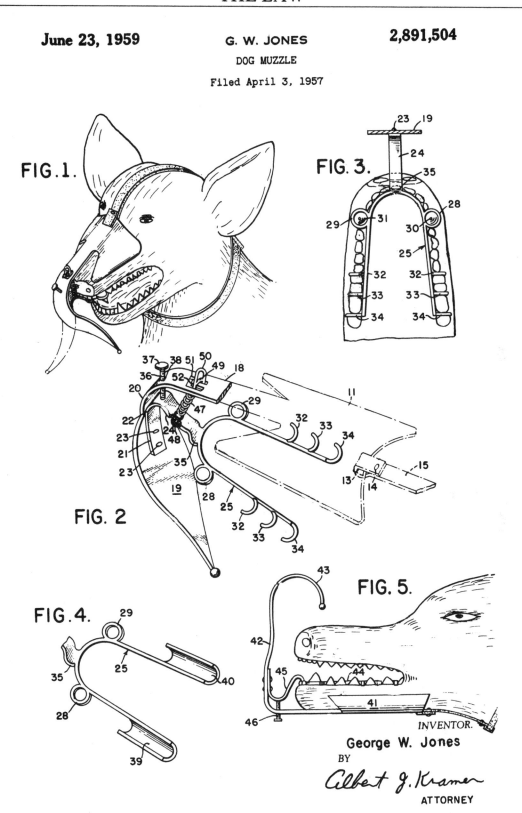

INVENTOR.

George W. Jones

BY

Albert J. Kramer

ATTORNEY

This inventor was striving for a humane means to restrain a chronic biter. To prevent bites, dogs are required to be muzzled in some communities when they are on the street.

An attack dog too easily provoked can cost his owner plenty. Lodi, a training academy graduate, has survived a shooting and a mugging and is still placid enough to work with different masters.

Judicial opinion began to change, however, when scientific breeding, especially in the 19th century, created a class of dogs that commanded high prices, even if the purchasers did pay them out of "whim and pleasure." If a dog were trespassing or threatening sheep, direct action against the intruder might be imprudent because its owner could sue for the price of the dog.

When disputes arise, the courts follow the principle of "relative value." It the dog worth more than the livestock? The principle appears straightforward, but applying it often requires subtle judicial reasoning. In 1976, for example, the Oregon Supreme Court was called upon to decide a case involving two Labrador Retrievers and 23 ducks and geese. The dogs had killed the domestic fowl and were about to kill five or six more, when the owner of the birds shot and killed the dogs. He and the dogs' owner then sued each other for the value of their animals. The court relied on a favorite legal character, the "reasonable man." It said that for the dog owner to collect, it had to be "reasonably apparent . . . at the time of the killing" that the dogs were worth more than the ducks and geese who were to be protected. Since the birds' owner knew they were valued at about $50 to $60 but did not know that the dogs were purebreds worth a total of $5,000, it was reasonable for him to conclude that he should shoot the dogs to save the birds.

A principal protection that humans have against canines is the right to sue the owner of a dog that bites. As a rule, however, the owner is not liable unless he had reason to know that he was harboring an animal with a "vicious propensity." The saying that "every dog is allowed one bite" supposedly expresses a legal rule that only by biting someone does the dog

How to Choose at the Pound

Adopting a dog from a municipal pound or voluntary shelter is an inexpensive way of acquiring a pet — and perhaps saving a doomed animal. A pound may charge an adopter only a few dollars for the license; a shelter may ask for a donation of $15 to $25, depending upon the size of the dog. Here are a few hints from Sid Weber, eastern director of the American Humane Association, the federation to which many shelters belong, on how to choose a dog:

1. Try to judge the dog's true character. Those that seem too frisky may merely be eager to get out of confinement, which is only natural. Do not be put off by dogs that cringe in the corner or whimper chronically. Many animals have been abused by previous owners and have become fearful, but a little love will soon restore them to a normal disposition. For good advice on a dog's temperament, ask the kennel attendant who feeds and cares for it every day.

2. Ascertain the state of the dog's health. Do not be wary of a dog whose ribs are showing or who otherwise looks malnourished. Regular feeding will return the animal to proper weight. Ask the shelter which vaccinations the dog has had and which it still needs. Although shelters generally examine dogs, you should take your choice to a veterinarian soon after adoption to have it checked to your own satisfaction. Most shelters will take the dog back if there are signs of ill health, but ask about time limits.

3. Determine the shelter's population control policy. Many wil not release an animal unless it has been neutered or the adopter promises to have the operation performed. If you are interested in a purebred, ask whether the shelter provides the pedigree papers when available. Some do not pass the papers on with the dog because they believe that a pedigree encourages owners to breed dogs.

To find a municipal pound that takes in stray dogs, look under the name of the town or county governmnt in the white pages of the telephone directory. To find a voluntary shelter, check the listing for an organization that uses one of the following in its name, usually in combination with the name of the community:

Society for the Prevention of Cruelty to Animals

Humane Society or Association

Animal Welfare League or Society

Animal Rescue League

Animal Protective Association or League

Animal Shelter

Animal Refuge

League for Animals or Animal League

Animal Havens League

Dumb Friends League

Animal Friends

Bide-a-Wee Home Association

Animal Aid Association

serve notice on its owner that its propensities are suspect. But teeth need not pierce flesh to demonstrate latent ferocity. A judge in a Missouri case wrote:

The dog is entitled to his first bite, provided he conceals his intention and makes no manifestation of his purpose, in such manner as to impart notice to his owner or keeper, but if the dog's vicious propensities be shown, or his inclinations to want to bite be manifested, then he is not permitted to carry out his designs before being recognized as a dangerous, vicious, or ferocious animal.

The courts do allow owners of biting animals to escape damages if they can prove "contributory negligence" on the victim's part, much as in automobile accident claims. But the owner must prove quite clearly that the biter was deliberately antagonized by the bitten. In a Florida case, a 5½-year-old girl accidentally rode a bicycle over the tail of a dog. When she tried to console the animal, it bit her. The court found the owner liable for damages because the girl had not mischievously provoked the dog.

Tagging Along

In one respect, at least, the owner stands in the same relationship to his dog as to his car: by law, a license tag signifies that a dog has, both. A license tag signifies that a dog has, somewhere, an owner who thinks enough of it to pay the annual fee, and it identifies dogs that have roamed.

But licensing has sometimes had an effect opposite from that intended. In Britain, where dog registration fees have been exacted since the 18th century, law-abiding poor persons at times have turned their dogs loose rather than pay for a renewal. Since the licenses expired in December, the annual unleashing occurred during the winter, when shelter was most needed.

In the early 1930s, the Depression years, many British households were so strapped for funds that the family dog seemed likely to become the victim of a budget cutback. But a group called the Tail-Waggers' Club devised an ingenious scheme for buying a license on the installment plan. The club purchased the license, and each week an owner would buy a "Tail-Wagger Stamp" for two pence from pet shops or branches of the humane society. When 45 stamps were pasted on a card, the license was paid off. During the first four years that the plan was in effect, 30,000 persons participated.

In the United States, state and local licensing

"The more I see of the representatives of the people, the more I admire my dogs."

ALPHONSE DE LAMARTINE
(1790-1869),
French statesman and poet

The Dog Catcher: Vanishing American

The laudable but often laughable municipal office of dog catcher, long a part of grass roots government in the United States, is becoming extinct, a victim of professionalization. In the old days, any citizen of good character might be appointed to patrol the town for strays, but the modern man with the net is an Animal Control Officer, or someone bearing a similarly august title, who has probably passed a Civil Service examination on catching dogs.

The dog catcher was always the butt of jokes — "he couldn't get elected dog catcher" was the utimate in political disparagement — and some municipalities tried to dignify the post by changing the name to to "dog enumerator" or "dog warden." But euphemisms did not suffice, because dog catchers were not only risible figures but objects of hostility from the owners of unlicensed dogs taken to the pound. Dog catchers have even had their lives threatened. In one place, Waukomis, Oklahoma, (population 300) the dog catcher went underground in 1977; his identity was kept secret by city officials to protect him from abuse.

The Animal Control Officer is in a more secure position, because often he has peace officer status, can issue summonses and may even carry a gun. A municipality with such an officer is more likely to have its dog licensing requirements clearly defined by law, reducing friction with the citizenry. Many officers have gained extensive dog handling experience by working at kennels and shelters, and proposals have been put forward to give them formal education at police academies or schools training veterinary assistants. In the future, the patrol van may be driven by a Bachelor of Dog Catching.

has sometimes been challenged by dog owners, who objected that it was unfair taxation. Certainly, from the dog's point of view it is taxation without representation. The courts have held, however, that licenses are not revenue-raising measures but legitimate exercises of the state's police powers to control the canine population— "a method adopted by the Legislature of regulating the keeping of a dog," as one judge put it.

Not all dogs are equal in the eyes of the law, for licensing purposes. Under early British regulations, a dog kept inside the house required a higher fee than one kept outside. Presumably, the rationale was that the owner should be willing to pay more for an animal that sleeps on the family hearth than one kept chained in the yard, although the differential may have exiled some dogs to the outdoors. The fees also differed according to what the dog did. Sporting dogs were charged higher rates, which discriminated against hunters, except that those who hunted foxes or hares could get group discount rates for packs of hounds. Sheep and cattle herding dogs received special exemptions in recognition of their service to agriculture.

In most places in the United States today, all dogs over six months of age must be licensed, although the fees are often higher for unspayed females than for males. That kind of sex discrimination has not been found to violate the Constitution, although there are many who believe that male dogs should be held equally responsible for unchecked population growth. In a few places the law discriminates against sexuality in general; the owner must pay more for dogs of either gender if their reproductive organs are in working order.

The state also trammels the liberty of dogowners in other ways. In most communities, there are "leash laws," requiring dogs to be leashed or muzzled on the street or kept in custody during prescribed curfew hours. Leash laws are even more ancient than licensing requirements, dating back at least to the time of the English King Canute. One of his statutes, enacted in 1031, required Greyhounds be kept more than ten miles from the royal forest to pre-

A Different Breed of Thief

Stealing a pet dog is a form of larceny whose effects are primarily emotional, but for the thieves it is purely a matter of money. There are nefarious hunters who make a practice of stealing a sporting dog each fall rather than bear the expense of supporting one all year. Other dognappers concentrate on small, easily concealed dogs like Dachshunds and Miniature Schnauzers, offering to return them for a "reward" — ransom is more like it — when an ad appears in the lost-and-found columns of the newspaper.

Dognappers have also made money by selling stolen goods to research laboratories, although that black market has been inhibited by Federal law. In 1966 Congress passed the Laboratory Animal Welfare Act, probably its first enactment dealing with dogs (and cats.) The law requires laboratories to buy their animals from licensed dealers, who can be fined or lose their license for handling stolen animals. The law is a serious impediment to theft, as is the preference of most laboratories for dogs whose health and heredity has been certified — by professional breeders — rather than off-the-street specimens.

Tattooing serial numbers on dogs, either on the ear with a clamp or on the inside of the leg with an electric tattooing pencil, has been recommended as another deterrent, since the dog is readily identifiable. Tattooing is probably helpful in making positive identifications of lost dogs, but it is questionable whether the dognapper will take the time or trouble to check the dog over for serial numbers before stealing it.

A major difficulty with tattooing is that the numbering systems and the methods of registering them have not been standardized. Some persons brand the dog with their Social Security number; others have used the American Kennel Club registration number. Various private organizations and some state agencies operate registries, but no central repository of numbers exists, making it difficult for the finder of a dog to know where to start looking. There is another difficulty: as one humane society official put it, "No one is going to get their head bitten off trying to turn over a Doberman to look for a tattoo."

serve the deer for the king's own hunting. The penalty clause provided that:

...if they do come any nearer to the forest they shall pay 12 pence for every mile; but if the Greyhound be found within the forest, the master or owner of the dog shall forfeit the dog and ten shillings to the King.

Forest denizens were permitted small dogs that were unlikely to bother the deer. The standard of measurement was a dog gauge, a loop of wire. If a dog could pass through it, it was allowed. But large dogs, such as Mastiffs, could be kept only if lamed by cutting the hamstrings of the back legs or by expedition, the removal of claws on the front legs.

Modern leash laws vary greatly in their severity. Some lay down minimal requirements, such as wearing a collar and identification tag away from home; others are so draconian that they permit the killing of an unaccompanied dog trespassing on another's property. Some communities, not content with muzzle mea-

In the Pit, the Odds Are Against the Fighters

Although banned in every state, dogfighting, one of the most ancient bloodsports, has experienced a resurgence in the 1970s. Investigations by the *The New York Times* and other newspapers have disclosed that clandestine matches are held regularly in at least a dozen states. Texas, especially, is a center for dogfighting.

The sport is well organized. National matches draw entrants from throughout the United States, and there are even two fan magazines: *Texas Pit Dog Reports,* published in Dallas, and *Pit Dogs,* published in Florida. (Their subscriber lists are kept secret). To prevent police raids, notices of events, mailed to dog owners, give only the date and the name of the city; participants have to find out the exact location via the grapevine.

In many localities, though, the police have displayed little interest in breaking up dogfights, possibly because of bribes by promoters, who stand to gain substantial sums from matches in which $500 bets are not uncommon. The illicit dogfight industry also attracts other forms of crime, including prostitution and armed violence. The fans are often pistol-packers with short tempers. Two persons prominent in Texas dogfighting were found murdered in gangland style in 1973, and even dogs have been shot to death — apparently by jealous owners of rivals.

(The lack of mutual trust among the enthusiasts is demonstrated by the practice of bathing each dog before a fight to wash off any poisons that might have been applied to kill the opposing dog when it bites.)

The dogs are either Staffordshire Bull Terriers or crosses between that breed and the Bullmastiff. The most aggressive puppies are selected and put through an athletic training course that consists of killing kittens for practice; later they graduate to mauling small dogs.

Owners of fighting dogs bring them to the match in crates loaded on trucks or campers. The fight takes place in a "pit" assembled of plywood sheets — although sometimes even a spare bedroom may be pressed into service as an arena.

A fight lasts from a half hour to 2½ hours, the end coming when one of the opponents "curs out" (shys away from the opponent) or dies. If death does not occur in the ring, it may occur later as a result of fight injuries or because the owner wishes to rid himself of a "loser."

Because of the inhumanity of the sport and the potential for fostering other crimes, Congress in 1976 prohibited the transporting of animals across a state line for activities such as dogfights. One effect of the law has been to bring the Federal Bureau of Investigation into the enforcement effort, but it is far from clear that the law will eradicate the sport. It may be difficult to prove that dogs came from another state, and penalties under state and local law for cruelty to animals can be as low as $25 — hardly enough to discourage the highrollers of the dogfight game.

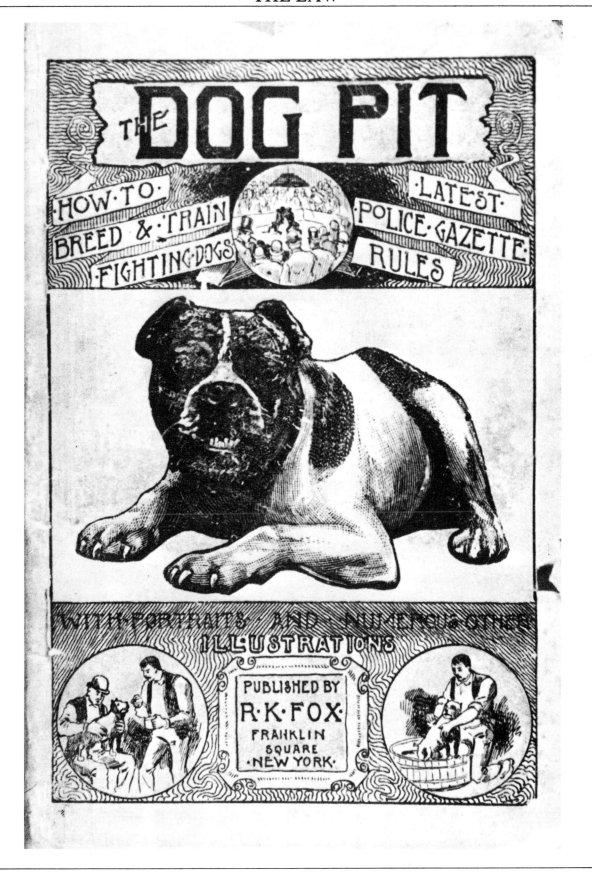

Legal protection has been extended to dogs mistreated by man, but enforcement is often lax. An Iowa "puppy mill" imprisoned St. Bernards in pens like these to produce puppies for quick profit.

sures, have simply banned the keeping of any dog that shows a "disposition" to attack humans. Other jurisdictions have used their zoning powers to prevent residents from getting so carried away with their love of dogs that they keep too many for the neighbors' comfort. Zoning ordinances might, for example, ban the presence of more than four dogs in one household — and make no exceptions even for the occasional large litter.

Communal Discord

Most towns also have laws against keeping dogs that present a nuisance. It is these enactments that cause so much strife among neighbors, for one man's nuisance is another man's Newfoundland. In the era of thin apartment walls, excessive barking has become the flashpoint for many a feud, followed by a complaint

*A **fire spaniel,** in 19th century British military slang, was a soldier who enjoyed lingering around the fireplace in the barracks.*

to the authorities. There is a story told of an apartment dweller who stayed up late one night recording the serenade of the dog next door. On the succeeding night he played the tape back with the speaker turned toward the adjacent apartment. As a result, upon a complaint filed by the neighbor, he was duly convicted of disturbing the peace. Although the story may be apocryphal, it well illustrates the point that in many instances of nuisance complaints, the parties do not need the ministrations of the law but a mediator.

Dogs that annoy people are one thing. But what about dogs that annoy dogs? The Commonwealth of Massachusetts has provided for such occasions. In 1976, the state legislature made it possible to file a complaint if a dog bites another dog. (The next step, presumably, is to provide legal aid so that the dog can file the complaint itself.) Otherwise, the law generally refrains from trying to regulate the relationship of dog to dog—except for one curious municipal ordinance in California that forbids breeding on public property.

The state does embrace dogs with the arm of the law to protect them against humans with vicious propensities. Cruelty to animals is an offense almost everywhere, although the definitions and the penalties vary considerably. The City of San Francisco goes so far as to prescribe a minimum standard of living for pets, which must be given "proper and adequate food, water, shelter, care, exercise, and attention." The commandment is backed up by the possibility of a $500 fine and a six-month jail sentence.

Perhaps the outstanding contribution that statutes have made to dog welfare has been the prohibition of organized fighting, the exploitation of animals for amusement and profit. Animal combats date back at least to classical

Strays are an increasing problem in poorer areas of cities like New York. The ASPCA is empowered to roundup unlicensed or unleashed dogs but says it lacks the resources to deal with the problem.

Curbing the Strays

Many cities and rural areas in the United States are troubled by an uncontrolled population of dogs and cats, a phenomenon that taxes the resources of both local government agencies and voluntary humane societies. Although accurate statistics are lacking, a national conference of animal welfare and medical specialists in 1974 concluded that there is "an overabundance of dogs and cats relative to the number of responsible people willing to provide these animals with adequate homes and care."

Dogs are probably the greater menace because roving canines increase the threat of bites, spread rabies, and foul the public pavements. Dogs also do extensive damage to wild and domestic animals. They have attacked rare birds in zoos, outdone the coyote as a livestock predator is some places, and caused the deaths of many wild deer.

The dogs often attack in packs. A report by the American Humane Association has compared the pack "to human mob psychology or hysteria . . . . Town and country canines of otherwise respectable ownership band together like 'boys out on the town for a night of fun.' Dogs which normally or individually would not chase or assault become gripped by the pack mania of the chase and once blood has been drawn all inhibitions are gone."

Many of these destructive canines are pets allowed to run loose. Others once were owned but have been abandoned or become lost. Some, the so-called "feral" dogs, have lost all traces of domestication and merged with the wildlife population.

Municipal agencies try to control the dogs by searching for strays and trucking them to the pound, where they are generally kept for a maximum of five to seven days. If no one can be found to adopt the dog, it is destroyed to make room for the next wave of homeless animals. Adoption is the exception rather than the rule. Purebreds and young dogs might find favor among visitors, but for most dogs, especially the aged and sick, which constitute much of the intake, euthanasia is unavoidable. Only about 10 percent of the dogs taken to the pound ever leave.

Helping carry out that final solution to the pet problem has created qualms in the nation's humane societies. The humane movement began with the founding of the American Society for Prevention of Cruelty to Animals in New York in 1866. Its aim was to promote kindness to animals by their owners, but the movement now finds itself dealing out death to large numbers of animals who have no owners. Gerald R. Dalmadge, a California humane worker, has remarked, "Some of us, in fact, would be delighted and surprised to hear the average citizen of our home town describe our society as a shelter or placement agency. We have become more accustomed to hearing it called a 'slaughterhouse' or an 'Auschwitz for animals'."

Humane society shelters—there are about 1,500 in the United States, some of them operating under contracts with local government—generally do afford a dog a better chance of survival. There may be no legally fixed maximum stay, as in the pound, and more effort may be devoted to locating a home. But even the societies find themselves pressed for space and faced with clearly unplaceable animals. Some shelters — those that do not destroy healthy animals on principle — may take only dogs with a good chance of adoption.

The humane societies have also come under attack because one of their most commonly used modes of euthanasia—the decompression chamber, which simulates the effect of high altitudes—is considered cruel by some persons. However, a study panel commissioned by the American Veterinary Medical Association endorsed the method in 1972 as rapid and painless.

The societies have tried to reduce the stray population by sponsoring neutering programs. Often they provide the operation free or at low cost. But some animal welfare specialists are convinced that widespread surgery is impractical or medically unsound and that they need a chemical method — perhaps an injection to create long-term infertility — that would be cheap and easy to administer in quantity.

times, when dogs and other species were used to stage spectacles in the arena. In the Middle Ages, bullbaiting was a popular sport. According to one account, the sport was invented when a nobleman standing on the parapet of Stamford Castle in 1209 saw butchers' dogs chasing bulls through a meadow. He thought it such an amusing sight that he ordered bulls and dogs assembled regularly in the meadow for combats. The rules varied. In some places, the dog was supposed to pull the bull once around the ring by the ear; in others it had to pull the bull off his feet. The sport called forth a new breed, the Bulldog, designed with a low center of gravity and jaws powerful enough to move a bovine mass. Dogs were also set against each other in pit fights. Animal fighting of all kinds was banned in the 19th century in England and most other countries, but it seems to live on in places as an underground sport, testifying to the law's inability at times to suppress the crueler impulses.

Quarantine Notice

ATTENTION DOG OWNERS

D. L. 47

A NIGHT QUARANTINE for dogs is in force in this county. It was laid at the request of the county board of supervisors to help protect livestock from dog damage.

Dogs must be securely confined between sunset and one hour after sunrise. Any peace officer shall kill on sight any dog at large in violation of such order. A dog shall not be deemed to be at large if accompanied by and under the full control of the owner.

Any owner of a dog who shall neglect to confine his dog shall be subject to a penalty of $10.00.

Please cooperate and take care of your dog.

NEW YORK STATE
DEPARTMENT OF AGRICULTURE AND MARKETS

ON THE TRAIL.

11

The Last Mile Is at Least a Walk
THE AFTERLIFE

The Afterlife

Leaving the Survivors in Limbo

In life a beloved pet; in death, what? That question confronts anyone bereft by the loss of his dog because, while the animal is special to its owner, the surrounding culture does not recognize the death of a dog as an event of much significance. A dog owner may consider the pet part of his immediate family, yet requesting a day off from work to mourn would certainly raise an employer's eyebrows—as well as questions about the employee's mental balance. The same dilemma presents itself when the owner must decide how to dispose of the dog's remains. He might prefer a dignified burial, perhaps with a ceremony, but he must be prepared to suffer the derision of those who regard a canine corpse as a simple public health problem, solved by a plastic bag and a trip to the incinerator.

These disparate attitudes toward the death of dogs suggest an underlying difference of opinion about whether canines have an immortal soul. Apart from some Hindu concepts of reincarnation, most modern religions do not grant souls to animals, and even the dog's long association with soulful mankind apparently did not earn him a place in the hereafter. Indeed, after centuries of trying to repress idolatrous animal worship cults, the Judaeo-Christian faiths are unlikely to start making exceptions for the family dog. It is clear, however, that, despite the absence of the religious sanction, there are those who firmly believe that their dog has a soul whose departure ought to be commemorated.

Some dogs, perhaps sensing their owners' embarrassment, take themselves off to die like elephants going to the burial ground. But when a dog is killed in an accident or simply expires on the doorstep, it is up to the owner who believes in the uniqueness of his pet to devise some sort of appropriate rite of passage. The traditional ceremony has been burial in a corner of the yard in a grave marked by a stone cairn or a little wooden cross erratically assembled by childish hands. Prayers are optional, but often a few words reminiscent of a burial service, recalling the dog's virtues, are pronounced. Sometimes grave goods, such as an old sock that the deceased was fond of chewing, are interred with the body, much as a sword and shield were buried with their Viking owner so that implements would not be lacking for the next life. Dog owners desiring a more elaborate funeral may purchase a child-size coffin from an under-

Smokey   Spunky
Jesus Walks With You
Get The Bone   Get The Ball

Tombstone Epitaph

My Ostey
Itsy-Betsy
Diddy Bop
My Baby Ostey

Tombstone Epitaph

taker and have a tombstone engraved. Some dig the coffin up and take it with them when they move to a new house.

A few dog owners insist that the only proper place for the dog is alongside their own final resting place, but they usually have difficulties with the religious authorities, who are not keen on using consecrated ground for members of the wrong sect, let alone the wrong species. A

In Search of Pootzy

The eternal resting place of dogs was the subject of a radio play by Norman Corwin broadcast in 1941. Entitled "The Odyssey of Runyon Jones," it portrayed the efforts of a dog owner to contact his pet, Pootzy, who was killed in a car accident, by going through celestial channels. A scene from the play follows.

RUNYON. Is this the Department of Diseased Dogs?

SECOND CLERK. *Deceased,* not diseased. Let me see that slip.

RUNYON. Yes, sir.

SECOND CLERK. Mm. Pootzy. Are you Runyon Jones?

RUNYON. Yes, sir.

SECOND CLERK. Just a minute; let me look at the file.
Sound of file case opening, cards flipped.

SECOND CLERK. *(to himself; scarcely audible, mumbling).* Pootzy Jones . . . one and a half years old . . . inveterate auto chaser . . . leash . . . attitude . . . mm. *(To Runyon.)* Young man, I don't think there's anything we can do for you.

RUNYON *(terribly downhearted).* You can't find Pootzy?

SECOND CLERK. Ordinarily, in a good many cases, when a boy's dog dies from old age or natural causes, or is merely run over while chasing a cat in line of duty, or is fatally wounded in a fight with other dogs, we can make arrangements with St. Bernard, the head of Dog Heaven, for the return of the animal on a limited basis.

RUNYON. What's a limited basis?

SECOND CLERK. *But* — in the case of Pootzy, he is down in the files as an inveterate auto chaser and tire nipper, Class 4. Also, it is known that he has resisted leashes, that he bit a dog catcher on August eleventh last, and that he stayed out all night on three separate occasions. I'm sorry to say he's *not* in Dog Heaven.

RUNYON. *(freshly disappointed).* No? Gosh! *(Almost at point of tears.)* Are you sure, Mister? Couldn't he have snuck in when nobody was looking?

SECOND CLERK. *(firmly).* He is not in Dog Heaven, and that settles that.

RUNYON. Well, where is he, then?

SECOND CLERK. In the place where all ill-behaved curs are punished. Curgatory.

doctrinal controversy erupted among theologians, lawyers and philosophers in France a while ago when someone proposed placing his dog in the family burial vault. One side in the dispute maintained that he had no right to impose the presence of an animal on human dead. The argument of the other side was summed up by a French official who said, "I would prefer the company of my dog to that of a human being that I despised."

Those who are satisfied with a quasi-human burial for their dog turn to the pet cemetery, an institution almost indistinguishable in appearance from its non-animal counterpart. Pet cemeteries are by no means a symptom of modern decadence. They have existed at least since ancient Egyptian times, and the oldest in the United States, the Hartsdale (New York) Canine Cemetery was founded in 1896. There are more than 400 pet cemeteries in the United States today, varying in appearance and tone as much as other cemeteries do.

Hartsdale has the mellow, steeply rolling landscape of a 19th-century churchyard, lined with tombstones of varying size and even mausoleums. The only details that remind the visitor he is not in a regular cemetery are the epitaphs. Rather than formal first names and family names, there are one-word appellations like "Pal," lifespans briefer than on most tombstones and variations on the theme of "gone but not forgotten."

Other pet cemeteries follow the latest fash-

Skippy
Duke
Buried Here Two Buddies
Proven True,
One Small And White The
Other Big And Blue,
Faithful To Their Masters
Returning Our Memory And Love,
Mom And Julia We Do.

Tombstone Epitaph

NOTICE

1 Headstones must be granite.

2 No fences, frames or slabs permitted

3 Ivy, artificial grass, chipits, (wooden or granite) not permitted.

4 Bushes, plants, etc. no higher than 2 feet and must be planted within 1 foot from base of monument.

5 Cemetery cannot be responsible for vandalism, damage to monuments and headstones, theft of bushes, figurines, etc.

6 All Christmas decorations must be off the graves by February 10th.

7 No artificial flowers permitted on graves from May 1st. to October 1st.

8 Live pets must be kept on a leash when visiting the Cemetery.

9 2nd. Sunday in September is Pet Memorial Day.

10 No bicycle riding.

Witch-finders in the New World thought dogs represented evil spirits at the bidding of witches.

*Black Pomeranian
Rags
Only A Dog, But Such Love He Gave
Cannot Have Perished In The Grave
So Constant And Faithful And True A Heart,
Must In Eternity Have Some Part
And I Sometimes Fancy
When I've Crossed Life's Sea
I'll Find Him Waiting To Welcome Me*

Tombstone Epitaph

ions in "grief management" for humans. Paw Print Gardens in West Chicago, Illinois, for example, is the embodiment of the fully developed California-style garden of remembrance. The lighted grounds are decorated with large cement statues of dogs and "reminiscing benches." There is also a place for religious observance, reverently described in the cemetery brochure:

The Chapel in Paw Print Gardens is dedicated to "God's Little Ones." It sits near the entrance to the gardens. From the steeple of the Chapel melodious music flows to all corners of the gardens. At designated times, chimes can be heard ringing throughout the gardens. Funeral services and private viewings are held in the Slumber Room of the Chapel.

Dog funerals can also be similar to human ones in another way: they can be expensive. The thought of economizing on the last rites of a relative leaves most people ridden with guilt, and so it is with dog owners. They are willing to pay rather dearly to see their pet off

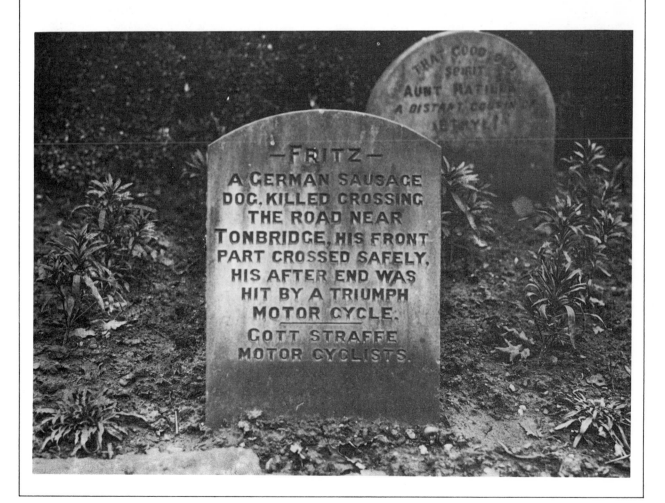

His Blind Implicit Faith In You
Is Matched By His Great Love . . .
The Kind That All Of Us Should Have
In Our Master, Up Above!
When Everything Is Said And Done
I Guess This Isn't Odd
For When You Spell "Dog" Backwards You
Will Get The Name Of God!

Tombstone Epitaph

in a manner that leaves no doubts about the family's gratitude for years of faithful service. The cemeteries offer a wide selection of conscience-salving services to the bereaved. At Paw Print Gardens, for example, a burial can cost as much as $500, although cheaper ones are available. The price includes $55 for the burial plot, almost $200 for the coffin, $165 for the memorial marker, and $50 for a light that is turned on at Christmas, Easter, Memorial Day, the dog's birthday, the anniversary of its burial or any special occasion designated by the family.

Optional services include embalming, the placing of flowers on the grave for special occasions, and "winter blankets" to protect the grave from the cold. The cemetery grants special veterans benefits: members of the K-9 Corps of the United States Army receive a free burial site, as do seeing-eye dogs — a reward for loyal performance of duty.

Many cemeteries advise dog owners to purchase a burial plot "in advance of need," as the undertakers say, when decisions may be made unclouded by emotion. Usually there is a discount for doing so, and some cemeteries offer family plots that will accommodate more than one pet. The Bide-a-Wee Memorial Park in Wantagh, New York, sells a plot for about $150 to $250 that will take two pet bodies and the ashes of a cremated animal.

Cremation is the cheapest professional way of disposing of a dog's remains. The cost varies considerably, depending upon how ceremoniously the ashes are treated. The American Society for the Prevention of Cruelty to Animals runs a free disposal service in New York City. Dogs must be brought to the ASPCA by the owners, but some commercial establishments, such as the Pet Crematory Service of America in Farmingdale, New York, offer pickup of

ILLUSTRATION BY DEBBIE HALL

Where to Bury a Dog

From an editorial in the Portland *Oregonian:*

There is one best place to bury a dog. If you bury him in this spot, he will come to you when you call—come to you over the grim, dim frontiers of death, and down the well-remembered path, and to your side again. And though you call a dozen living dogs to heel they shall not growl at him, nor resent his coming, for he belongs there. *People may scoff at you, who see no lightest blade of grass bent by his footfall, who hear no whimper, people who may never really have had a dog. Smile at them, for you shall know something that is hidden from them, and which is well worth the knowing. The one best place to bury a good dog is in the heart of his master.*

You Have Returned To Outer Space,
Among The Stars To Roam,
Gone Is The Magic Of Your Faces,
And Sadness Fills Our Home

Tombstone Epitaph

the body and delivery of the ashes. The charges: $33 for up to five pounds, rising with the weight of the dog. Pickup is extra. Many cemeteries also perform cremations and may have special sections for ashes. At Paw Print Gardens, cremation costs about $25 to $75 and urns from $15 to $75. The ashes can be taken home or left at the cemetery for "inurnment."

Obituary

This is E. B. White's tribute to Daisy, which appeared in the *New Yorker* magazine in 1932:

Daisy ("Black Watch Debatable") died December 22, 1931, when she was hit by a Yellow Cab in University Place. At the moment of her death she was smelling the front of a florist's shop. It was a wet day, and the cab skidded up over the curb— just the sort of excitement that would have amused her, had she been at a safer distance. She is survived by her mother, Jeannie; a brother, Abner; her father, whom she never knew; and two sisters, whom she never liked. She was three years old.

Daisy was born at 65 West Eleventh Street in a clothes closet at two o'clock of a December morning in 1928. She came, as did her sisters and brothers, as an unqualified surprise to her mother, who had for several days previously looked with a low-grade suspicion on the box of bedding that had been set out for the delivery, and who had gone into the clothes closet merely because she had felt funny and wanted a dark, awkward place to feel funny in. Daisy was the smallest of the litter of seven, and the oddest.

Her life was full of incident but not of accomplishment. Persons who knew her only slightly regarded her as an opinionated little bitch, and said so; but she had a small circle of friends who saw through her, cost what it did. At Speyer Hospital, where she used to go when she was indisposed, she was known as "Whitey," because, the man told me, she was black. All her life she was subject to moods, and her feeling about horses laid her sanity open to question. Once she slipped her leash and chased a horse for three blocks through heavy traffic, in the carking belief that she was an effective agent against horses. Drivers of teams, seeing her only in the moments of her delirium, invariably leaned far out of their seats and gave tongue, mocking her; and thus made themselves even more ridiculous, for the moment, than Daisy.

She had a stoical nature, and spent the latter part of her life an invalid, owing to an injury to her right hind leg. Like many invalids, she developed a rather objectionable cheerfulness, as though to deny that she had cause for rancor. She also developed, without instruction or encouragement, a curious habit of holding people firmly by the ankle without actually biting them — a habit that gave her an immense personal advantage and won her many enemies. As far as I know, she never even broke the thread of a sock, so delicate was her grasp (like a retriever's), but her point of view was questionable, and her attitude was beyond explaining to the person whose ankle was at stake. For my own amusement, I often tried to diagnose this quirkish temper, and I think I understand it: she suffered from a chronic perplexity, and it relieved her to take hold of something.

She was arrested once, by Patrolman Porko. She enjoyed practically everything in life except motoring, an exigency to which she submitted silently, without joy, and without nausea. She never took pains to discover, conclusively, the things that might have diminished her curiosity and spoiled her taste. She died sniffing life, and enjoying it.

CHECKERS
1952 ——— 1964

NIXON

Checkers helped Richard Nixon survive one crisis; it was unavailable to help with the last one.

Terry Boy
May You Be A King
In Little Dog's Heaven
And Fill Their Hearts
With Joy And Happiness
As You Did For Us On Earth
We Love You And Miss You
So Much
Mommy And Daddy

Tombstone Epitaph

Although dogs may die of their own accord, in many instances the owner makes a conscious decision to end the dog's life, an act that often produces severe guilt feelings. There are, of course, many valid reasons for opting for euthanasia. The dog may be too sick to move or eat, experience severe pain, or require so much care that the family's life is disrupted. The decision might even be a simple matter of economics; a dog may need extensive medical treatment that is beyond the family's means. It can be argued, after all, that a pet exists to

Hachiko
the Faithful

A statue of an Akita in the Shibuya train station in Tokyo commemorates canine fidelity that survives the death of the owner. The dog, named Hachiko, would go to the station each evening to greet its owner, a university professor, upon his return from work. One evening in 1925 the professor failed to return, having died during the day. But until the dog's own death almost nine years later, Hachiko went to the station every day at the usual time to wait for the homecoming. Admirers of Hachiko's devotion contributed money to raise the statue.

give the family pleasure, and that when it becomes a burden, doing away with it is only logical. But many owners balk at using cost-benefit analysis to determine whether a pet should live or die. And they are willing to make extreme sacrifices of time or money to avoid the gnawing feeling of having been ungrateful.

Veterinarians are often called upon for counsel, although an owner may abandon the vet rather than the dog if the medical opinion is not what he wants to hear. The practitioners have a number of standard arguments. They may point out that the dog will die someday anyway and that euthanasia is painless. Sometimes the arguments rise to the level of existential philosophy. One veterinarian, Leon F. Whitney, has written, "An animal does not miss tomorrow . . . If he dies, his existence merely terminates. He is being deprived of nothing, for he has no conception of the future." (Of course, it can be argued that no one who is dead misses anything.) But there are times when ending a dog's life is emotionally difficult for the professional medical man even when his judgment dictates that it should be done. James Herriot, the author of *All Creatures Great and Small,* recalled a trying moment when he told a wretchedly poor old man that his dog and only companion had to be killed: "I always aimed at a brisk, matter of fact approach, but the old clichés had an empty ring."

On the other hand, veterinarians sometimes find themselves asked to perform euthanasia on a healthy animal because the owner has somehow convinced himself that the dog is terminally ill or because the dog has become an inconvenience, or has developed some annoying habit. Since most veterinarians entered the profession to preserve the life of animals, not end them needlessly, they may try disabusing the owner of the notion that death is the only alternative.

Choosing euthanasia is somewhat less grim now than it was in the past, when the meaning of the word (Greek for "an easy death") was belied by the grim methods used. The dogs were gassed, shot, electrocuted or given the

Skippy Girl
The Happy-Hunting Ground
Is A Nicer Place By Far
In Having Added
A Bright New Star

Tombstone Epitaph

poison strychnine, methods that sometimes produced terror and struggle. In most private veterinary clinics today, the dog is injected with an overdose of an anesthetic drug; it is literally "put to sleep" and never wakens. However it is done though, the owner often is left with the haunting sense of having "pulled the plug" on his companion.

Irish
Our Pal

Tombstone Epitaph

12

He Has Learned to Adjust

THE DOG'S BEST FRIEND

The Dog's Best Friend

Life at the Upper End of the Leash

Although dogs have certainly not outlived their practical usefulness to mankind as a whole, the canine's contribution to the well-being of urban and suburban dwellers is, to say the least, intangible. Millions of metropolites give up some of their valuable living space and wealth to canines having no flocks to tend, no foxes to chase, and no ducks to retrieve. What is it that they receive in return?

A dog's services are basically at the emotional level, and emotions are difficult to fathom. But it is safe to assume that, in a society suffering from anomie and loneliness, the dog is valued because it offers friendship for reasons that, if not totally altruistic, are at least aboveboard and mutually understood. (Recognizing that, social workers now speak of providing "pet therapy" to lonely invalids or aged persons.) A dog may also restore contact with the natural world to those who are cut off from the earth by a layer of road tar and cement.

Canines stimulate healthy human interaction. In some discordant homes, mutual concern for the dog's welfare is the last remaining thread of the ties that bind. Dogs may substitute for children, unborn or grown up, or for parents. Dr.

ILLUSTRATION BY KIMBLE P. MEAD

Boris M. Levinson, a psychologist who specializes in human-pet relationships, maintains that "the child needs love, affection and nurturant care, and when such care is not available from a succorant parent or is in short supply, a pet can partially fill the void."

A dog may also symbolize a person's self-image. It may give its owner a reassuring sense of power that he lacks in his dealings with other people and with society at large. When the dog is the follower, every man can be a leader. Dr. Bruce Max Feldmann, a veterinarian, has argued, "Pets can be extensions of how pet owners see themselves or would like to be seen: swift, athletic, physically well-proportioned, attractive, masculine, feminine, virile, intelligent, clever, courageous, etc."

The choice of a dog as pet thus involves deep-seated nonrational forces, but there is evidence that the choice makes sense from a strictly economic point of view. In 1977, the Consumers' Association in Britain applied its testing standards to the question of which pet gives the purchaser the most for his money; the dog emerged as "Best Buy." The association took into account the relatively high purchase price and "operating" costs of dogs compared to cats, but it concluded that they were worth the extra expense because most dog owners surveyed reported actively enjoying their animals' company an average of four hours each day. Cat owners reported a mere hour and 40 minutes a day of consumer satisfaction, Cats, in fact, ranked a poor third behind horses. Equine pets cost much more to own and maintain but their durability — a 25-year lifespan — compensated for the high initial outlay. (Tortoises were found to be very durable, but they were rather impassive, as were goldfish.)

Whether done for emotional reasons or because it is the best buy, acquiring a dog has serious repercussions. It may even determine where the owner lives. Dog owning predates cities, and there is much debate about whether canines and urban civilization are compatible. In the minds of nonowners, dogs in cities are misfits responsible for the many bite cases each

year and the mounds of feces on street corners and park paths. (More than 40,000 bites are reported in New York City alone each year, and, by one ingenious estimate, more than 20,000 tons of dog excrement are deposited there.) The opponents of dogs might one day form a political movement powerful enough to prohibit dogs within city limits altogether or regulate their size. The adoption of a state law imposing heavy fines on New York City owners

Abby's Advice

DEAR ABBY: Am I wrong for refusing to sleep with the man I love because he wants his dog to sleep on the floor of our bedroom?

When I walked out, he said the dog always slept on the floor in the same bedroom with him and his first wife, who is now deceased.

Abby, I have never had dogs and I am not used to them. I told him he could put the dog in the other bedroom, but he said he wouldn't do it—that next to his deceased wife, the dog came first. So where do I stand?

NO DOG LOVER

DEAR NO: Right behind his dog.

Two Ways to Show a Dog Your Appreciation:

Charles F. Levine lives in Montreal with his wife, Carol, four dogs and 20 cats. He makes this modest proposal to cat-less dog owners.

1) Get It a Cat

Not all dogs and cats, obviously, are destined to be friends. Some dogs even kill cats. My experience with a number of cats and dogs living in close proximity suggests, however, that the possibilities for friendship are much greater than those of enmity. My advice to one-pet families, in fact, is: get your dog a cat.

Many people, having bought a dog, find that it develops rather obvious neurotic tendencies, such as perpetual barking and chewing of furniture. In general, this behavior takes place when no one is at home and is clearly a form of punishment imposed on the masters for the loneliness they force upon their pet. Providing the dog with the companionship of a cat may well curb some of its more odious habits. The arrival of a kitten may also perk up an elderly dog that has lost its get-up-and-go.

Some people are deterred from getting a cat because their dog chases cats, which they take as a sign of hostility. But dogs chase cats because of a reflex that impels them to pursue moving objects. A great many children get bitten because of the same reflex. Even my dogs, who live whisker by jowl with felines, still try to chase cats when they see them on the street.

There are some basic rules for selecting the kitten or cat. If possible, bring your dog along to meet the kitten in its present home. There are kittens who take immediately to dogs (we have one who playfully twitted a large dog minutes after meeting it) and others who will run and hide. Try to choose a cat that has a positive attitude toward your dog. Remember that most dogs are much larger than cats, so it is not necessarily a

bad omen if an eight-ounce kitten gets its back up when sniffed by a 100-pound canine.

Keep the cat and the dog in separate rooms for the first few days or, better still, leave the cat in a cage. The cat and the dog should be able to sniff each other, so they can become accustomed to their respective scents. Then open the door and watch what happens. At best, the dog and cat will immediately begin a friendship; at worst, the cat may still be unnerved by the dog and leap on a table for a safer look.

Once the animals have become accustomed to each other, you will find that their relationship will enrich your appreciation of both dog and cat. Cats can, for example, bring out the tender, protective instincts in dogs. Our dogs have been mother, father, brother, sister and friend to a succession of cats found on the street in various states of hunger and disrepair. One December night, Paquie, an unpretentious mutt, saved a tiny black-and-white kitten from freezing to death by locating it in a snowbank and digging it out. Paquie was trained to be cat-oriented by our first dog, Ming, a Malamute. (Cat affinity is obviously learned, not inherited.) Whenever her muscles tensed in preparation for a playful cat chase, Ming would bowl her over with a shoulder block worthy of the National Football League.

Although usually not serious about it, cats will sometimes take out on their canine roommates their aggressions against other cats. When our cat, Houdini, was getting old and beginning to get the worst of his fights, he would come home and swat the Malamute on the nose. Just like anyone else who had had a bad day at work, he felt like kicking the dog.

2) Remember It in Your Will

Dogs, it has often been said, are surrogate children, and there is no better proof of that than the proceedings in Surrogate Court. Many persons, including some who were very wealthy, have made or attempted to make dogs their heirs. In 1968, for example, Eleanor E. Ritchey died, leaving $14.5 million to her 81 dogs, who could thus afford to hire a veterinarian and four other employees to look after them at their ken-

nel in Deerfield Beach, Florida.

Some states, however, have prohibited such testamentary indulgence by pet owners. Under New York State's Estates, Powers and Trusts Law, only a "person" can inherit property, and dogs do not meet the legal definition of a person. But, as usual, there is a loophole. A dog owner can leave his money to set up a trust to care for animals, of which his dog naturally would be one.

The legitimacy of such a will was upheld in 1946 by the Appellate Division of New York State Supreme Court in a case involving Bertha L. Hamilton, who left her house and more than $400,000 to found a home or hospital "for the care, comfort and benefit of dumb animals." The bequest was challenged on the ground that it was not charitable because it was not for the welfare of humans. The court held that creating a home for animals was a charitable use of funds, taking note of the "common view that the care and comfort of animals are generally beneficial to mankind.... In the modern view consideration for dumb animals is regarded as commendable, and encouraged and promoted by numerous societies which are organized for this purpose." The decision split the court and drew a sharp dissenting opinion. It contended that "the arguments and logic which sustain the desirability and legality of the perpetual application of income . . . for relief and aid to the unfortu-- nate of the human race . . . do not apply to the benefaction, care and relief of dumb animals." Fortunately for dogs, the animal lovers had a majority on the bench.

who fail to scoop up their pets' droppings suggests that such a movement might have broad support from the man in the street, especially if he is on foot.

Some dog owners have exacerbated the situation by buying so-called "guard dogs" or "attack dogs" for the specific purpose of defending themselves against their fellow city dwellers. Often these dogs are bought from unscrupulous trainers — sometimes doing business by mail order — who have failed to insure that the dog has the proper temperament and responsiveness. The result is scared or even scarred neighbors who wonder whether an innocent social call will be misinterpreted by the dog as an attempted burglary. The neighbors may become even more concerned when, as often happens, the owner is bitten by his supposed guardian. Some cities and states have begun regulating and licensing guard dogs and their professional trainers to control the abuses of the canine protection fad.

Even if they are not finally banished by law from the city, dog owners will continue to suffer severe restrictions on their choice of dwelling. Many apartment buildings forbid dogs, and some of those that have tolerated them in the past prohibit new pets. Where they are allowed, dogs may create friction, especially if their size and temperament arouse hostility among the neighbors. Roger Caras, a vice pres-

A female bulldog is called a **bullbitch.**

ident of the Humane Society of the United States, has cautioned owners that inexperienced persons may "buy Rottweilers, Old English Sheepdogs, Vizslas and Irish Setters for apartment living. There is no way that these animals left untrained are not going to offend non-dog lovers who try to get on the elevator with them . . . . No one who has been knocked down by a flaked-out field dog that has gotten ten minutes of exercise (a stroll to the curb and back) a day for six months, and no one who has had five hundred stitches and six major plastic surgery operations will stop and evaluate your manners or your dog's. You are the enemy."

For dog owners, it is often their urban lifestyle rather than their pet that ultimately gives way. A canine fancier who took refuge in the country described to the readers of *Dog World* magazine how she decided that city life had become unbearable:

> *The day we looked around our downstairs five-room apartment in the two-family house we owned in the residential area of a small Massachusetts city and saw nearly wall-to-wall West Highland White Terriers was the day we decided a move to the country was of top priority . . . . The feeling of freedom living in a rural area is enormous. No fears of complaints about the noise or of a man in a blue uniform knocking on the door to say "Now, ma'am, about all these dogs . . .".*

She made the happy discovery that the countryside is "animal-oriented."

Owning a dog may condition the choice of an occupation or place of work as well as a place of residence. Many corporate executives, shaking off the inhibitions of the past, are taking their dogs with them to the office, where the pets crouch beside the desk or curl up on a

Reykjavik: The Pedestrian's Paradise

If you see a dog on the streets of Iceland's capital city, Reykjavik, you know that it is a stray or that someone is about to get a summons. The keeping of dogs is banned by law within the city limits because, according to an official of the Icelandic consulate, dog ownership "was found not suitable for sanitary reasons." As a result, the condition of the streets in that city of 85,000 is, in the words of the official, "wonderful." When they get nostalgic for the sound of dogs barking, the residents of Reykjavik make excursions into the country.

ILLUSTRATION BY KIMBLE P. MEAD

chair from nine to five. Some businessmen, in fact, have refused to locate their offices in buildings that will not allow dogs, and executives have quit their jobs because the boss thought a dog detracted from the hard-working atmosphere. Of course, when the boss himself brings in a dog, it is a signal to the employees; the next day there may be a pet stationed at every typewriter. Dogs even share after-hours entertainment. The smaller breeds may be carried in a satchel to dinner and the theater.

Various reasons are offered for taking the dog along to work. Some owners contend that the dogs are lonely when left home alone, others that it is good exercise for the dog to be walked to and from work (although many dogs just share the taxi ride). But it is also possible that the owner, not the dog, feels the separation most and finds that canine companionship makes the daily grind a bit less abrasive.

At home and at work the dog is a conditioning factor in human relationships, but on the street the dog's presence dominates them. Urban dog walkers tend to congregate, perhaps for the safety of numbers, in a few recognized drop zones, where an informal etiquette develops. In New York's Central Park, there are definite rules of the road. When two walkers meet on a narrow path, the person with the bigger or fiercer dog is usually allowed to pass, although the walker giving way may mischievously permit his dog to tease the other so that the owner of the big dog has to struggle to restrain him.

The etiquette also prescribes what to say after one says hello to a fellow walker; the proper ice-breaker is to inquire about the condition of the other dog's stools and whether they are worm-free.

Under the rules, walkers may challenge each other to an unspoken obedience trial. By casually giving commands like "Come" and eliciting instant responses, a dog owner effects a subtle put-down over the other person — unless there is a similar demonstration in reply. (If his dog does not respond, the challenger is similarly considered to have lost face.) Dogs may also be used as a pretext to introduce oneself, partic-

ularly to those of the opposite sex, and stroking the head of the other person's dog may be used to demonstrate affection for its owner.

City dogs walk, but in the suburbs, where man drives, dogs ride. Suburbanites have become accustomed to driving with their dogs to show them off, to avoid leaving them home alone and to have some company during the many hours — perhaps 25 percent of their waking life — they spend in cars. Businesses have accommodated their customer's habits; some drive-in banks slip a dog biscuit into the money tray along with the deposit receipt.

Suburban dogs become so used to riding that they often get excited at the sound of the ignition. When in a parked car, they may exhibit protective feelings that they do not show toward the house, even though dogs have been asphyxiated by carbon monoxide or succumbed to heat prostration when the car windows were left closed. The reason for the devotion to riding is fairly simple: the destination. Dogs often end up with their owners dining on hamburgers at the fast-food stands.

Dog owners do more than local traveling with their pets. They go on vacation trips with them and even on intercontinental journeys. When he took "an old French gentleman Poodle known as Charley" on the cross-country trip that inspired *Travels with Charley,* John Steinbeck was emulating many other campers. Most dog owners, of course, are not seeking literary inspiration when they move about with their pet; they are merely following the traditional American practice of going new places without leaving the comforts of home. The pets do not only go on road trips; most airlines, responsive to their customers' wishes, will fly a dog anywhere, and the premier ocean liner, the Queen Elizabeth 2, has a kennel for 35 animals. (The dogs also need not leave the comforts of home; the ship's kennel area is equipped with a street lampost.)

Long distance traveling, especially in a plane's hot, stuffy cargo hold, can be so stressful that the dog has to be tranquilized, but then so may its owner, giving them another shared experi-

Many dogs are automobile addicts, but precautions must be taken to prevent windblown dust and dirt from damaging their eyes. In non-convertibles, the dog should be kept from hanging its head out the window.

The Nixon family poses with Checkers. The public's sentimental attachment to dogs saved Nixon from a disastrous scandal while he was running for Vice President.

ence. Occasionally a traveler has been unworldly enough to check his pet through to the final destination, realizing after several plane changes that losing a piece of luggage is much more serious when the contents have to be walked three times daily. (Humane societies have reported cases in which a dog sat for days in a crate at an airport waiting for its owner to be located.)

Travelers often burden themselves with the dog's luggage as well. One guidebook for pet travel recommends taking, among other items: a blanket, chewing toys, cans of food, a can opener, food and water bowls, comb and brush, eyewash, mineral oil and a rectal thermometer. After properly equipping himself, the traveler may find that, with a dog, there are fewer places where he can go. Some countries, like Britain, require protracted quarantining of imported animals, and not all hotels will look kindly upon guests arriving with a potential carpet-chewer in their party.

Presidential Pets

Few persons have adapted their lifestyles to include dogs as carefully as politicians, particularly those of presidential caliber. Photographs of the candidate with wife, children and dog are obligatory in campaign literature, proving that the aspirant is a responsible family man. Presidential candidates have found pet dogs to be useful image-builders. As the *American Kennel Gazette* put it in 1924, "The country at large takes a natural interest in the President's dogs and judges him by the taste and discrimination he shows in his selection . . . . Any man who does not like dogs and want them about does not deserve to be in the White House."

The gazette approved of President Harding's choice, an Airedale named Laddie Boy, who, it said, "could win the hearts of thousands where he had only time for hundreds." In any event, Laddie Boy was considered an improvement over Theodore Roosevelt's pets, a collection of lizards, rattlesnakes, wild turkeys and kangaroos.

Despite the publicity advantages of dog own-

Liberty matched her owner, Gerald Ford, in disposition. She was friendly, outgoing and occasionally a bit slow to respond.

Pushinka, the daughter of a Russian Cosmodog, was a gift to the Kennedys and bore four puppies while in the White House.

The Fala File

A former President usually has his correspondence enshrined in official archives, and sometimes the President's dog does too. The "Fala file" at the Franklin D. Roosevelt Memorial Library in Hyde Park, New York, comprises 11 boxes filled with the dog's papers: Christmas cards, letters from admirers and proposals from female dogs seeking to be mated with the celebrated Scottish Terrier. Often the letters were accompanied by photographs. (The proposals were routinely but politely turned down, on Fala's behalf, by a Presidential assistant.) The collection also embraces more than 100 periodical articles and cartoons about Fala, a photograph collection and an MGM movie entitled *Fala at Hyde Park*.

These are excerpts from two of the letters Fala received:

July 2, 1942

Dear Fala,

I saw your picture last week, and I certainly think you have set a splendid example for the rest of us doggies to follow in contributing our rubber toys to the nation's drive for scrap rubber. . . . I gladly gave them up for doggies can help your grand pop, our beloved President, in his great effort to collect rubber.

P.G.

August 21, 1942

My Dear Fala,

Just a line on a subject I think is important because I believe we Scotties ought to stick together. My name's Johnny, and I own an actor by the name of Lionel Barrymore. He's all right and does the best he can, but sometimes he goes haywire, as when he took all my rubber toys, including a mouse I could never get the squeak out of, and sent them away with a lot of old hose and rubber matting.

I enclose a picture of myself and the guy I own.

Johnny

Fala accompanied F.D.R. even to delicate international conferences.

ership in general, individual dogs have sometimes been sources of embarrassment to chief executives. Calvin Coolidge's Terrier, Peter Pan, had to be exiled for harassing the White House employees, and Franklin D. Roosevelt's German Shepherd, Major, once bit British Prime Minister Ramsay MacDonald. Roosevelt's later pet, the Scottish Terrier Fala, was a colorful prop for the President, who took the dog with him for comic relief at international conferences. In 1944, however, Republican politicians accused the President of having dispatched a destroyer to the Aleutian Islands to retrieve Fala, who had been left there accidentally, at great cost to the taxpayers. Roosevelt, executing a brilliant tactical maneuver, turned the charge to his advantage. In a dinner speech, he complained with mock gravity:

These Republican leaders have not been content with attacks on me, or my wife, or on my sons. No, not content with that, they now include my little dog, Fala. Well, of course, I don't resent attacks . . . but

Fala does resent them . . . . I think I have a right to resent, to object to libelous statements about my dog.

Almost a decade later, in 1952, then vice presidential candidate Richard Nixon also defused a political accusation by using his dog, not to lampoon his opponents as Roosevelt had, but to wring sympathy from the voters. Nixon had been accused of taking clandestine gifts. In a radio broadcast, the candidate said that the only gift he had received after his nomination was "a little Cocker Spaniel . . . black and white, spotted, and our little girl, Tricia, the six-year-old, named it Checkers." The Checkers Speech, as it came to be called, saved Nixon's political career for the time being, but years later, as the shadow of Watergate began creep-

Heidi was the Eisenhowers' Weimaraner. No media lover, she had to be coaxed for hours by Mamie before posing for pictures.

Alaska's Iditarod Trail:
The Polar Derby

In the nineteenth century, when miners sluiced for gold near Nome, Alaska, their main connection with the outside world in winter was the sled dog highway called the Iditarod Trail. The trail snaked for 1,050 miles, along the Bering Sea coast and the Yukon River Valley, toward Anchorage. In 1973, Alaska's sled dog racers realized their dream of reopening the whole trail, part of which was covered by brush, with the help of the United States Army Corps of Engineers and volunteers. In early March, 34 "mushers" and their dog teams glided out of Anchorage and made for Nome in the world's longest sled dog race.

The obstacles were formidable. Blizzards dumped mountainous snow drifts onto the trail, and temperatures plunged to as low as 50 degrees below zero. When it warmed up, puddles of water a yard deep formed over the ice. The drivers were even harassed by nosy moose. There were some encouragements, though. Villages along the route hung out signs like "Nome or Bust" to cheer the teams onward.

After 20 days, the winner, Dick Wilmarth, pulled into Nome, greeted by a sizeable (for northwest Alaska) crowd. He gave all credit to his team leader, a dog named Hotfoot. But the hazards of the trail had obviously taken their toll. Neither Wilmarth's nor any other team completed the race with all dogs still in harness, and more than a third of the sleds had to drop out along the way.

The hazards, however, did not end in Nome. The winner was apparently unaware that an old local ordinance required lead dogs to be equipped with a bell to warn pedestrians, and Wilmarth might have been given a summons for his pains. He was saved by a fan who came forward to hang a victory garland - made of bells - on Hotfoot.

Saved by the Sleds

Among the most critical sled dog missions in history was the 1925 "serum run," in which 19 drivers and their teams saved the people of Nome from a diphtheria epidemic by bringing antitoxin from Anchorage. Because the weather was too severe for the fragile planes of the era, the territorial governor telegraphed drivers along the route to set up relays. Crossing mountains and heaving ice floes, mostly in the dark, the sleds took seven days, from January 25 to February 2, halving the previous record time for the journey, even though the men, the dogs and even the serum were in danger of freezing for most of the way. The lead dog for the last 50 miles was Balto, a Siberian Husky upon whose instincts the team and driver relied to guide them through a blinding snowstorm.

LBJ's public ear yanking of Him and Her prompted an immediate mass protest by the nation's dog lovers.

ing over him, Nixon found himself again in trouble, in part because of a dog, this time an Irish Setter named King Timahoe. He was criticized for using official limousines to transport the dog to Camp David because it became air-sick flying with the President in his helicopter.

King Timahoe's predecessors in the White House, the Johnson Beagles, created a dog lovers' backlash against their owner when he allowed himself to be photographed picking one of them up by its ears. Johnson apparently was deeply offended by the outcry from dog fanciers unfamiliar with Texas Beagle-lifting techniques.

Former President Ford, who has a reputation for likableness and ineptitude, acquired a dog that suited that image. Liberty was as kindly as most Golden Retrievers, but she was a failure at obedience and had to be taken for remedial training.

Although Mr. Ford's successor, Jimmy Car-ter, recalled hunting with dogs in Georgia in his autobiography, the only canine in the Carter's Presidential household is a dog with the suitably Southern name of Grits, a gift to Amy Carter from her teacher. Grits' presence exemplifies, in a way, the American dream: from humble, mixed breed origins to the White House in one generation.

Names People Play

Throughout history dogs' names have reflected the character of their owners. The Assyrian Emperor Assurbanipal gave his dogs names like Biter of Enemies, which summed up that bellicose monarch's main interests. Queen Victoria, the epitome of stuffiness, was so impersonal that she often gave her dogs last names, like Waldman and Kilburn, rather than first names. President Lyndon Johnson, exhibiting the simplicity of folks along the banks of the Pedernales, dispensed with personal names entirely, referring to his Beagles by their gender: Him and Her.

Show and stud dogs tend to have impressively long, exotic names, as aristocrats are wont to, suggestive of the breed's country of origin. There is a German Shepherd boasting the name of Xaver vom Fourniermuhlenbach, an Afghan called Samir of Scheherezade, and a Hungarian Komondor named Marossentgyorgi Elod Miklos. (A nickname, presumably, is used for whist-ling them in.) Alternatively, show dogs may be given bold, brassy names that sound like those of racehorses: Golden Spike, Flying Colors or Hot Wheels.

Which are the most popular names? The American Kennel Club, which permits no more than 37 dogs of each breed to register under the same name, reports that may appelations are vastly oversubscribed. Among them, predictablly, are Spot, Snoopy, Lassie and Pierre. The AKC regulates naming behavior rather strictly. Names may not be "disparaging or obscene": Runt is not allowed. Nor may they be too flattering: Champ and Winner are also forbidden.

Modern names may be intended to display the sophistication and wit of the owner. A deep-voiced dog, who in the old days might have been just plain Boomer, is now Basso Profundo, and a light-hearted owner is apt to name his Gordon Setter Flash. Dogs are also billboards for political statements. An owner may name it "Yankee" just to have the pleasure of shouting "Yankee, come home!"

A TRIBUTE TO THE DOG
(BY SENATOR GEORGE GRAHAM VEST)

OLD
DRUM

The Jury Was Convinced

When Charles Burden's dog, Drum, was killed by Leonidas Hornsby, Burden brought suit for damages. The trial, held in Warrensburg, Missouri, in 1870, resulted in a damage award to Burden, but a more intriguing offshoot of the case was a persuasive speech to the jury by the plaintiff's lawyer, Senator George Graham Vest. The speech is remembered as the classic statement of the qualities of dogs that men admire. An excerpt follows.

The one absolutely unselfish friend that a man can have in this selfish world, the one that never deserts him, the one that never proves ungrateful or treacherous, is his dog. A man's dog stands by him in prosperity and in poverty, in health and in sickness. He will sleep on the cold ground where the wintry winds blow and the snow drives fiercely, if only he may be near his master's side. He will kiss the hand that has no food to offer, he will lick the sores and wounds that come in encounters with the roughness of the world. He guards the sleep of his pauper master as if he were a prince.

When all other friends desert, he remains. When riches take wings and reputation falls to pieces, he is as constant in his love as the sun in its journey through the heavens. If misfortune drives the master forth an outcast in the world, friendless and homeless, the faithful dog asks no higher privilege than that of accompanying him to guard against danger, to fight against his enemies.

And when the last scene of all comes, and death takes the master in its embrace, and his body is laid away in the cold ground, no matter if all other friends pursue their way, there by the graveside will the noble dog be found, his head between his paws, his eyes sad but open in alert watchfulness, faithful and true, even in death.

13

Going Bare Is Hardly Essential

GOODS AND SERVICES

Goods and Services

To Buy
Or
Not to Buy

Buying a dog is like buying a luxury car in some respects. The basic price is only a downpayment entitling the purchaser to enter the world of options, extras and accessories. Owning a dog makes a person a potential buyer of thousands of products and services intended to keep the dog healthy, good looking, well-behaved and amused. Some of these commodities are necessary or ingenious; others are frills. The characteristic that most have in common is that they are merchandised with a typically American feel for a rich and seemingly limitless market. The purveyors to the dog fancy evidently know their customers well.

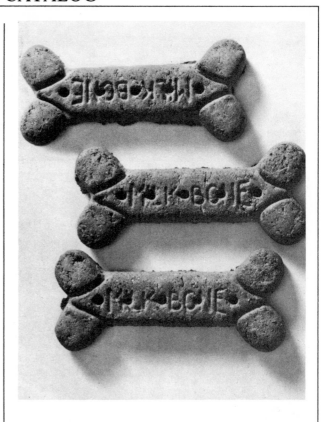

*A **dog in a doublet** is an old British expression for a daring person. It derives from the practice of clothing boar-hunting dogs in leather doublets for protection.*

The consumer's decisions start with the choice of dog itself. The choice may seem easy and pleasurable, but it is often hastily made and soon regretted. A survey of dog owners and former owners taken by the Pet Food Institute in 1975 found that more than a third of them had voluntarily given their animals away to another person or to a shelter. A variety of reasons were offered: the dogs became uncontrollable, the living area proved too small, the family had moved to a no-pet apartment, or caring for the animal was financially burdensome.

Much of the disillusionment probably results from poor planning. Acquiring a dog, after all, is not primarily a calculating decision. The peak buying period for dogs, as for many other goods, is Christmas, which suggests that many dogs are bought on impulse in the full flush of Yule cheer and perhaps even on the way home from the office party. People pick the type of dog that they had in childhood, that they have seen in movies, or that sustains their fantasies. Getting a ferocious animal may satisfy the owner's need

Owners often convince themselves that a dog's craving for luxury matches their own. Some provide their pets with stylish wardrobes and custom protection against the elements.

to compensate for a Milquetoast disposition, a sporting dog his desire to emulate the he-men in *Field and Stream*. It is the romantic who finds himself encapsulated with a St. Bernard in an efficiency apartment—so far from the Alps, so close to the delicate vases.

The first step toward rational buying is to cooly assess whether one has enough *Lebensraum* to house the dog without filling in all the spaces between the furniture and to give it the proper amount of exercise. Obviously, a Maltese will find it easier to get a good workout by running laps around the coffee table than will an Irish Wolfhound. It requires time and effort to exercise adequately the larger sporting and working dogs—a mile run daily is often recommended —so the would-be owner should consider carefully whether he is willing to take up jogging on behalf of his dog's health.

The type of dog chosen should also be compatible with the owner's other interests in life. It would not be wise to allow a Dachshund, carefully bred over the centuries to dig for badger, to live in close proximity to a garden, nor would it be prudent to keep rodent-hunting Terriers within reach of gerbils.

Children are always a principal consideration. Getting a dog "for the kids" is the great rationalization of the canine trade, although the purchase is often quite clearly a case of the adult buying himself electric trains by giving them to his youngsters. Dogs can be either too big or too small for children. A five-year-old could not easily stay on his feet while walking a 175-pound Great Dane, and a Pekingese might be too small to defend itself against infantile but

A choice of edible rawhide chew bones. Some dogs like chomping on one big one . . .

lethal pranks.

Temperament is less easy to judge than size. Ads for almost all breeds carry the obligatory assurance "good with children," the equivalent of the used-car salesman's guarantee that a vehicle is a creampuff. Most dogs of appropriate size are probably suitable for children, but personality can vary widely. Nasty quirks, unfortunately, do not really show themselves until the animal has matured somewhat, which means that the seven- to 12-week-old puppies that most people prefer are an unknown quantity temperamentally. The breed itself, of course, is a general indicator of character. Those who like their dogs affectionate to the point of soppiness could not go too far wrong with a Golden Retriever, but they would have to turn elsewhere, perhaps to a Bouvier des Flandres, for something with a bit more protective instinct. Many of the toy breeds are alert watchdogs, alhough they lack the deterrent effect of a Mastiff. An owner with an aversion to slobberingly friendly dogs might try an Afghan Hound or a Saluki, both of which tend to be aloof even towards their owners. For phlegmatism, a good choice might be the Basset Hound. Buyers should bear in mind that some breeds are associated with various unpleasant traits: St. Bernards drool copiously, Bulldogs snore raspingly and many Terriers and toy dogs bark compulsively.

Longevity may be a factor. Some breeds live longer than others, and, crass as it may seem, anyone who wants to get more years for his money should buy those dogs that live to a riper old age. Many of the larger breeds generally have lifespans of a decade or less; the

. . . others will chew on dozens. Many will also play fetch with them when sticks are in short supply.

Leashes are available in vary lengths of leather, nylon and chain — some with light-reflecting trim for safety during the nightly walk.

smaller dogs may live to about 15 years. To many owners, of course, the quality of their years with a dog is likely to be more significant than the number of them.

Another important element in the decision is the dog's coat. The white dreadlocks of a Komondor are sure to impress the neighborhood, but they are also certain to press the owner into the slavery of a coat care. Long coats in general need more brush, comb and scissors work than short coats, and white hair does as well in slush as whitewall tires. Some dogs, notably the Poodle, may commit the owner to regular payments for professional grooming services. Many dogs with profuse coats shed hair profusely, requiring the home as well as the dog to be groomed often. Shedding may provoke allergic reactions among humans, although the severity of the reaction can vary markedly with the breed. Some dogs, like the Irish Water Spaniel, shed virtually nothing at all, and most wirehaired dogs shed little. Obviously, choice of coat is one decision in which the practical and perhaps medical realitities must be balanced against the desire for a pet with panache.

Many owners prefer males to females in any breed because they are bigger and usually considered more representative of the ideal type. The official American Kennel Club standard for the Bulldog, heedless of possible accusations of sexism, states bluntly that in judging "due allowance should be made in favor of the bitches, which do not bear the characteristics of the breed to the same degree of perfection and grandeur as do the dogs."

Statistically, the owners of males are less likely to perceive that neutering is necessary (the Pet Food Institute survey found that only 12 per cent of males compared to 51 percent of females were neutered by their owners), but many fanciers contend that females are gentler and more tractable. (The same was once contended of human females.) Of course, when puppies are desired, having a male poses disadvantages.

There has been a traditional prejudice against

females on the ground that their twice yearly period of fertility, the estrus or "heat," attracts the male dogs in the neighborhood and requires that they be locked up for about three weeks each time. But if the female is kept in an apartment anyway, there is little difficulty unless the males learn how to use the elevator.

Cost is another factor. Most purebred puppies are priced from about $100 to $500—or more, especially if it is one of the exotic breeds.

If a purebred is not essential, the buyer can take advantage of the wide selection at the pound or shelter, the bargain basement of the dog market.

In assessing the value of purebred puppies offered for sale by breeders, the initials "AKC" in the ad should by no means be taken as a guarantee of quality. The letters merely signify that the puppies have been produced by dogs registered with the American Kennel Club and

that the puppies themselves are eligible for registration. (If so, the breeder ought to be able to supply the buyer with a properly filled out application for registration, containing the serial numbers of the litter and of the parents.) No buyer should delude himself into thinking that any puppy that can be registered can be turned into a show champion. As the AKC points out in its general information booklet,

Breeders breeding show stock are attempting to produce animals closely resembling the description of perfection in the breed standard. Many people breed their dogs with no concern for the qualitative demands of the breed standard. When this occurs repeatedly over several generations the animals, while still purebred, can be of extremely low quality in terms of their breed standard.

The worst breeders are the "puppy mills," which deliberately aim for quantity rather than quality and which often supply dogs to pet shops. For that reason, most knowledgeable buyers avoid shops in favor of reputable breeders, whose names can be obtained from local dog clubs or the national "parent club" of each breed.

Truth in advertising is not unknown. Many breeders distinguish in their ads between the more expensive "show quality" and the cheaper "pet quality" dogs. Magazines advertising white German Shepherds usually disclose that they are ineligible to be shown. But there are always some who do not scruple to sell a puppy known to have a disqualifying fault by promising the buyer a triumph in the show ring. Some buyers have successfully sued to recover their money because they contracted to buy a "show dog" and were given one that the seller knew was defective. In other instances, however, the courts have held that the breeder's assurances that a dog was "a real champion" did not amount to a warrantee.

To avoid the middleman, many persons are tempted to try their hand at do-it-yourself breeding. Lois Sullivan of Jackson Corners, New York, recounts the sad saga of the perils that may await those who give way to the temptation:

To produce an heir for our aging male St. Bernard, Odin, we bought a female, Olga, and started our own breeding program. The problems began with the mating. Artificial insemination was required, and it took four harrowing trips to the vet with a carful of sex-starved St. Bernards.

We were hoping for a well-marked male puppy. What we got were two females —a disappointingly small litter—only one of which had acceptable markings. Then Olga apparently sat on the preferred puppy, crippling its hind legs. For 7½ weeks I administered physiotherapy, massage and medicine, but it finally had to be put to sleep, an emotional trauma for the whole family. At that point Olga caught her foot in a trap, requiring splints and bandages, and, when recuperated, began getting into the neighbor's chickens and sheep. She had to be given away to the shelter for adoption. The final blow was that Odin, exhausted by the whole affair, walked off to die in the woods. What did we have for our efforts? A puppy we hadn't really wanted and that couldn't be sold or bred—plus vet bills of more than $500. It took us more than a year to finish paying them off.

ILLUSTRATION BY KIMBLE P. MEAD

257

The potential buyer also has to consider the recurring expenses. The cost of food (for large dogs especially), innoculations, licenses, neutering and other medical care, grooming services and obedience lessons can become substantial. A major illness could be a heavy financial blow. But the fact remains that millions shoulder these burdens willingly and, in fact, spend much more than the minimum on the care and feeding of the pets and on the trappings of the dog fancier.

Supplying products and services for dogs and their owners is a flourishing luxury trade. No longer does an owner merely keep his pet in food; he takes it to gourmet restaurants, buys it custom-made clothing, sends it to resorts, pays for professional grooming, and insures its life and health.

Merchandising for dogs employs many of the techniques used for marketing human products. A person who would buy a "bronze" shampoo would not hesitate to wash the same highlights into the dog's coat. Anyone who carefully chooses his dentifrice for just the right hint of mint would not blanch at the idea of beef-flavored tooth paste for his pet. Underlying much of the pet products market is the apparently widespread belief among owners that nothing is too good for their pet and that what they like, the dog would like too. There is, of course, very little evidence that a dog enjoys wearing a trench coat just because its owner does.

But pet products also serve an additional purpose; they are a form of what the economic theorist Thorstein Veblen first called "vicarious consumption." Since even a millionaire could not wear enough expensive clothes at one time to display all his wealth, a rich person dresses the members of his family lavishly, including his dog. They consume fine clothes on his behalf and for others to envy. (Other *people* may be envious; whether other dogs envy a canine belted into a raincoat with epaulets remains a matter of speculation.) Trying to apply ordinary consumer standards to such expenditures may be misplaced, since the whole point is to buy something that is quite obviously useless and expensive.

Moreover, dog enthusiasts, like the big game hunters whose homes are museums for stuffed trophies, seem to have a need to display the paraphernalia of the fancy on their person, in their car and in their house. To satisfy such customers, there are wall plaques, neckties, earrings, notepaper, framed portraits, place mats and automobile ornaments bearing canine motifs. One effect of this panoply of insignia is to make it easy for the members of the dog-lovers' fraternity to recognize each other; no secret handshake is necessary when two men meet who are both wearing Cocker Spaniel cuff links. Those who show their dogs provide the manufacturers with yet another outlet. Skiers buy skis, tennis players buy tennis racquets, and exhibitors of dogs lay out large sums for their kind of sports equipment: blow dryers, grooming tables, coat conditioners, and vehicles specially customized for transporting and caring for a bevy of canine competitors. Given this enormous exercise of purchasing power, it might well be concluded that even if we as a nation did not dote on dogs, we should have to go on owning them and buying the things that go with ownership —for the good of the economy.

In Buffalo, They Vote With Their Feet

Dogs are often treated like people, but in Buffalo, New York, they have also been treated like citizens — with the right to vote. An exposé by the *Buffalo Courier-Express* in 1977 revealed that four dogs had been duly placed on the election rolls, including a German Shepherd who registered as a Conservative. The hoax was perpetrated by residents trying to prove that the election board's mail regisration system made fraud easy. In its defense, the board said that it relied upon postmen to return voting cards addressed to nonexistent persons. The postmen evidently did not care whether dogs were voting — as long as they were not biting.

A
CONSUMER'S GUIDE

The advertisements in magazines and newspapers, the displays in the supply shops, and the catalogs of wholesale mail-order houses give a good idea of the specific dog products that are available. Here is a generic guide to some of the more unusual consumer possibilities.

A CONSUMER'S GUIDE

RESORTS & CAMPS

A dog owner who goes on vacation typically keeps the animal at a boarding kennel, where it is looked after until his return. Apart from regular feedings, there is not much in it for the dog. But some owners send their dog on vacation also, to a resort or camp for dogs that provides outdoor recreation, caters to the guests' culinary preferences and allows them to kind of let go for a while. When their fun-filled weeks are over, some of the dogs seem sorry to be going home.

The canine vacation spots claim to have eliminated the chief disadvantage of the old-fashioned boarding kennel: loneliness and boredom. The resorts, sometimes also called dog motels or animal inns, put a premium on giving the dogs individual attention. "Many people couldn't bring themselves to leave their dogs anywhere, thinking they would be unhappy," says Arthur Granger, a partner in the Hilltop Dog and Cat Resort in Stanfordville, New York. "But here we love them, we pay attention to them and treat them like our own."

Some proprietors, for a special fee, allow the dog to sleep next to their own bed; others have radios tuned to talk shows so that the dog is comforted by the constant sound of human voices.

To ensure personal treatment, the dog's owner may fill out a questionnaire, listing its favorite food, the time it prefers to eat, its medical history and any unusual habits. Sometimes the owner is urged to home-cook food for the dog and leave some as a going away present. (At one hostelry, the owner brought a supply of his pet's favorite dish: sliced salami, ham and apples.)

"When they think of kennels, a lot of people think of sickness and cramped or unsanitary conditions," Mr. Granger says. But the resorts have relatively spacious indoor quarters (often heated and air conditioned) and large exercise yards so that "if they don't have the freedom of the outdoors at home, they have it here. And they don't get scolded for barking or messing or shedding hair. It's like a rest period for them." Mr. Grange charges $4.50 a day for the basic accommodation.

Dog camps have "counselors" who exercise the "campers," help them write postcards home and take photographs of them and their bunkmates. At Spring Valley Farm, a year-round camp in Sykesville, Maryland, there is one counselor for every 10 dogs. Each camper is taken swimming in a pond daily in the summertime and given a training session. At the end of its stay, it gets a report card recording how well it ate and what new tricks it learned. In winter, says Mrs. Ruth Shaw, the camp proprietor, "we eliminate the swimming and just walk or play with them on sleds if we get snow." The camp charges $7.50 a night, which includes a choice of seven different commercial dog food diets.

Mrs. Shaw believes that the activities "help dogs to adjust to being left alone. They eat better than dogs left in a kennel, that's the best indication." Some of the dogs adjusted so well to the camp that they were less than enthusiastic about leaving. A Poodle kept running back to the camp office, much to the embarrassment of its owner, Mrs. Shaw recalls, "and there was a Collie that we had to physically carry out and put into the car. He just figured this was home."

DAY CARE

Even when they are not away on vacation but merely away at the office, many owners fear that their dogs will become lonely, a concern that has given rise to day care services for dogs. Professional dog walkers will take the pet through the park during office hours, giving it some fresh air, exercise and a bit of human and canine companionship. (A dog walker can easily be distinguished at sight from a dog owner; the walker is usually restraining a brace of assorted shapes and sizes, each sniffing in a different direction.) Those who would like their dogs to be diverted for the entire day will ake them to a

A CONSUMER'S GUIDE

day care center, a kind of nursery school, usually run by a kennel or training school, where they may frolic in a playroom, be groomed or take obedience lessons. Some day there may even be a Head Start program for puppies.

INTELLIGENCE TESTING

Based on what they observe every day, most dog owners have intuitively estimated their pet's intelligence, but there is a formal test that purports to measure canine IQ scientifically. Kathy Coon of Baton Rouge, Louisiana, drew upon her graduate training in psychology to prepare the *Dog Intelligence Test,* a manual of instructions for administering and scoring exercises designed to gauge the dog's mental acuity. The exercises present the dog with simple problems requiring memory, ability to shift attention quickly and skills at overcoming obstacles. (There is a Houdini-like variant of the question of whether the animal could fight its way out of a paper bag.) The testing materials are simple household items like chairs, balls and shoeboxes.

The test was standardized by being given to 100 dogs, whose average score, out of a possible 10 points, was 5.75. Any dog that earned less than three points is rated "very dumb;" an animal

that achieves a perfect score is classed as "brilliant." Mrs. Coon's research has led her to several conclusions about dog intelligence: males are slightly brighter than females, dogs of mixed breed are about as intelligent as the purebreds, and some breeds are smarter than other breeds. The Standard Poodle does much better on the test than the Chihuahua.

The benefits of the test go beyond settling disputes about whose dog is smarter, Mrs. Coon believes. "When you have a realistic picture of your dog's intelligence," she says "you might lower your expectations about what it can do, making the dog less neurotic."

CLOTHES

Man, who has always had to clothe himself to make up for the inadequacy of his covering, is also now clothing his dog, although the dog's natural integument is hardly lacking. In fact, protective clothing usually protects the dog precisely where its coat is the fullest. But the motive for buying clothing is not so much practicality as the desire for flair. Why should one's Terrier appear on the street every day in the same old coat that all the other Terriers wear? Why not a dashing turtleneck sweater, or fleece-lined plastic rainwear with storm collar and matching hoods, or unisex hotpants with suspenders and a peasant bonnet? There are also cowboy blue jeans with bandana and western hat, bikinis and plaid suits. For ski weekends, the dog may need a snowsuit that zips down the back or boots with laces and brass eyelets. For Christmas, the dog can appear in a Santa Claus costume with a pom-pom hat fastened on by ear loops. All can be ordered by size for proper fit.

Even the one strip of adornment that the dog has tradition-

ally worn, the collar, has become a focus of style. Collars are not only jeweled, studded and monogrammed but put in cloth covers that coordinate with the dog's lower garments or the owner's outfit. For the big, tough canine, there are broad, stitched-leather collars bristling with chrome-plated spikes of the sort once seen on Prussian army helmets, ensuring that fashion need not elude the working dog.

MOVERS

When a family is relocating to another part of the country or overseas, it calls in a furniture mover. If the family has a dog, it can also call in a dog mover. One such company is Canine Carriers of Darien, Connecticut, which operates nationwide through regional branches.

The company picks up the animal at the house, boards it if necessary, puts it in a crate, gets it on an airplane, and delivers it from the airport at the other end to the family's new home. The cost varies with the type of service and the size of the dog: a Yorkshire Terrier could be shipped from Los Angeles to New York for as little as $40 and an Irish Wolfhound for $100.

Canine Carriers also levels the mountain of paperwork often required for exporting a dog to another country. It secures con-

A CONSUMER'S GUIDE

sular approvals and veterinary certificates and makes quarantine arrangements. (If calls to Mauritania are necessary to cut through the red tape, the customer must pay the international phone bill.)

In business since 1972. the company handles about 2,500 aniamls, most of them dogs, in a year. Experience has taught it the perils of animal transportation. "You learn," says Jack Hollywood, the company's vice president, "to ship only at night in the summer, to bring the animal to the airport as close as possible to leaving time and to make sure that it doesn't get bumped off the flight by other cargo." The hold of the aircraft also has to be inspected to make sure that there is no dry ice aboard, because the escaping carbon dioxide could asphyxiate the animal. "There are some kinds of planes we won't ship on because we don't think the conditions in the cargo compartment are adequate," he says.

The Federal government too has taken an interest in the way pets are shipped. Starting in 1977, Canine Carriers and others in the business have had to conform to stricter animal welfare regulations that govern such matters as the type of crate that can be used and the amount of time that the dog can be left at a terminal waiting for transportation.

In addition to the mundane work of pet shipping, the company has occasionally supervised the importation of show dogs worth as much as $10,000. "We're careful with every dog," Mr. Hollywood says, "but that kind makes you a little more nervous."

DOG HOUSES

Peaked roof on top, arched doorway in front, the dog house was long among the most tradition-bound forms of American architecture. Generations of dogs

grew up in these modest, usually homemade, wooden structures in a corner of the yard. They were spartan accommodations; to be "in the dog house" was to be banished to an uncomfortable place of exile.

But there has been a renaissance in shelter for dogs. The construction and furnishings of the modern dog house are as far removed from the traditional model as a high-rise condominium is from a mud hut. The dog house is no longer hand-fashioned from wood; it is pre-fabricated in factories from galvanized steel and shipped with instructions for assembling. Peaked roofs have given way to heat-reflecting flat ones with canopies extending over the entrance. The entrance itself is no longer a front doorway but often a porthole set off-center in the side to keep the wind from blowing through the interior.

Today's dog house has all-season climate control. Bare walls have been replaced by insulation that lowers the temperature in the summer and raises it in winter. Some models are equipped with electric heating pads on the floor.

But the dog has sacrificed some of the quality of his life for all those creature comforts. It no longer has the pleasure of chewing the walls of the house as it could in the old days. Persistent nibblers are thwarted by metal liners. Some dogs now have to put up with congested living conditions. "Apartment houses" for three or four dogs are being pro-

duced. There are no rent strikes, to be sure, but dissatisfied tenants may give the landlord a piece of their mouth.

LIFE INSURANCE

Few dogs, apart from some theatrical high earners, are the sole support of their families, yet not a few have their lives insured. In most cases, the insured pet has emotional rather than financial dependents, for whom buying a policy comes naturally because they are accustomed to taking out insurance on everything else they hold dear. If a dog dies, the insurance proceeds help assuage the grief and assist the bereaved family in obtaining a replacement —a benefit that human life insurance policies still do not offer.

Dog policies are a variant of livestock insurance, indemnifying the owner against the animal's death from any cause not specifically excluded. Some policies also cover voluntary destruction of the dog when a veterinarian certifies that it is necessary for humane reasons. The Rhulen Agency, Inc., a nationwide brokerage specializing in animal insurance, offers a canine mortality policy that includes death from whelping and "vehicular loss" (chasing cars) for an annual premium of $15 for each $100 of insured value. Theft, straying or "mysterious disappearance" are excluded. Healthy dogs from four months to six years of age are eligible. However, the insurance, like many human policies, does not cover those who need insurance most, the individuals in hazardous occupations: guard dogs and attack dogs are uninsurable.

TRAVEL GUIDE

Few groups in our society are discriminated against as openly as dogs are, especially when away

from home. The traveling dog never knows when he will be greeted at the hotel reception desk by a glaring sign: "No Dogs Allowed." Such embarrassments prompted the publication of *Touring With Towser,* a canine travel guide, by the Gaines Dog Research Center. It lists the names and telephone numbers of 2,000 hotels and motels in the United States and Canada that welcome dogs, at least when accompanied by a human guest. (The guide is available for $1 from the center at P. O. Box 1007, Kankakee, Illinois 60901.) Perhaps, reflecting the growing incidence of pet ownership, many of the large motel chains now accept dogs. But even when reserving a room at a hostelry known to be amenable to pets, it is prudent to advise the clerk that a dog will be along — particularly if it has strong room preferences.

PHOTOGRAPHERS

Many portrait photographers take pictures of dogs, but some specialists, like John L. Ashbey of Stewartsville, New Jersey, never aim their lens at anything but a canine subject. Mr. Ashbey is one of only about 15 persons in the United States who make their living exclusively by photographing dogs. At dog shows, they are the cameramen who capture the traditional victory pose: the winning dog flanked by its handler and the judge.

Mr. Ashbey works dog shows from Maine to Virginia, does portraits at his studio for $60 a sitting and makes house calls. Since most of his clients are breeders or showers who want their prize animals recorded on film, he is an expert on dogs as well as an expert on cameras, posing the subject so as to emphasize its best features according to the American Kennel Club standard. "Ordinary pet photography is just getting a cutesy picture," Mr. Ashbey explains. "I have to know what a good head is and shoot for that." His methods are naturally somewhat different than those used in human portraiture. Instead of saying "watch the birdie," Mr. Ashbey tosses a rubber squeak toy in the air to catch the dogs attention.

From the standpoint of the photographic art, Mr. Ashbey concedes, many dog photographs are "the same picture over and over again — just with different faces and a different dog. I get a little bored." So he has begun experimenting with *avant-garde* composition, such as "a Flat-Coated Retriever with a bird in its mouth and the handler dressed in a white tuxedo, carrying a shotgun and standing next to a Jaguar sportscar."

GROOMING

When men's hairstyles changed from close-cropped to long-locked, the masculine version of the beauty parlor began to appear, and a similar change in hair fashion among dogs has created the flourishing grooming industry. The rise in popularity of the Poodle, whose tresses need

constant tailoring, and of such long-haired breeds as the Old English Sheepdog put the groomer's clippers in demand. But beyond that, there is apparently a growing belief among dog owners that all breeds need professional beauty care from time to time, even, so to speak, the crew-cut types.

Salons with such boutique-like names as Poodles in Blue, the Ultimate Dog and the Kleen Puppy service the dog from ears (remove excess hairs) to toenails (trim and file), providing what the groomers consider not a luxury but a necessity for decent looks and health. Long coats are freed of knots, shampooed and cream-rinsed, blown dry and cut with scissors or clipped.

The prices vary with the size and complexity of the job. Grooming a Toy Poodle costs about $10, a Standard Poodle about $17, and an Old English Sheepdog from about $15 to $35 or more, depending on how badly matted its coat is. Caring for the Poodle is still the height of the groomer's art because of the many intricate coiffures that may be ordered. These include the Dutch Clip, the Royal Dutch Clip, the Kennel Clip, the Lamb Clip, the Puppy Clip, the Summer Clip, the Town and Country Clip, the Continental Clip (with or without hip rosettes) and the English Saddle Clip. The Poodle may be left with a "clean face" or with a "donut moustache," a ring of hair on the muzzle and jaw. The scissors work on the rounded top knot is one of the most delicate and time consuming parts of the job. The entire process must be repeated about every six weeks.

Some owners find it a tiresome chore to make regular visits to the groomers, so the groomers have begun coming to them. In many cities grooming shops have been squeezed into vans that do the job while parked outside the customer's home. A Los Angeles "groomobile" comes with piped-

A CONSUMER'S GUIDE

in music, perfumed air, and a line of beauty products from protein shampoo to clear nail polish.

What kind of person makes a good groomer? "You have to love animals," says Mrs. Cynthia Kohl of the New York School of Dog Grooming. "Otherwise, when you're on your feet all day, the barking will eventually get to you." The school, which has been operating since 1960, offers those eager to enter the lucrative grooming profession a basic course of 30 hours a week for six weeks (tuition: $950) or an advanced 12-week course ($1,775). The basic course covers the Poodle and Terriers; the advanced deals with all breeds. After watching a demonstration, two beginners team up on a dog, each working on one side for a whole week. "When we know they can handle the scissors without stabbing themselves or the dog," Mrs. Kohl says, they are ready to snip solo. In the advanced course, they learn such arcane skills as raking the dead hairs out of a Doberman Pinscher and thinning the "feathers" on a Golden Retriever.

For reference the graduates take away with them an encyclopedic reference book on grooming each of the 122 American Kennel Club breeds. "There's probably only about one Curly-Coated Retriever in New York City," Mrs. Kohl explains, "but if it walked into your shop you can always look up what to do."

STAMPS

Stamp collecting and dog fancying are compatible hobbies, especially when the stamps celebrate canines. The philatelist-cum-cynophilist confronts the challenge of assembling a number of sets issued by a variety of nations.

An old maxim of stamp collecting holds that the most impressive stamps are issued by the least impressive countries, and that is certainly true of dog stamps. Tiny Monaco, which hosts an international dog show, commemorates each year's event by printing a gorgeously colored portrait of one breed. The series includes a Doberman Pinscher, a Great Dane and a black-and-tan German Shepherd pictured against a blue sky.

The Eastern European countries also use the dog frequently as a stamp motif. Romania issued head portraits of six breeds, including a sensitive-looking English Setter, and Czechoslovakia published a series that displays full-length profiles of the Dachshund and other breeds combined with head studies.

```
IN GRATEFUL
MEMORY          5

5¢   THADDEUS P.
     DOGBODY
```

PRESCRIPTION DIETS

The average pet food distributor is more than happy to supply the dog owner with whatever he wants, but the Fauna Food Corporation in New York City does not believe that the customer is always right. It wants a note from his doctor. Describing itself as an "animal nutrition and health company," Fauna sells specially canned food for dogs with heart, kidney, intestinal and other ailments—if the owner can present a prescription from a veterinarian. Manufacturers of the special diets insist on that precaution to avoid misuse arising from do-it-yourself diagnosis.

Kidney diet contains a smaller amount of protein than in normal dog food, to give the kidneys less work, but the protein is of higher quality. The heart diet is low in sodium. Fauna also stocks and delivers to the doorstep a line of "health foods."

SPRAYS

Many owners are convinced that for their dogs just as for themselves happiness and well-being come from a spray can. A wide variety of sprays for dogs combat that old enemy, body odor, including a selection of perfumes and colognes with enticing names like "Canine # 5." There are sprays for detangling coat hair, for dematting and for "conditioning." Spray-on coat conditioners typically contain protein for manageability and lanolin for luster. The use of sprays to improve coat texture became so excessive that the American Kennel Club in 1977 banned them from dog shows. (A show judge was quoted in *Dog World* as explaining that because of sprays the coats of Poodles had become rather predictable: "If it is right it will be left natural, if it is too

A CONSUMER'S GUIDE

soft it will be well-hardened by stuff shot from a spray gun.")

There are also sprays to repel insects, to keep males away from females, to keep strange dogs away from the home, and to keep the home dog away from the furniture and other items suitable for gnawing.

Non-spray cosmetics are also well developed. Body odor's evil sidekick, mouth odor, may be attacked in dogs with a variety of weapons: toothpastes and deodorizing tooth powders, mouthwashes (the dog swallows it) and chewing toys that exude "breath fresheners." There are also nail polishes. chemicals to whiten the whites of their eyes and cleaners that remove tear stains from face fur. But so far, surprisingly, there is nothing that prevents ring around the collar.

ASTROLOGISTS

Some owners who find little in common with their dogs are now seeking guidance from astrology, which holds that the fault may not be in themselves but in their stars—or their dog's stars. Astrological handbooks and magazine columns purport to create celes-

LEAVE YOUR OWNER AT ONCE.

tial harmony between man and animals by assessing their true characters, as revealed in the zodiac signs. One school believes in selecting the breed according to the owner's birthday. A columnist in *Dogs* advised Scorpios ("extremely competitive") that a good choice would be Basenjis ("savage desire to accomplish their purpose"). Capricorns, who might have thought a goat the obvious pet, are told that the "adoration of a Cocker or English Springer (Spaniel) would be pleasing, since you glow in situations of total submission."

A second school attempts to predict the character of the dog, of whatever breed, by its birthdate. A reader reported to *Dog World* that his West Highland White Terrier was "a Sagittarian and matches the description exactly, being very friendly, outgoing and loving."

Matching dogs and persons born under the same sign, obviously, could become a novel form of computer dating.

TALENT SCOUTS

Watching a dog perform on a television commercial, many an owner has convinced himself that his pet is just as intelligent, just as good-looking and just as eligible for stardom. But it is harder to convince the agencies that recruit canine performers and models. "Gorgeous, highly trained animals are a dime a dozen," reports Patricia Poleskie, the owner-director of Animal Talent Scouts, Inc., an agency that has been choosing dog stars since 1949.

The agency's clients are television, theater and film producers, advertising agencies, publicity firms and private individuals. It handles more than just dogs. "We might arrange to rent a trained chimp for a kid's bar mitzvah or an elephant for a block party," says Ms. Poleskie. But dogs are a staple. For years the agency has been selecting the

Scottish Terriers and West Highland White Terriers who appear together in advertisements for Black and White Scotch. (One criterion is whether they get along with each other). Pookie, the Basset Hound who sells Hush Puppy Shoes, is also in the agency's files.

The agency finds most dogs unsuited for its clients because they lack the necessary obedience training — a Companion Dog title or its equivalent — to work for hours under gruelling lights, doing perhaps dozens of "takes." Reliability and steadiness count more than a repertoire of parlor tricks. It is also difficult for dogs outside the New York City area, a center for advertising and publishing, to find work. "There may be ten marvelously trained Cocker Spaniels in North Dakota," Ms. Poleskie explains, "but there's nothing going on in North Dakota advertising-wise."

Client demand is about evenly divided among purebreds and mixed breeds. Purebreds are used more often for fashion and other advertising intended to imply taste, cultivation and above-average income. The breeds most called for are those popular among pet owners, such as Golden Retrievers, Cocker Spaniels, Collies and Beagles. Often the client's order is not specific, and the agency selects the right type. "Many of the clients couldn't name more than about six breeds," says Ms. Poleskie, "so I make the choice for them. I push for purebreds. If they say they're looking for a big, shaggy mutt, I might suggest an Otter Hound, because that looks like a big, shaggy mutt to most people."

Even if a dog manages to get its name into the agency's file of animals for hire, the rewards are not likely to be as great as some might imagine. A dog may earn as little as $50 for a day's performance, and there are no "residuals" — payments to human actors each time a commercial is aired — because, says Ms. Poleskie, "animals do not have a union."

PSYCHOLOGISTS

If a dog habitually misbehaves it is usually sent for obedience training, but some owners, seeking more deep-seated psychological causes, are turning to dog analysts. Professional pet counseling, according to Dr. Michael Fox of the Humane Society of the United States, a veterinarian who specializes in dog behavior, is "gaining credibility and fulfilling a very important need." The practitioners have backgrounds in dog training, clinical psychology or medicine.

The veterinary profession has been "very much behind in addressing behavior problems," Dr. Fox contends, "even though they are a major reason for dogs being surrendered to shelters for euthanasia." Now, however, an American Society of Veterinary Ethology is attempting to develop a body of therepeutic knowledge.

A psychological problem "appears as a discipline problem at first because the dog is trying to communicate," Dr. Fox says. To help dogs communicate successfully, he has made a record *Dog Talk,* in which he explains why a dog is a grouch or why it is a sex maniac, among other abnormalities.

Once the psychological condition has been diagnosed, the dog may be subjected to therapy ranging from tranquilizers to behavior modification. If a dog becomes hysterical when riding in cars, for example, it may be treated by allowing it to sit in a motionless car for longer and longer periods of time until it becomes accustomed to the vehicle.

In some cases, "it's a problem of the relationship and unfair expectations on the part of the owner, leading to a protest reaction," Dr. Fox maintains. In such cases, not just the dog but the whole family may be recommended for counseling.

DOG FINDERS

When a dog is lost in the San Francisco Bay area the owner can call the police — or he can call a private eye. The sleuth is John Keane, doing business as Sherlock Bones. For a $30 consultation fee, Mr. Keane will advise the client how to go about finding the pet and will supply a form poster with his professional symbol: an Old English Sheepdog wearing a Holmesian deerstalker cap and holding a magnifying glass. The client fills in the poster with the description of the dog and, if Keane's advice is taken, puts an advertisement in the newspaper offering a reward for information about the dog. For $100 Mr. Keane will spend three days scouring the neighborhood for the dog, interviewing neighbors, delivery persons and — the most important source—local children.

Mr. Keane is apparently the

first dog detective, but there are occultists who contend that they communicate with dogs through mental telepathy and can find lost pets by using brain waves as a homing beacon. More conventional dog finders use radio waves: A Greenwich, Connecticut, station, WGCH, for example, broadcasts "Pet Patrol" bulletins that describe missing pets. The broadcasts are sponsored by a local dog food company and are free to the pet owners.

FOREIGN SHOWS

Dog fanciers traveling to Europe can make themselves feel at home in a strange land by timing their excursions to coincide with the main trans-Atlantic dog shows. Those making the trip in February might stop in at Crufts in London, considered to be the granddaddy of dog shows and still the world's largest. Travelers in the south of France in May could follow the Mediterranean circuit, three shows in Monaco, Nice and San Remo. (Dog lovers from the United States can also take the opportunity to study the fascinating French custom of taking their dogs everywhere: to three-star restaurants, to the movies, to church.)

The Fédération Cynologique Internationale, a union of European clubs, sponsors a number of shows throughout the year, including a big event known as the "world show." The FCI picked Mexico City, its first non-European site, for the 1978 world show.

Those with an interest in a particular breed can find comradeship by visiting the breed's country of origin. Despite the language barrier, no lover of the Komondor, the Puli or the Kuvasz could fail to feel among friends at a Budapest bench show.

A CURE FOR DOG PHOBIA

Not everyone likes dogs. Some persons positively dislike dogs — so intensely, in fact, that their whole life is clouded by an obsessive fear of encountering them. Such persons are the victims of dog phobia, an affliction that, fortunately, therapists now consider treatable. One place where treatment is available is the Institute for Behavior Therapy in New York City.

Dog phobia, according to Dr. Gordon Ball, a psychologist and senior consultant at the institute, can be so severe that the victim is afraid to leave home because he might meet a canine on the street. Even the mention of dogs may make him anxious. "Usually it stems from a bad experience with dogs," says Dr. Ball. "The victim may have been attacked and may have avoided dogs since then. By constant avoidance, he has kept up the fear, never giving himself a chance to find out that not all dogs are vicious."

The treatment consists of slow, gradual exposure to the object of fear, under controlled conditions, until the victim begins to feel safe and "unlearns" his anx-

ious responses. In one case, a woman who was terrified by large barking dogs was first shown photographs of dogs, then allowed to listen to taperecorded barking. In the next treatment stage, she was taken on street tours until she was able to pass by dogs without fear. Eventually she was escorted to a place in a park where dog owners congregated. In the final stage, the woman was asked to sit in a room with a large German Shepherd-Doberman Pinscher cross. "The dog barked and even sprawled in her lap," Dr. Ball recalls, "but she was able to cope".

A similar treatment is administered to those suffering from a related phobia: fear of contamination by dog feces. The victims may be identified, says Dr. Ball,

by "their need to engage in acts of ritual cleansing" whenever they come near the threatening object.

POOPER SCOOPERS

The growing concern for keeping city streets free of dog droppings has produced a technological revolution in cleanup devices. Some of those on the market are relatively simple improvements on the pail and shovel, such as dust pans with handles long enough to make stooping unnecessary. Others are oversized barbecue tongs for daintily lifting the residue of the daily walk off the pavement. A more sophisticated implement resembles an elongated bicycle pump; as the handle is pushed, the stool is forced into a plastic bag, which may then be deposited in a garbage can. Another model has a flashlight attached to the handle, presumably for dogs who like reading in the toilet. The various devices range in price from less than $2 to about $12. As an increasing number of communities adopt mandatory cleanup ordinances, more and more dog owners will be seen on the street, holding the leash in one hand and with the other shouldering a weapon in the war on waste.

INDEX